The 1993 Book of Jewish Thought

The 1993 Book of Jewish Thought

קובץ עיונים בפרשנות המקרא ובמחשבת ישראל

A Journal of Torah Scholarship

Editors:

Chaim Sh. Eisen
Moshe Ch. Sosevsky

Editorial Committee:

Nachman Bulman
Yehudah Copperman

Menachem Genack
Hillel Goldberg

**Orthodox
Union**

**Yeshivat
Ohr Yerushalayim**

ISBN 1-879016-10-9

Phototypeset at Targum Press, Inc.
Produced by Olivestone Print Communications, Inc.

PRINTED IN THE UNITED STATES OF AMERICA

CONTENTS

> The Midrash depicts Elkanah as the central figure in the events leading
> up to the birth of the prophet Shemu'el. The author demonstrates how
> Chazal were attentive to a broader issue that preceded the birth of
> Shemu'el and served as background to it: the abandonment of Shiloh
> and the overall deterioration that took place during the period of Sefer
> Shofetim. The opening verses of Sefer Shemu'el suggest the transforma-
> tion wrought by Elkanah to reverse this tendency. Properly analyzed
> through the Midrash, they serve as a key to understanding the period as
> a whole and Elkanah's role in it.

> The Mishnah states that on Rosh HaShanah, "all mankind pass before
> Him like *benei maron*." The expression *"benei maron"* is sufficiently ambig-
> uous to be expounded in three alternate manners by the Gemara. Based

on the commentary of Maharal MiPrague, the author attributes to these interpretations varying perceptions of the judgment of man on Rosh HaShanah. In the process, the essay outlines classic approaches to Aggadah.

The apparent ambivalence of the Torah's description of Eli'ezer, slave of Avraham, is reflected in numerous Midrashic and Talmudic sources, where he is alternately cast as a righteous Torah scholar and as a faithless, accursed slave. By grappling with these divergent sources, the author creates a coherent picture of the man entrusted with perpetuating the spiritual legacy of our forefather Avraham. In doing so, the essay illustrates how seemingly inconsistent and contradictory sources can ultimately prove to be components of the same composite portrait.

Historical accounts, Biblical allusions, Talmudic sources, Midrashic narratives, Halachic dictates, and teachings of the Chasidic masters are among the many sources that imply a connection between Sukkoth and Chanukkah. After exploring these diverse sources, the author suggests philosophical concepts and themes that may provide a basis for the links that abound between the two holidays.

King Sha'ul's visit to a necromancer seems to constitute a blatant violation of the Torah's prohibitions against witchcraft and other forms of divination. The author attempts to establish possible rationales for Sha'ul's seemingly unpardonable sin. In the context of defending Sha'ul, the essay explores the approach of Chazal toward the wrongdoings of personalities in the Bible and the general nature of Biblical narratives.

While Chazal's analysis of Scripture primarily involved derivation of the Halachah through Midrashic expositions, they nevertheless taught us that "Scripture does not depart from its plain meaning." But what function are we to ascribe to this "plain meaning," considering that the Halachah frequently does not at all accord with this meaning? Through numerous citations from classic commentaries on the Torah, the author demonstrates that the "*peshat*" of Halachic statements in the Torah does indeed play a crucial role, comprising various levels of meaning that might otherwise have remained concealed from us.

According to the Talmud, the *shekalim* that were contributed by Yisra'el to the sanctuary served as an antidote for the *shekalim* offered by Haman to Achashverosh in exchange for permission to exterminate the Jewish people. The association between the two sums of money appears elusive. In clarifying the Talmud's intent, the author provides insight into the *mitzvah* of *machatzith hashekel* and various dimensions of Purim. Through these, the essay presents an incisive analysis of the Torah's view of the relationship between the individual and the community and its ramifications regarding the Jewish concept of personal responsibility.

In the bible's description of the anointment of King David, difficulties abound. Why does Shemu'el "the seer" initially fail to discern which of Yishai's sons is or is not fit for royalty? Why does Yishai seem to withhold his son David from the prophet? And why — after G-d's reproach to Shemu'el that "man sees the external appearance, but G-d sees the heart" — is David introduced with a detailed *physical* description? Weaving together varied statements by Chazal and later commentators, the author analyzes this glimpse of King David that the bible offers and its implications for understanding his complex character and singular greatness as G-d's chosen anointed.

One of the most enigmatic *aggadoth* in the Talmud juxtaposes Mosheh Rabbeinu and Rabbi Akiva, the two greatest historic figures in the infusion of Torah into the world. Mosheh is shown Rabbi Akiva's Torah — as an incomprehensible discourse — and Rabbi Akiva's "reward" — as his flayed flesh being weighed in the meat market. Through both examination of textual subtleties and comparison with parallel sources, the author proposes a comprehensive analysis of this *aggadah*'s underlying meaning and message. By doing so, the essay not only clarifies the distinct roles of Moshesh and Rabbi Akiva but also suggests important insights into Torah's relationship with man and the world — and into man's dual struggle as receiver of the Torah of G-d and innovator in the Torah of man.

THE EMERGENCE OF MAN: *Hillel Goldberg*   243
A Musar Approach to
Mizmor 19

Reared on the teachings of the Musar movement, one learns to respond to the emotional-spiritual power of Tehillim. In applying this approach to Mizmor 19, the author offers a subjective commentary on the flow of the *mizmor* and insights into the unspoken spiritual ascent to which it alludes. In so doing, the essay traces the *mizmor*'s development from a seemingly universal approach expressed in its opening declaration — *"The heavens tell the glory of the L-rd"* to an intensely personal conclusion — *May the words of my mouth and the meditation of my heart be pleasing before You, G-d, my Rock and my Redeemer."*

TRANSLITERATIONS:

Phonetic transliteration is used throughout, without recourse to anglicized forms or conventional English spelling. Transliterations are italicized, except proper nouns and books of the Bible. Several specific conventions employed in transliteration are listed below.

1. א and ע are ignored, except where interposing between two vowels, whereupon א is indicated by ' and ע by ' to prevent erroneous pronunciation of the vowels as a diphthong.
2. ב and ו are both transliterated as *v*.
3. ח and כ are both transliterated as *ch*.
4. י is usually transliterated as *y*. However, where it follows *kamatz gadol*, *patach*, *tzeirei*, and *segol*, at the end of a syllable, it is transliterated as *i*, and where it follows *chirik* at the end of a syllable, it is ignored.
5. כ and ק are both transliterated as *k*.
6. *Dagesh chazak* (forte) is indicated by doubling the letter, except ש (*sh*) and צ (*tz*) and where the letter is a capital.
7. *Dagesh kal* is indicated in ב (*b* vs. *v*), כ (*k* vs. *ch*), פ (*p* vs. *f*), and ת (*t* vs. *th*).
8. *Tzeirei*, *segol*, and *sheva na* (the vocalized *sheva*) are all transliterated *e*. *Tzeirei* at the end of a word is transliterated *ei* to prevent confusion. *Sheva nach* (the silent *sheva*) is ignored.

ABBREVIATIONS USED IN REFERENCES:

Ag.	— *Aggadah, Aggadath*	*Peth.*	— *Pethichta*
b.	— bar, ben, ibn	*Pir.DeR.E.*	— *Pirkei DeRabbi Eli'ezer*
BeM.R.	— *BeMidbar Rabbah*	R.	— Rabbeinu, Rabbi, Rav
BeR.R.	— *BeReshith Rabbah*	R.	— *Rabba, Rabbah*
ca.	— *circa* ("about")	*Ru.R.*	— *Ruth Rabbah*
ch., chs.	— chapter, chapters	*Sh.HaSh.R.*	— *Shir HaShirim Rabbah*
com.	— commentary	*Sh.R.*	— *Shemoth Rabbah*
Dev.R.	— *Devarim Rabbah*	*T.DeV.Eli.R.*	— *Tanna DeVei Eliyahu Rabba*
Eich.R.	— *Eichah Rabbah*		
Est.R.	— *Ester Rabbah*	*T.DeV.Eli.Z.*	— *Tanna DeVei Eliyahu Zota*
Hil.	— *Hilchoth*		
ibid.	— *ibidem* ("in the same place")	*Tan.*	— *Tanchuma*
		Tar.	— *Targum*
Koh.R.	— *Koheleth Rabbah*	*Tos.*	— *Tosefta*
lit.	— literally	trans.	— translated
loc. cit.	— *loco citato* ("in the place [passage] cited")	*VaY.R.*	— *VaYikra Rabbah*
		vol., vols.	— volume, volumes
Mid.	— *Midrash*	*Yal.*	— *Yalkut*
Mish.	— *Mishnah*	*Yal.Sh.*	— *Yalkut Shimoni*
n., nn.	— note, notes	*Yer.*	— *Yerushalmi*
p., pp.	— page, pages	Z.	— *Zota*
Pes.	— *Pesikta*		

PREFACE

Since our *aliyah* to Israel, we have become increasingly aware of a great amount of highly original yet fully traditional scholarship in the fields of *parshanuth HaMikra* and *machsheveth Yisra'el* being taught and published in Israel today. With few exceptions, this scholarship is virtually unknown to the American Jewish community. In addition, there are a number of *rabbanim* and *mechanchim* in America and elsewhere who are both knowledgeable and talented in the fields of *parshanuth* and *machshavah*, who do not presently have an appropriate forum in which to publish their scholarship. It is primarily to fill these voids that *JEWISH THOUGHT: A Journal of Torah Scholarship* is being inaugurated.

In undertaking this project, we considered the fact that the religious Jewish population today is far more learned than it was even a mere generation ago. An ever-increasing number of Jews are *yeshivah*-educated, and a consistently growing percentage of both men and women have studied Torah in Eretz Yisra'el, in its various *yeshivoth* and *michlaloth*. Many have been exposed to this new scholarship in *parshanuth* and *machshavah* and should feel particularly attracted to a journal dealing with these issues, as a stimulant to their ongoing Jewish learning. More generally, we feel that *JT* will provide a vehicle for enhancing the level of Torah study in the wider Jewish population, beyond serving its natural constituency of *rabbanim* and *mechanchim*. In the process, we hope not only to elevate the quality of Torah learning but to stimulate excitement about Jewish observance in general, by providing a forum for quality scholarship in topics related to Jewish practice, prayers, and beliefs.

As we go to press, and our dream begins to become a reality, we wish to take this opportunity to express our heartfelt appreciation to a number of individuals whose assistance was instrumental in producing this journal. Rabbi Menachem Genack, rabbinic administrator of the Orthodox Union, greatly encouraged this project from its initiation to its realization (his position as editor of *Mesorah* — another worthy OU publication — notwithstanding). Mr. Sidney Kwestel, president of the Orthodox Union, gave of his valuable time on a number of occasions both in the United States and in Israel to help formulate the nature of the OU's involvement in producing *JT*. Rabbi Pinchas Stolper, executive vice president of the Orthodox Union, provided valuable advice on various aspects of the publication and dissemination of *JT*. Targum Press assumed responsibility for all technical aspects of publication. The attractiveness of the final product is a tribute to its dedicated staff. We are especially gratified that Feldheim Publishers undertook the distribution of *JT*. A particular note of thanks is due Yaakov Feldheim for giving of his valuable time to provide a number of practical suggestions concerning the publication and distribution of the journal. Finally, special thanks are due our wives and families, who encouraged this project in spite of the enormous pressures and constraints that it placed upon all of us.

We believe that *JEWISH THOUGHT: A Journal of Torah Scholarship* can potentially fill a significant void in Jewish learning in both America and Israel, by responding to, and encouraging, a thirst for quality Torah scholarship in the fields of *parshanuth HaMikra* and *machsheveth Yisra'el*. In doing so, it is our fervent hope that *JT* will help to enhance and beautify this unique sphere of Torah learning and ultimately have significant impact on the Jewish community at large, "להגדיל תורה ולהאדירה": to magnify Torah and make it glorious.

— Eds.
Tammuz, 5750
Yerushalayim

INTRODUCTION

Defining Jewish thought seems like a deceptively simple and superfluous enterprise. But in a world in which philosophical jargon is bandied about so frivolously, it seems prudent to attempt to define at the outset exactly what we mean by "Jewish thought." One might also wonder what connection exists between the two principal domains of inquiry in this journal: *parshanuth HaMikra* (Biblical commentary and exegesis) and *machsheveth Yisra'el* (classic Jewish philosophy). It appears that certain definitions are in order. First, what *is* philosophy?

In contemporary parlance, "philosophy" is used principally to denote *the investigation of causes and laws perceived as underlying reality*. In this sense, we may characterize the pursuit of philosophy as the endeavor to produce a coherent system through which man may confront and attempt to apprehend reality. Of course, this definition describes all philosophies, Jewish and otherwise. By what standard, then, are we to designate a given philosophy Jewish?

In R. Yehudah HaLevi's classic treatise on Jewish philosophy, when the legendary king of the Khazars asks his Jewish mentor to explain through what natural course of sociopolitical evolution Judaism arose, the latter responds:

> In such a manner indeed systems that are based on human reason are

established and born, since they are innovated by people.... Not so regarding the system that has its origin in G-d: it arose at once. [G-d] said to it, "Be!" And it was — just as in the creation of the world.

(*HaKozari* 1:81)

Among the most essential creeds of Judaism is the belief in revelation: *that G-d revealed Himself and His will to man.* Both historically and religiously, this is the starting point of Judaism. Recognition of this principle is essential, because it strikes at the heart of what we as Jews mean by "reality." Accepting the definition of philosophy as a quest for a system with which to come to terms with reality, we must define what "reality" means to us.

From the perspective of general philosophy, the parameters of life in this world may be taken as the axioms of reality. In these terms, a so-called philosophy that ignores the experiential realities of life is by definition not a philosophy. Essentially, the same approach may be employed in defining a Jewish philosophy, with the additional qualification that in Judaism, "reality" encompasses more than merely the given realities of life in this world. An additional set of "givens" is assumed: *the Torah, that was given to us by G-d.* From this perspective, a philosophy that denies this additional, *Jewish* set of "givens" may be an acceptable philosophy in a secular sense. But it cannot, by definition, be regarded as a *Jewish* philosophy.

This principle is of paramount significance to us, not only as a means for distinguishing a philosophy as Jewish, but also as a basis for recognizing what sort of method we should expect from Jewish thought and what sort of conclusions it may be expected to furnish. Obviously, since Jewish philosophy is predicated upon Torah as given, we must first consider the nature of Torah. "*Torah*" means "teaching," and it is clear that what the Torah predominantly teaches is a way of life. The "givens" of Jewish philosophy, then, are collectively the G-d-given realities of the world *plus the G-d-given Jewish way of life.* This observation is particularly significant in contrast with other philosophies. For example, we usually expect a philosophy to deduce from the realities of life certain principles that can then be applied as practical guidelines to proper conduct in life. The process then is from the philosophical ideas to the way of life. Given our definition of *Jewish* philosophy, we will expect the progression in Judaism to proceed in the opposite direction. In Jewish thought, the philosophical ideas are not the basis of the way of life, but its conclusion.

In light of this recognition, the synthesis of *parshanuth* with *machshavah* as the two domains of a single journal is not at all surprising. Indeed, such a synthesis is practically unavoidable. Most of the essays in this issue are in fact syntheses in some way of both domains within themselves. Ultimately, all *machsheveth Yisra'el* must spring from the truths of G-d revealed to man in Scripture as illuminated by Jewish tradition. And ultimately, the lessons we can glean from these G-d-given truths through classic *parshanuth HaMikra* must serve as the foundation for *machsheveth Yisra'el*.

Finally, we recognize the proper role of Jewish thought in the larger framework of Torah scholarship in general: it comes not to suggest a way of life but to help us relate to the way of life that was already revealed to us at Sinai. Jewish law — Halachah — provides us with the "raw materials" for the edifice that we are to construct with our lives. Jewish thought is the quest for "building plans" to instruct us how to put the raw materials for construction into their proper places in that edifice. While wood and bricks provide the substance of the home, piles of wood and bricks unorganized in a building do not provide a home in which to live. Building plans on paper are also insufficient. Both aspects together are vital. It is through the synthesis of Jewish law and Jewish thought that we can truly aspire to internalizing Torah as the guide to illuminate and sanctify our lives, and ultimately to realizing "לתקן עולם במלכות ש־די": perfection of the entire world under the sovereignty of G-d. It is our prayer that *JEWISH THOUGHT: A Journal of Torah Scholarship* will help to advance this goal.

כי מציון תצא תורה, ודבר־ה' מירושלם:

Ch.Sh.E.
Tammuz, 5750
Yerushalayim

Jewish Thought is privileged to present to its readers an essay by Rav Yehoshua Bachrach. Hebrew-speaking students of the Tanach have derived immense benefit and pleasure from the works of Rav Bachrach for over two decades. As the esteemed author of several major works on Nach, his impact on study of the Tanach in Israel has been profound.

In order to appreciate fully Rav Bachrach's approach, it should be noted that Rav Bachrach was a student of the famous Yeshivah Sha'arei Torah of Grodno (headed by Rav Shimon Shkop, *z.tz.l.*) and other elite Lithuanian *yeshivoth*, before arriving in Eretz Yisra'el and studying in its hallowed institutions of Torah learning. As such, his approach to study of the Tanach is pre-eminently that of an erudite *talmid chacham.* Just as the Torah scholar develops his *chiddushim* in the realm of Halachah by attempting to consolidate his varied sources into a unified Halachic principle, so Rav Bachrach presents to the reader diverse Midrashic sources and proceeds to weave them carefully into a unified picture of the Tanach personality or event that he seeks to portray.

More precisely, however, Rav Bachrach presents his varied sources and then proceeds *to allow the reader* to weave them carefully into a unified picture. Rav Yehudah Copperman, in his foreword to *Mother of Royalty* (the English translation of Rav Bachrach's אמה של מלכות), summarizes Rav Bachrach's style:

> Bachrach does not attack his reader nor push nor force nor cajole him. He merely reads the verse again and again asking question after question, until the intelligent reader is forced to raise his hands in despair if he thinks to find satisfaction in grammar, history, or archaeological excavations. Bachrach leads the reader to the conclusion that, in order to understand *peshat* in its depth, one must of necessity have recourse to *derash*. *Derash*, as he presents it, seems the simple logical answer to the problems left unresolved.
>
> (Foreword to *Mother of Royalty*, Jerusalem: Feldheim, 1973, p. X)

Because of Rav Bachrach's unique style, the reader ought not to anticipate from him a typical scholarly essay, methodically appointed and thoroughly formulated. He should rather read along and think along with the author until they *both* arrive at the implied conclusions. To the uninitiated reader this role may appear daunting.

To facilitate the reader's task, explanatory headings and subheadings have been interpolated throughout the essay and many explanatory notes have been furnished in the end matter. These should help to clarify Rav Bachrach's intentions as he proceeds through the thicket of Midrash and commentaries. It is hoped that these emendations will assist the reader in joining with Rav Bachrach in his quest to elucidate the character and role of Elkanah, father of Shemu'el the prophet.

MIN HARAMATHAYIM TZOFIM:
Elkanah and the Sanctuary of Shiloh

Yehoshua Bachrach

The essay that follows is based upon the sources provided below:

There was one man	ויהי איש אחד
from Ramathayim Tzofim,	מן־הרמתים צופים,
from the hills of Efrayim,	מהר אפרים,
named Elkanah	ושמו אלקנה
son of Yerocham son of Elihu	בן־ירחם בן־אליהוא
son of Tochu son of Tzuf,	בן־תחו בן־צוף,
an Efrathi.	אפרתי:
And he had two wives,	ולו שתי נשים,
one named Channah,	שם אחת חנה,
and the second named Peninnah,	ושם השנית פננה,
and Peninnah had children,	ויהי לפננה ילדים,
and Channah was childless.	ולחנה אין ילדים:
And this man ascended from his city	ועלה האיש ההוא מעירו
year by year,	מימים ימימה,
to worship and sacrifice	להשתחות ולזבח
to the G-d of Hosts, in Shiloh,	לה' צבא־ות, בשלה,
and there the two sons of Eli,	ושם שני בני־עלי,
Chofni and Pinchas,	חפני ופנחס,
were priests of G-d.	כהנים, לה':

(Shemu'el I 1:1-3)

"*Min HaRamathayim Tzofim*" is based upon an essay first published in Hebrew by the author in *Peri HaAretz* (Jerusalem), vol. 1.

1. INTRODUCTION

We read in *Tanna DeVei Eliyahu*:

> Elkanah would go up to Shiloh four times a year: three times as enjoined by the Bible and once of his own volition.
>
> And he would take with him his wife and sons and daughters and brothers and sisters and all his relatives. And they would stop in cities along the way and spend the night in the city square, the men congregating alone and the women congregating alone (for men talk with men, women with women, adults with adults, and children with children). And the people of the province would be excited and ask them, "Where are you going?"
>
> And they would reply, "To the house of the L-rd in Shiloh, whence Torah and commandments and good deeds emanate. Why not join us? Let us go together!"
>
> Immediately the people would weep and say to them, "We will go up with you."
>
> Five households went up with him, the next year ten households, and the next year all were inspired to go up. And the route he traveled one year, he would not travel the next year, but an alternate route, until all of Yisra'el would go up.
>
> The Holy One Blessed be He, Who assesses man's innermost thoughts, said to Elkanah, "Elkanah, you have brought merit to Yisra'el and educated them in the commandments, and many have benefited because of you. Upon your life, I will give you a son who will bring merit to Yisra'el and educate them in the commandments, and many will benefit because of him." *Thus, we learn that the reward for Elkanah's deed was — Shemu'el.*
>
> (T.DeV.Eli.R. 8)

We have studied the first chapter of Sefer Shemu'el many times. It is the *haftarah* on the first day of Rosh HaShanah, following the Torah reading, "And G-d remembered Sarah" (BeReshith 21:1), for "on Rosh HaShanah, Sarah and Rachel and Channah were remembered" (*Rosh HaShanah* 10b). We have studied and read, but never did we perceive Elkanah as so central a figure, or of such stature, as depicted in *Tanna DeVei Eliyahu*. Perhaps we read the opening verses too cursorily, drawn to the interesting topics that follow: the sorrow of Channah, whose womb was closed by G-d, whose rival wife angered her so; the power of her whispered prayer, while Eli mistook her for a drunkard; her extraordinary vow in which she promised her son-to-be-born completely to G-d, for his entire life.

Chazal were more attentive and saw a broader issue here, preceding the story of Shemu'el's conception and birth and serving as background to it. This issue is the transformation wrought by Elkanah in preparing the people's hearts to love the sanctuary in Shiloh. Shemu'el, his son, then proceeded to prepare the people for the concept of a consolidated monarchy, and ultimately for the building of the Beith HaMikdash. Indeed, in order to understand Sefer Shemu'el, we must first attempt to fathom the magnitude of the transformation that this involved.

2. SEFER SHOFETIM AS PRELUDE TO SEFER SHEMU'EL

The Abandonment of Shiloh

In Sefer Shofetim, it did not seem that the sanctuary of Shiloh served as a center for the nation. Not a single judge gathered the nation there for prayer or sacrifice. On the contrary, there were numerous indications that the people who entered the Land forsook G-d's commandment to build the Beith HaMikdash. "The division of the Land was inordinately agreeable to them" (*Ru.R. Peth.*:2).[1] Therefore, all the generations of the judges were deemed as "one generation of utter nothingness" (*Babba Bathra* 15b). Consequently, the roads to Shiloh were mournfully untrodden. The text hints at this at the end of Sefer Shofetim, by noting numerous landmarks of the route to Shiloh: "North of Beith-El, east of the highway that rises from Beith-El to Shechem, and south of Levonah" (Shofetim 21:19).

> R. Yochanan b. Torta said: We have found that Shiloh was destroyed solely because the people desecrated the holidays and profaned the sacrifices [for they did not go up there for the pilgrimage festivals[2] (*Korban HaEidah*)].
>
> (*Yer. Yoma* 1:1 [4b])

> They regressed and betrayed, like their ancestors;
> they became like a bow of deceit.
> They angered Him with their private altars,
> and with their idols they would provoke Him to jealousy.
> The L-rd heard, and He was angered,
> and He was greatly disgusted with Yisra'el.

And He forsook the sanctuary of Shiloh,
the tent in which He dwelt among men.
(Tehillim 78:57-60)

The final chapters of Sefer Shofetim relate two solemn events, the idolatrous image of Michah and the concubine at Giv'ah, which indict the "bow of deceit" of all these generations.[3]

"Each man did as he saw fit."

In the case of both the idolatrous image of Michah and the concubine at Giv'ah, as preface and afterword, the prophet bemoans the absence of monarchy and Beith HaMikdash:

In those days, there was no king in Yisra'el;
each man did as he saw fit.
(Shofetim 17:6, 18:1, (19:1), 21:25)

The statement, "each man did as he saw fit," should not be taken literally, implying a general lawlessness. We find this phrase in the Bible once before, specifically in connection with the Beith HaMikdash and the sacrifices:

But to the place that G-d your L-rd
will choose of all your tribes, to place His name there,
you shall seek His residence and come there....
You should not do, as all we do here, today,
each man as he sees fit.
(Devarim 12:5,8)

Rashi explains:

When you cross the Yarden, you are immediately permitted to sacrifice on private altars for the entire fourteen year period of conquest and division [of the Land]. On private altars you may not sacrifice all that you sacrifice here today in the sanctuary which travels with you and is anointed, which alone is suitable for sacrifice of sin and trespass offerings, vows and voluntary offerings. On private altars only vows and voluntary offerings may be sacrificed. That is the meaning of *"each man as he sees fit"*: vows and voluntary offerings — which you volunteer as you see fit to bring and are not obligated to bring — these you shall sacrifice.
(Rashi on *Zevachim* 117b)

When, however, "they came to Shiloh [and the sanctuary was erected there], the private altars were proscribed" (*Zevachim* 112b).[4]

The idolatrous image of Michah is a symbol of the "bow of deceit," which originates with a forbidden private altar and terminates in idol worship, as a direct affront to the sanctuary.

> They maintained the idolatrous image of Michah, which he had made, all the time that the house of G-d was in Shiloh.
>
> (Shofetim 18:31)

> It has been taught, R. Nathan says: From Garev to Shiloh was a distance of three *mils* [Michah's image was located in Garev (Rashi)], and the smoke of the altar in the sanctuary and the smoke of Michah's image intermingled. This was the reason that the men involved in the concubine of Giv'ah incident were punished. The Holy One Blessed be He said to them, "For My honor you did not protest, but for the honor of flesh and blood you did protest?"
>
> (*Sanhedrin* 103b)

The idolatrous image of Michah was the sin of that generation, and the debacle of the Giv'ah incident was its consequence:

> Should you ask: why were those 70,000, who were killed at Giv'ah of Binyamin, killed? Because there was a Great Sanhedrin that Mosheh and Yehoshua and Pinchas the son of Elazar left with them. The members of the Sanhedrin should have girded their loins in iron and made preparations, and traveled to all the towns of Yisra'el: one day to Lachish, one day to Beith-El, one day to Chevron, one day to Yerushalayim, and so, over the course of a year or two or three, teach Yisra'el proper behavior, until Yisra'el would settle the Land, in order to glorify and sanctify the name of the Holy One Blessed be He throughout the world which He created, from one end of the world to the other. But they did not do so. Instead, when they entered their land, every one of them became involved with his vineyard and his wine and his field, indifferent to his fellows, in order to avoid any extra effort.
>
> (*T.DeV.Eli.R.* 11)

In dramatic contrast with this background of decadence and general torpor, we begin to appreciate the greatness of Elkanah as he emerges with his unique mission.

3. THE TRANSFORMATION WROUGHT BY ELKANAH

Elkanah's Mission

> For he will remember the days of his life, which were not many;
> for the L-rd will answer him, in his heart's joy.
>
> (Koheleth 5:19)

> *"For he will remember the days of his life, which were not many"* — This
> [refers to] the generation of Eli.
>
> *"For the L-rd will answer him, in his heart's joy"* — This [refers to]
> Elkanah, who would guide Yisra'el and bring them up to Shiloh by
> a different route each year.[5] Therefore Scripture distinguishes him:
> "There was *one man* from Ramathayim Tzofim."
>
> Another interpretation:
> Therefore Scripture *praises* him: "And this man *ascended* from his city."
>
> (Koh.R. 5:18, Ag. Shemu'el)

What basis did *Tanna DeVei Eliyahu* have for such an elabora-
tion on the story of Elkanah? Is all this implied in our chapter?
More properly, the Midrash perhaps implies to us how we
should study this chapter.

In the ascent of Elkanah and his family to Shiloh, we hear a
hymn of adoration for the house of G-d, a vivid portrayal of one
family's pilgrimage, the men and women, the sons and daugh-
ters and little ones: how they gather to eat from the sacrifice in
sanctity, how they come to pour out their hearts and their woe
before G-d, and how they make their vows there.

From this description we sense the transformation that Elkanah
and his family wrought in Yisra'el. This, then, provides the
introduction to Sefer Shemu'el, and to Shemu'el himself, who
created a unified nation in its land, in anticipation of the monarchy and the Beith HaMikdash.

"Thus, we learn that the reward for Elkanah's deed was — Shemu'el."

Indeed, we appreciate what a great reward Shemu'el represents. He is none other than the perpetuation of his father's deed.
For of Shemu'el it is said:

And he went year after year,
and made the rounds of Beith-El and Gilgal and Mitzpah;
and he served as judge for Yisra'el, in all these places.
And his return was to Ramah for there was his home....
(Shemu'el I 7:16-17)

R. Yochanan said: Every place he went, his home was there with him
[for everywhere he went, he would carry all his household utensils and
his tent with him, in order not to derive benefit from others (Rashi)].
(Berachoth 10b)

Longing for the Beith HaMikdash

In the description of Elkanah's efforts in *Tanna DeVei Eliyahu*,
we find all the elements of longing for the Beith HaMikdash —
that Elkanah ultimately instilled in the hearts of all Yisra'el —
that are set forth in the Torah and reiterated in the Nevi'im:

You shall seek His residence and come there.
(Devarim 12:5)

"You shall seek His residence" — This [refers to] the sanctuary of Shiloh.
(Rashi, ibid., citing *Sifrei*)

And the meaning of *"you shall seek His residence"* is that you should
set out from distant lands and ask, "Where is the route to the house
of G-d?" And one may say to the other, "Let us ascend to the
mountain of G-d, to the house of the L-rd of Ya'akov" (Yeshayahu
2:3). As in, "They shall seek Tziyyon; their faces will turn in that
direction" (Yirmeyahu 50:5).
(Ramban, ibid.)

Thus said the G-d of Hosts:
Nations and inhabitants of many cities will yet come.
The inhabitants of one will approach the other and say,
"Come let us go to entreat the favor of G-d
and seek the G-d of Hosts; I will go too."
(Zecharyah 8:20-21)

Compare, too, the procession of bringing up the First Fruits:

How were the First Fruits taken up? All the cities of the district would
gather in the [main] city of the district and spend the night in the square
of the city, without entering the homes. Early in the morning the official

would say, "Arise and let us ascend to Tziyyon, to G-d our L-rd"
(Yirmeyahu 31:5).

(Bikkurim 3:2)

"Therefore Scripture distinguishes him."

Chazal taught us to read the text attentively. Why is it written
this way and not otherwise? Why is it expanded here and abbre-
viated there? And why are seemingly redundant matters recorded? The scant verses about Elkanah distinguish and praise
him as expounded by Chazal, with allusions that are reminiscent
of the description in *Tanna DeVei Eliyahu*.

4. MIDRASHIC ANALYSIS OF THE TEXT

1:1. There was one man from Ramathayim Tzofim, etc.
(ויהי איש אחד מן־הרמתים צופים וכו')

> *"There was one man"* — Wherever *"one"* is said, greatness is implied,
> as in the case of Elkanah, where it says *"one man"*: in his generation
> there was no other like him.
>
> (BeM.R. 10:12)

> *"From Ramathayim Tzofim"* — R. Elazar says: There were two heights
> ["רמה" means "height"; "רמתים" is the plural]: one of David and one
> of Shemu'el.
>
> (Mid. Shemu'el, ibid.)

> [Elkanah was] one of two hundred seers ["רמתים" is expounded as
> "מאתים" ("two hundred"); "צופים" can mean "those who see"] who
> prophesied for Yisra'el.
>
> R. Shemu'el b. Nachmanei said: [Elkanah was] a man who comes
> from two heights ["רמתים" meaning "heights"] which face [lit. see,
> from "צופים," meaning "see"] one another.
>
> R. Chanan said: [Elkanah was] one who is descended from men who
> stand at the height ["רומו," from "רמה"] of the world. And who are
> these? [These are] the sons of Korach.[6]
>
> (Megillah 14a)

To this Scripture referred:
"What my soul sought and I did not find; one man in a thousand I found"
(Koheleth 7:28). — To what does this refer? When the Holy One

Blessed be He sees that a generation is culpable, He searches once more to find even a single righteous man, for whose sake He will suspend [judgment]. Why? For one righteous man supports the world on his foundation, as Shelomoh says, "When the storm passes, the wicked man is no more, but the righteous man is the world's foundation" (Mishlei 10:25).

They sinned in the days of Michah and burned incense to the idolatrous image of Michah. And the smoke of [the sanctuary at] Shiloh rose from sacrifices to G-d, and the smoke of the image of Michah rose from the hills of Efrayim, from the house of Michah. And they intermingled, as it is written, "smoke arose in His nose" (Tehillim 18:9). And afterwards He found Elkanah, *one man*: *"There was one man."*

(Ag. BeReshith 49a)

The verse citing Elkanah's lineage is perceptibly lengthy. It is best to read it immediately after the opening verses of the last two stories in Sefer Shofetim, which serve as an epilogue for that wicked generation[7] in which "each man did as he saw fit [lit. did what was upright *in his eyes*]." And let us preface this with the opening of the story of Shimshon, "who followed *his eyes*" (*Mish. Sotah* 1:8) — "for she is right *in my eyes*" (Shofetim 14:3). Introducing the story of Shimshon, we read:

There was one man from Tzor'ah from the family of the Dani named Manoach.

(Shofetim 13:2)

Introducing the story of the idolatrous image of Michah, we read:

There was a man from the hills of Efrayim named Michayehu.

(ibid. 17:1)

Introducing the story of the concubine at Giv'ah, we read:

There was a man of Levi living on the far side of the hills of Efrayim.

(ibid. 19:1)

Finally, in contrast, introducing the story of Elkanah, we read:

There was one man from Ramathayim Tzofim, from the hills of Efrayim, named Elkanah son of Yerocham son of Elihu son of Tochu son of Tzuf, an Efrathi.

Recall also that the text tells of two Levis who abused their place in the house of G-d in Shiloh, whereas Elkanah, a Levi as well (Divrei HaYamim I 6:1-13), aroused his generation to love the house of G-d.

> The memory of the righteous will be for a blessing,
> and the name of the wicked will rot.
>
> (Mishlei 10:7)

R. Shimon said: Mention and praise; mention and efface [the root "זכר" in different conjugations can mean either "זכר" ("memory") or "להזכיר" ("to mention")]:

"Mention and efface," as in, "There was a man from the hills of Efrayim named Michayehu."

"Mention and praise," as in, "There was one man from Ramathayim Tzofim, from the hills of Efrayim, named Elkanah."

(VaY.R. 32:6, Mid. Shemu'el 1:4)

Another interpretation:
"One man in a thousand I found" (Koheleth ibid.) — This [refers to] Avraham. It was foreseen that one thousand generations would arise preceding Avraham, as David says, "The word He commanded to a thousand generations with which He wrought a covenant with Avraham" (Tehillim 105:8-9). And since He saw that there was no benefit to be derived from them since all were wicked, He condensed them into twenty generations. And then He created Avraham. Therefore it is said, *"One man in a thousand I found"* — [I] found "the man great among the giants"[8] (Yehoshua 14:15).

Elkanah too was a single righteous man in his generation, and all his deeds resemble Avraham's.

Avraham was called a man, as it is written, "And now return the *man's* wife" (BeReshith 20:7). And of Elkanah it is written, "There was one *man.*"

Avraham was called a prophet, as it is said, "for he is a *prophet*" (ibid.). And Elkanah is called a prophet, as it is said, "A *man of G-d* came to Eli"[9] (Shemu'el I 2:27).

Avraham attributed heaven and earth to the Holy One Blessed be He, as it is written, "Blessed be Avram to the Supreme G-d, *Possessor of heaven and earth*" (BeReshith 14:19). And Elkanah attributed heaven and earth to the Holy One Blessed be He, as it is said, "named *Elkanah*" [expounded here as קנה + א-ל ("G-d possessed")].

Avraham was called "one," as it is written, "Avraham was *one*"

(Yechezkel 33:24). And Elkanah was called "one," as it is written, "There was *one* man."

(Ag. BeReshith, ibid.)

Another interpretation:

"*There was one man*" — To this Scripture refers in saying, "For My thoughts are not your thoughts" (Yeshayahu 55:8). The attributes of G-d are unlike the attributes of flesh and blood. In the case of flesh and blood, no one may use his [the king's] scepter nor ride his steed nor be called "Augustus" as he is. But the Holy One Blessed be He is not like this; He is not jealous of His creatures.

Said the Holy One Blessed be He:

"I have a scepter; when will Mosheh come and use it?" As it is said, "And Mosheh took *the staff of the L-rd* in his hand" (Shemoth 4:20).

"My steed is a whirlwind, as it is written, 'G-d's path is in storm and whirlwind' (Nachum 1:3); let Eliyahu come and ride in it." As it is said, "When G-d took Eliyahu up to heaven *in the whirlwind*" (Melachim II 2:1).

"[Regarding] My throne, let Shelomoh come and sit upon it." As it is said, "Shelomoh sat *on the throne of G-d* as king" (Divrei HaYamim I 29:23).

"[Regarding] My name, as it is said, 'Hear, O Yisra'el ... G-d is One' (Devarim 6:4), let Elkanah the righteous come and be so called." As it is said, "*There was one man.*"

(Ag. BeReshith ibid.)

Son of Tochu (בן־תחו)

R. Yochanan said: In numerology [*gimatrikon*, in which the first letter of the *aleph-beith* is exchanged with the last, etc.], Tochu is Asaf.[10]

(Yal.Sh. 77)

An Efrathi (אפרתי)

"*Is Efrayim my dear son*" (Yirmeyahu 31:19) —

R. Yehoshua b. Levi said: Noble [important and honored as the son of royalty].

R. Yehoshua b. Nachman said: Honorable [of distinguished lineage].

"An Efrathi" —

R. Yehoshua says: Noble [that he is an honored and important man].

R. Yehudah b. Pinchas said: Courteous.

R. Nachman said: Honorable [of distinguished lineage].

R. Pinchas said: Efrayim was crowned with this crown by our father Ya'akov on his deathbed. He said to him, "My son Efrayim! Leader of the *yeshivah*, leader of a tribe, superior and praiseworthy of my children, let him be called by your name: [Elkanah was the son of Yerocham son of Elihu] 'son of Tochu son of Tzuf, *an Efrathi*'; 'David was the son of *an Efrathi man*' (Shemu'el I 17:12)."[11]

(*Yal.Sh. 77, VaY.R. 2:3*)

1:3. And this man ascended from his city year by year
(ועלה האיש ההוא מעירו מימים ימימה)

The man was honored in his home; the man was honored in his city, honored throughout Yisra'el. And all his honors were on his own account.

(*Mid. Shemu'el*, ibid.)

The words "from his city," seemingly superfluous, hint at the ascension of Elkanah and all his household, which made an impression upon his city and thence upon all Yisra'el. Similarly, Rashi adduces from the otherwise superfluous words, "Ya'akov left Beersheva" (BeReshith 28:10), that "the departure of a righteous person from a certain place leaves an impression" (Rashi ibid.; see also *BeR.R. 68:7*).

Year by year [lit. days by days]
(מימים ימימה)

Targum translates, *"from one holiday to the next."* And the literal meaning appears to be *"from one year to the next."* It seems that he had vowed to ascend there every year, he and his family, to sacrifice there, in addition to the three [mandatory] pilgrimage festivals. For on the three pilgrimage festivals, the men are obligated and not the women. As it says, *"The man Elkanah ascended with his entire household to offer the annual sacrifice and his votive sacrifice to G-d"* (Shemu'el I 1:21).

(R. Yeshayah of Terani)[12]

The phrase "מימים ימימה" (here trans. "year by year") is cited in the Torah with regard to Pesach: "You shall keep this statute in its season *year by year* (מימים ימימה)" (Shemoth 13:10). The language implies loving anticipation. Thus, the Torah (ibid.) also employs the term "ושמרת" ("you shall keep"), which implies anticipation; it is used comparably regarding Ya'akov: "His father *kept the matter in mind* (שמר את הדבר)" (BeReshith 37:11), that is, "was *awaiting and anticipating* its fulfillment" (Rashi ibid.). Similarly, the Torah instructs us: "*Keep* (שמור) *the season of spring*, and make Pesach to G-d your L-rd" (Devarim 16:1). Through this, the Torah endears Pesach to us: we are to anticipate it as we anticipate the spring season. Therefore, it is also written regarding Pesach, "מימים ימימה," meaning "year by year" but literally "days by days," that we should consider the year as merely a few days, due to our love for this holiday.

We first learn that "מימים ימימה" means "year by year" from Rashi's commentary on the verse, "And her brother and her mother said, 'Let the young woman [Rivkah] sit with us *days or ten* (ימים או עשור)'" (BeReshith 24:55). Explains Rashi (ibid.), "'Days' (ימים) [means] 'a year,' as in, 'He may redeem it within *the year* (ימים)' [where 'ימים' appears as analogue to 'שנת ממכרו' ('the year of sale'), indicating that 'ימים' likewise means 'year'] (VaYikra 25:29)." Rivkah's brother and mother want Rivkah to stay with them for "ימים" ("one year"), but if this is difficult for Eli'ezer, they would reduce the period to "עשור" ("ten months"). And they diminish the year, as it were, by calling it "ימים" (lit. "days"). Similarly, in the chapter on redemption by the original owner of a sold house in a walled city (VaYikra ibid.), where the owner awaits redeeming his property, the entire year of his sale is referred to as "ימים" (lit. "days").[13] Here, too, Scripture did well to invest Elkanah's ascents with loving anticipation: "מימים ימימה," literally, "days by days."

And there the two sons of Eli, Chofni and Pinchas, were priests, of G-d.
(ושם שני בני-עלי, חפני ופנחס, כהנים, לה':)

Here again, the verse emphasizes the praise of Elkanah, albeit indirectly. Otherwise, what purpose would there be in supplying this additional information at the close of such a long and full passage? If it were important to notify us who the priests in

Shiloh were at this time, it would have made sense to mention Eli himself, especially since he will be discussed in this chapter. Why does the text inform us only of his sons, who are scoundrels? R. Yitzchak Abbarbanel interprets this to Elkanah's credit as well:

> [This is stated] to show us that even though Chofni and Pinchas, the two sons of Eli, were at the sanctuary, and took the sacrifice by force, as stated below ["And the sons of Eli were scoundrels, they did not acknowledge G-d" (Shemu'el I 2:12)], Elkanah did not refrain from coming there year after year to worship and sacrifice. For he was concerned about worship of the L-rd, Blessed be He, and not fearful of the corruption of the priests, in his great righteousness.

> (ibid.)

5. CONCLUSION: A TALE

The following tale is related by the Apter Rav:[14]

> One day, I realized that from the heavens they were not obeying me. I was discouraged and saddened. Still distressed, I saw that the earth was not listening to me, and not the earth alone, but all the towns in the vicinity of my city were not obeying me, and even the people of my city were not listening to me, and even the people of my household were not listening to me. I began to study the matter and did not cease until I had restored my wife's heart to me. Once my wife began to obey me, my son began to obey me. And once my son began to obey me, all the members of my household began to obey me. And once the members of my household were obeying me, the entire city began to obey me. And once my city obeyed me, all the other cities and places obeyed me. And once all the cities and places were obeying me, the earth listened to me once more. And once the earth listened to me, from the heavens they listened to me.

How well this tale summarizes the mechanics of the transformation wrought by Elkanah in the midst of Yisra'el. Indeed, what is implied in the scant verses that describe a family pilgrimage is the dedication that ultimately transformed the entire nation.

In the light of his selfless dedication to the sacred mission of uniting the nation of Yisra'el in its devotion to the G-d of Yisra'el and His sanctuary, we begin to comprehend Elkanah's pivotal role in linking the epoch of the judges with the epoch of his son, Shemu'el. Elkanah initiated and epitomized the evolution of the nation of Yisra'el from the spiritual and political fragmentation of Sefer Shofetim to the emergence of a unified monarchy and the erection of the Beith HaMikdash in Sefer Shemu'el and beyond. The content of Sefer Shemu'el is, in a sense, implied in its opening verses, for the transformation wrought by Shemu'el, about which Sefer Shemu'el revolves, was initiated by his righteous father, "one man from Ramathayim Tzofim, from the hills of Efrayim, named Elkanah."

"Thus, we learn that the reward for Elkanah's deed was — Shemu'el."

— Eds.

NOTES

1. *Ed. note:* This is perhaps an allusion to the licensed use of private altars during the period of division of the Land, an institution that the nation found so "inordinately agreeable" that it persisted for centuries even after it was proscribed. (See Melachim II 23:5-20 and Divrei HaYamim II 33:17 for indications of the prevalence of private altars — in spite of repeated attempts by the prophets and righteous kings to eradicate them — even at the end of the period of the first Beith HaMikdash.) As epitomized by the idolatrous image of Michah (see text below), the obsession with private altars and the consequent abandonment of Shiloh were among the principal degenerative forces that afflicted the period of the judges.

2. *Ed. note:* See *Korban HaEidah* commentary, ibid., who continues, "... for they did not go up there for the pilgrimage festivals [as demonstrated] by *Elkanah having to circulate among the cities of Yisra'el to instruct them to go up for the pilgrimage festivals.*" (Emphasis eds.)

3. *Ed. note:* It should be appreciated that, according to many commentaries, these episodes — the idolatrous image of Michah and the concubine at Giv'ah — did not occur chronologically at the end of the period of the judges, but at the beginning of this period. (See Rashi, Radak, and Ralbag on Shofetim 17:1.) Especially according to this perspective, the unchronological recording of these events and the conspicuously inconclusive ending of Sefer Shofetim are specifically intended to epitomize the period of the judges and provide background for Sefer Shemu'el. (See Radak, ibid. 21:25.)

4. *Ed. note:* Private altars were explicitly cited in Tehillim 78:58 (see text above) as one of the critical acts of betrayal by Yisra'el that precipitated the destruction of Shiloh (ibid. 60). The proscription, as demonstrated by the idolatrous image of Michah (see text below), was not universally observed. Indeed, this violation persisted as a principal corruption of the nation throughout the period of the first Beith HaMikdash. (See n. 1 above.)

5. *Ed. note:* Specifically in contradistinction to the indifference and inertia of the members of the Sanhedrin that were so indicted by the Midrash (see *T.Dev.Eli.R.* 11, quoted in text above), Elkanah's circulation among Yisra'el is especially

significant. This is particularly highlighted in the Scriptural and Midrashic description of his son, Shemu'el, who, in his role as judge, specifically "made the rounds" (Shemu'el I 7:16), throughout all Yisra'el (see text below).

6. *Ed. note:* Elkanah's descent from the sons of Korach is explicit in Divrei HaYamim I 6:7-13. It is noteworthy that one of the sons of Korach was also named Elkanah (Shemoth 6:24, Divrei HaYamim I 6:8). The sons of Korach figure among the ten authors of Tehillim. (See Tehillim 42, 44-48, 84, and 87, and various references in Divrei HaYamim. See also *Babba Bathra* 15a and n. 10 below.)

7. *Ed. note:* See Radak on Shofetim 21:25 (see n. 3 above).

8. *Ed. note:* This verse is understood by Chazal as a reference to Avraham. (See *Yer. Shabbath* 16:1 [46a], *Sofrim* 16 and 21, and numerous Midrashic references.)

9. *Ed. note:* This verse is understood by Chazal as a reference to Elkanah. (See *Sifrei* on Devarim 33:1, *Yal.Sh.* Devarim:951 and Shemu'el:91, and Rashi on *Megillah* 14a, ד"ה נבואה שהוצרכה לדורות. See also commentaries on the verse.)

10. *Ed. note:* Asaf was a Levi musician who was one of the ten authors of Tehillim. (See Tehillim 50 and 73-83, and various references in Ezra, Nechemiah, and Divrei HaYamim. See also *Babba Bathra* 14b and Rashi, ibid., ד"ה על ידי עשרה זקנים.) It is possible that the Midrashic association of Tochu with Asaf was mandated because of the absence of the name Tochu in the genealogy of Elkanah listed in Divrei HaYamim I 6:7-13. It is noteworthy that a tradition associating Asaf with Avi'asaf, the son of Korach, is recorded in the *Tosafoth* (in com. on *Babba Bathra* 15a, ד"ה ועל ידי שלמה ועל ידי בני קרח). (See n. 6 above.)

11. *Ed. note:* The Midrashic sources cited are constrained to interpret "Efrathi" as a character label (and not as a genealogical identity) because both Elkanah and David are called "Efrathi" and neither is descended from the tribe of Efrayim. (Elkanah is from the tribe of Levi, and David is from the tribe of Yehudah.) Compare Chazal's treatment of the analogous problem presented by Mordechai, who is called "Yehudi" but is described as descended from the tribe of Binyamin. (See Ester 2:5 and *Megillah* 13a, *Est.R.* 6:2.)

12. It is possible that this fourth voluntary pilgrimage took place on Rosh HaShanah. For according to the *Zohar*, it seems that Channah's prayer was offered on Rosh HaShanah:

> "*And on the day*" (Shemu'el I 1:4) — [This means] a day with sadness, and this is Rosh HaShanah: a day of harsh judgment, as in the story of the Shunammith (Melachim II 4:18) and of Iyyov (Iyyov 1:6).
>
> (*Zohar*, III, 231)

Note also that in the *Shulchan Aruch*, in the laws of Rosh HaShanah, regarding the law that "we eat and drink and are happy, and do not fast, on Rosh HaShanah" (*Orach Chayyim* 597:1), the *Be'er Heitev* commentary (ibid.)

notes, "This seems to be corroborated by Channah and Elkanah the prophet, who ate on Rosh HaShanah." This gives us another good reason for reading this chapter as the *haftarah* on Rosh HaShanah.

13. *Ed. note:* We find a similar usage in which the Torah explicitly describes years as "days" in characterizing the seven years of loving anticipation in which Ya'akov toiled for Lavan in order to marry Rachel: "Ya'akov worked for Rachel seven years, and they were in his eyes *like a few days* because of his love for her" (BeReshith 29:20).

14. See S.Y. Agnon, *The Fire and the Kindling.*

JUDGMENT ON ROSH HASHANAH:
Analysis of Content and
Process in a Talmudic Aggadah

Beryl Gershenfeld

The essay that follows is based upon the source provided below:

At four intervals the world is judged:	באַרבעה פרקים העולם נדון:
on Pesach, [the world is judged] regarding produce;	בפסח, על התבואה;
on Shavu'oth, [the world is judged] regarding fruit;	בעצרת, על פירות האילן;
on Rosh HaShanah, all mankind pass before Him like *benei maron*, as it is said, "He Who formed [them], [sees] their hearts together and understands all their actions;"[1]	בראש השנה, כל באי העולם עוברין לפניו כבני מרון, שנאמר, היוצר יחד לבם, המבין אל־כל־מעשיהם;

RABBI GERSHENFELD is one of the founders of Yerushalayim's Machon Shlomo - Heiden Institute. He is a member of the faculty of Neve Yerushalayim Seminary and of the summer faculty of the Torah Institute in Moodus, Connecticut. He wrote this essay לעלוי נשמת אביו ר משה אהרן בן ר יהודה אריה ז"ל

and on Sukkoth, [the world]   ובחג,
  is judged regarding water.   נדונין על המים.

(*Mishnah Rosh HaShanah* 1:2)

---

1. INTRODUCTION

Reading this *mishnah* awakens one's memories of Rosh HaShanahs past. Hearts and minds associate the *mishnah*'s image of *"benei maron,"* usually translated as "sheep," with Rosh HaShanah's stirring *"UNthanneh Tokef"* prayer:

> Let us relate the force of this day's holiness for it is awesome and terrifying.... *All mankind pass before You like benei maron....* As a shepherd examines his flock, passing each sheep beneath his rod, so do You pass, count, enumerate, and recall every living soul.
> (Repetition of *"Musaf"* on Rosh HaShanah and Yom Kippur)

We are touched and inspired. But our familiarity with the *mishnah* blunts our critical, inquisitive nature. Satisfied with our facile understanding, we proceed to the next *mishnah*.

Such a response is inappropriate to the intricacies of Mishnaic style. The words of the Sages are "like golden apples in mesh casings of silver" (Mishlei 25:11): from afar one sees the valuable silver, but the essential value of the golden interior is discovered only when one carefully peers through the external casings.[2] Only in the depths of the text will one discover the essential philosophical truths that are concealed within it.[3] We must therefore analyze this *mishnah* more thoroughly to understand Rosh HaShanah and the nature of the judgment of man on this day.

2. KEYS TO UNDERSTANDING THE LANGUAGE OF CHAZAL

Difficulties Raised by the Mishnah

Studying the *mishnah*, one immediately notes both its lack of parallelism and its extraordinary emphasis on Rosh HaShanah. After stating that on Pesach, the world is judged regarding produce and on Shavu'oth, the world is judged regarding fruit, one expects the literary form to continue with the succinct characterization that on Rosh HaShanah, the world is judged regarding man. Instead, there is an abrupt shift and the *mishnah* interjects "on Rosh Hashanah all mankind pass before Him like *benei maron*." Why does the *mishnah* abruptly shift its form? Furthermore, why does it select the obscure nomenclature, "*benei maron*"? Indeed, what does this term signify? Finally, why is a verse cited only with regard to Rosh HaShanah's judgment and not with regard to the other judgments enumerated in the *mishnah*? Far from irrelevant, these questions represent the "mesh casings of silver" through which we can peer to discover the hidden golden interior of the *mishnah*. They are hints from R. Yehudah HaNasi, the redactor of the Mishnah, to proceed cautiously and consider carefully the meaning of these words, for one senses that in these succinct terms the uniqueness of Rosh HaShanah is implied.

Probing the *mishnah*, the Talmud seeks a more precise definition for the crucial and obscure phrase "*benei maron*":

> What does "like *benei maron*" (כבני מרון) mean? Here we translate (תרגימו) "like a flock of sheep (כבני אמרנא)." Reish Lakish says: [It means] "like the ascent to Beith Maron (כמעלות בית מרון)." R. Yehudah says in the name of Shemu'el: [It means] "like the troops of the house of David ['מרון' related to 'מרות,' meaning sovereignty and lordship (Rashi)].

> *(Rosh HaShanah 18a)*

The Talmud's analysis appears to compound our difficulties. Why did R. Yehudah HaNasi employ such an ambiguous term that could justify so many opinions? Moreover, why did he employ a metaphor altogether, rather than stating explicitly that men pass before G-d one at a time? Finally, are Chazal only debating semantics, or do the various explanations of "*benei maron*" represent distinct perceptions of the day of judgment?

Our initial emotional response to the *mishnah's* graphic description of man passing before G-d like sheep is now superseded by intellectual wonder. Clearly, the essence of Rosh HaShanah is hidden in words too cryptic and subtle for us to grasp their meaning through cursory study. Before we begin to grapple with these textual difficulties, we must first understand the literary form through which Chazal chose to express their philosophy: the world of Aggadah.

Aggadah as a Distinct Medium

One cannot understand Aggadah with only the techniques of Halachic analysis, because Aggadah differs from Halachah not only in content (nonlegal versus legal) but also in form. The complexity of Aggadah caused Chazal to adopt a distinct mode of expression. Halachic discussions are explicitly detailed, while Aggadoth are written in subtle hints and riddles that conceal their essence.[4] Ramchal states:

> It is inappropriate that the esoteric dimension of Torah be transmitted [like the Halachic dimension] before anyone who wishes to seize it, both out of deference to the value of the concepts [involved] and because of their depth.... In consideration of their depth ... only those who are pure of mind and well learned in the ways of investigative analysis will succeed in mastering them. If a boorish or unlearned mind were to chance upon them, these true and valuable concepts would be perverted into errors and bad ideas. Therefore, while the Sages concluded that these concepts must be transcribed to prevent their being lost from later generations, [they transcribed them] in concealed ways and various riddles that would be incomprehensible except by those to whom the [oral] keys had been handed. These keys are the principles through which the allusions may be understood and the riddles elucidated.
>
> (Ma'amar al Aggadoth Chazal)

Sublime religious truths are meaningful only if one is sufficiently refined and learned to understand them correctly and integrate them properly into one's life.[5] To protect the uninitiated and to preserve the glory of G-d's Torah, these complex ideas were intimated in the subtle hints called Aggadah.[6]

As Ramchal warns, comprehension of Aggadah is impossible without the necessary "keys." To plumb the depths of Aggadah, one must learn from a mentor who possesses the keys to unlock Chazal's allusions and riddles. Our guide to this *mishnah* will be Maharal,[7] who is recognized as one of the classic expositors of Aggadah.[8]

Rosh HaShanah and the Purpose of Creation

The key to understanding our *mishnah* lies in Rosh HaShanah's selection as G-d's day of judgment. On Rosh HaShanah G-d completed His creation by forming man. Every year, on the anniversary of man's creation, G-d investigates to determine if man has fulfilled his purpose in creation.[9] But what, we may ask, is the purpose of man's creation?

This issue pierces the essence of existence; its complexity has inspired debate for generations. Is man's task to express creatively his own individuality, or is his purpose to sublimate his particular identity by submissively following G-d's commands? Is he to transcend his individual vision by identifying himself as a part of a broader community? Without answers to these classic questions, we cannot comprehend the judgment of Rosh HaShanah. We would stand before G-d without understanding the case against us; our defense would be haphazard and confused.

3. THE FIRST PERSPECTIVE: "LIKE A FLOCK OF SHEEP"

Man as a Follower with Common Obligations

The metaphor of a flock of sheep in relation to their shepherd suggests that man is judged by a single set of objective criteria. A shepherd does not require each animal to express unique individual strengths. He has only uniform tests for his flock: Are they healthy enough to walk to market? Are they heavy enough to be sold for meat? Specifically the metaphor of sheep (as opposed to another species) is employed because Chazal note that the nature of sheep is to follow faithfully.[10] While goats stray and make their own paths, sheep do not. The analogy to man is clear. Man was created with a uniform societal goal. He is not expected to express his unique personality or creative energies; his task is solely to follow the wise commands of G-d. What is deemed essential about mankind is not diversity but similarity. Everyone is endowed with the same 248 organs with which to fulfill the same 248 positive *mitzvoth*.[11]

From this perspective, man's role is to conduct himself in faithful harmony with G-d's will as it is manifest through Torah and *mitzvoth*. To prepare for Rosh HaShanah, one will seek to be more scrupulous in observing the mitzvoth, to follow G-d's "lead" more faithfully. Instead of seeking to express individuality, one will strive to discharge the uniform task of functioning as a good human being by obediently fulfilling G-d's commands.

While this analysis sheds some light on the mishnah, problems clearly remain. Why did the mishnah elaborate concerning the judgment of man? In addition, why did R. Yehudah HaNasi not state explicitly that mankind is judged like sheep? Why did he employ the cryptic phrase "כבני מרון," which is only vaguely related to the Aramaic "כבני אמרנא" ("like sheep")?

"These and those are the words of the Living G-d."

To respond to these difficulties a major axiom of Talmudic study must be introduced. Chazal state that when alternate opinions are expressed in Aggadah and the debate is not resolved, we conclude that "these and those are the words of the Living G-d" (Gittin 6b).[12] To comprehend Aggadah properly, one must recognize that all the opinions recorded contain aspects of truth. Before we proceed, further clarification of this principle is necessary.

One approach to harmonizing disparate opinions in Aggadah is to perceive them as varied facets of the same reality.[13] For example, imagine three viewers analyzing a book's exterior. One sees its front and describes the gold letters, one sees the back and states that there is just a blank cover, and a third viewer perceives the book from the side and describes the white pages. While no view is complete, none is wrong. Only by adding together all three perspectives can one properly understand the reality of the book.

A second approach to resolving conflicting opinions in Aggadah is to organize them as increasingly exact analytic formulations.[14] One opinion is a simple approximation that provides general insight. The second opinion is a more complex reiteration of the same idea that clarifies the subject matter more precisely by adding additional factors. The relationship between classical (Newtonian) physics and the theory of relativity (which offers a more precise approximation for the behavior of exceptionally fast-moving bodies by including relativistic effects) provides a useful analogy to this second approach.

The form of the Talmud's discussion of our mishnah appears characteristic of the second approach. The Talmud indicates this by introducing as the first explanation of *"benei maron"* the Aramaic translation — the *targum* — of the *mishnah*.[15] Targum, in its classic sense as the Aramaic translation of Scripture, expresses the simple understanding of the verse, enabling even the common unlearned man to grasp the basic meaning of the text.[16] Because of the limited intellectual sophistication of the audience, the exact meaning of the text with all of its nuances and connotations is not preserved.[17] Similarly, the first explanation of the *mishnah* is only its *targum* — its approximate translation. It does not resolve all of the essential problems in the text. To understand the text more precisely, we must analyze it more carefully and probe thoroughly the philosophical concepts involved.

4. THE SECOND PERSPECTIVE: "LIKE THE ASCENT TO BEITH MARON"

Man as a Unique Individual

To perceive men as interchangeable, having common divine obligations without individual distinctions, is too simplistic a vision to define the nature of man adequately. In fact, the greatness of G-d's creation is the uniqueness of every individual. The Mishnah states:

> Therefore man was created singly ... to proclaim the greatness of the Holy One Blessed be He: A person forms many coins with the same mold, and they all resemble one another. But the Supreme King, the Holy One Blessed be He, formed every man with the mold of the first man, yet not one of them resembles his fellow. Therefore, every single person is obligated to say, "For me the world was created."
> (*Mish. Sanhedrin* 4:5)[18]

Each man is unique and, therefore, must recognize that he has a special task in life that he alone can fulfill.[19] Man is obligated to recognize his individuality and the responsibility that it entails; he is obligated to say, "For me the world was created."

To view oneself as part of a flock in which only the group is significant and not the individual — the first explanation offered by the Gemara — is to diminish the greatness of G-d's creation and man's responsibility. Chazal set out to supplant this vision of a flock by emphasizing the uniqueness of each individual:

"One who sees a massive group of Jews should say, 'Blessed is He [G-d] Who knows the wisdom [in the heart of each individual (Rashi)]'; for their minds do not resemble one another nor do their faces resemble one another" (*Berachoth* 58a). In observing a large group of Jews one should not see a homogeneous mass: one should perceive the diversity and uniqueness of the individuals of which it is composed.

The second interpretation of *"benei maron"* in the Gemara — "like the ascent to Beith Maron" — embodies this more sophisticated vision of man's creation. The ascent to Beith Maron, narrowly winding through the mountains, was a famous landmark in Talmudic times. In Talmudic literature, "the ascent to Beith Maron" is used as the paradigm for a road traversable by only one person at a time.[20] As an explanation for *"benei maron,"* it expresses the individuality of G-d's judgment: that "all mankind pass before Him" *one at a time.* Unlike a shepherd who surveys his flock of sheep together relative to a uniform standard, an observer on the road to Beith Maron inspects each person separately as he files past. Likewise, G-d judges every person individually, in accordance with the principle of individual uniqueness. Each human being has his own special potential to develop, relative to which he is individually judged.[21] In contributing this second interpretation of *"benei maron,"* Reish Lakish also replaces the original subject of the metaphor — sheep — with a road traversed by *human beings*, implicitly emphasizing this additional human factor.

Recognition of individual uniqueness and G-d's individualized judgment will stimulate man to identify his own special capabilities in anticipation of Rosh HaShanah. Merely studying Torah and heeding G-d's commandments more diligently will not suffice. Man must introspect and apply his unique skills to each deed that he performs.[22] He will have to be sensitive to his intellectual inclinations, emotional responses, and physical needs. Indeed, nothing less than his unique worth must be discovered and actualized. He cannot copy other men — even great men — but must seek to sanctify G-d with his own unique heart and soul.[23]

This challenge confronts man in all arenas of expression. When one sits before a Gemara engrossed in study, one is not simply partaking of a routine deed already undertaken by countless Jews throughout history. It is a unique act, because one's own mind, shaped by one's particular milieu, is called upon to grapple with G-d's wisdom. We must strive to find our own special potential in Torah.[24] One's unique portion contains ideas that one can teach to the entire world; one's judgment on Rosh HaShanah must then depend on how faithfully one has expressed these crucial ideas. In a similar fashion, all of one's endeavors in life (e.g., prayer, mode of livelihood, and acts of charity) should reflect the unique capabilities and sensitivities that G-d has implanted within him.[25]

From this perspective, the lack of parallelism in the *mishnah* is understandable. The uniqueness of man is reflected in the uniqueness of man's judgment. Had the *mishnah* merely continued its literary form and stated that on Rosh HaShanah, the world is judged regarding man, this essential distinction of the role of man in creation would have been lost. The Gemara alludes to this implication in the *mishnah* by the shift in metaphor from a flock of *sheep* to a narrow path upon which *men walk singly*. While the *targum* provides a first approximation for explaining the *mishnah*, only by probing more thoroughly the nature of man through the insight of Reish Lakish does the deeper meaning of the text become evident. The anomalies of the *mishnah*, at first so mystifying, intimate its rich meaning.

The Dangers of Individual Creativity

Yet several difficulties still remain. According to Reish Lakish, why did the *mishnah* choose the ambiguous term, *"benei maron"*? Why did it not state explicitly, "G-d judges each man individually"? In addition, why did the Gemara first explain the *mishnah* according to the *targum* and not according to Reish Lakish's more sophisticated perspective?

In response to these questions, we note Ramchal's explanation that Chazal purposely expressed their ideas in the Aggadic form of hints and riddles because they realized that complex concepts are often misinterpreted and misapplied by the masses. Chazal feared that if they explicitly emphasized that man's judgment on Rosh HaShanah assesses his actualization of his own creative individuality, many errant notions and responses would develop. The Mishnah therefore opted to couch this idea in ambiguity. Similarly, the Gemara, in explaining the *mishnah*, initially provided a simple interpretation appropriate for the common man: "like sheep," emphasizing man's collective, uniform obligations to serve and heed G-d.

Why did Chazal avoid stressing the importance of man's individuality? They recognized that such emphasis would engender a lack of appreciation of both traditional, received knowledge and the need for uniform actions. Man would fail to recognize that such means are necessary in order to achieve the goal of true individuality. Indeed, if a person begins life by searching for creativity and individuality, he usually accomplishes little. Imagine, for example, an individual attempting to create modern physics without any recourse to the last millennia of scientific development. The sensible approach is for him first to study the accumulated scientific tradition of his predecessors and then to apply his own creativity to unsolved problems. R. Bachyei b. Pekudah notes that this confusion of goals and means applies equally in the religious sphere. For example, while personalized rational knowledge of G-d (the goal) is qualitatively better than accepted traditional knowledge (the means), one can rarely achieve the higher level without first integrating the more elementary level.[26] One must train and discipline one's mind before one can successfully seek creative expression.

Chazal recognized that emphasis on individuality may lead to mediocrity, because untrained minds tend to overlook the necessary preconditions of acceptance and discipline. To avoid such misunderstanding, the Mishnah did not explicitly state this rarefied goal of individuality but alluded to it in an ambiguous term that suggests two distinct facets. The initial understanding of *"benei maron,"* "like sheep," is the simple first step a person should seek to attain by recognizing his common obligations. The second more refined meaning, "like the ascent to Beith Maron," alludes to an additional dimension where the emphasis is on man's individual obligations. The wise student properly trained in analysis will grasp this dual-faceted expression correctly and develop both the common and unique aspects of his existence. The Talmud, similarly, first expresses the *mishnah*'s more simplistic face, and only subsequently provides Reish Lakish's deeper interpretation.

5. THE THIRD PERSPECTIVE:
"LIKE THE TROOPS OF THE HOUSE OF DAVID"

Individuals Integrated into a Community

While the intricacies of our *mishnah* are now in sharper focus, the verse cited by the *mishnah* still requires analysis: "He Who formed [them, sees] their hearts together and understands all their actions" (Tehillim 33:15). What is intended by "[sees] their hearts *together* (יחד)"? If the explanation of Reish Lakish — "like the ascent to Beith Maron" — is sufficient, then G-d should relate to every person individually. The statement that He relates to "their hearts *together*" seems incongruous. In addition, further analysis of the verse cited introduces a new complication; "המבין אל-כל-מעשיהם" (here trans. "understands all their actions") literally means "understands *to where* (אל) all their actions [reach]." The insertion of "אל" appears confusing and unnecessary.[27]

To resolve these difficulties a more complex vision of man's role in creation must be developed. Shemu'el provides an alternate explanation for the metaphor "*benei maron*": "like the troops of the house of David." According to this metaphor, man's purpose in creation is not limited to personal, individual development; he must also seek to develop the nation Yisra'el and ultimately to enhance all of human society.[28] An individual alone can achieve little, but as part of a group working together, his efforts can contribute to the accomplishment of monumental tasks. When Yisra'el fulfills the will of G-d, the Torah promises, "Five from among you will pursue one hundred [a ratio of one to twenty] and one hundred from among you will pursue ten thousand [a ratio of one to one hundred]" (VaYikra 26:8). From this shift in ratios, Chazal derive that the efficiency of large groups is incomparably greater than that of smaller units.[29] Indeed, such concerted action benefits both the individual and the larger community: "Ingathering...for the righteous is beneficial to them and beneficial to the world" (*Mish. Sanhedrin* 8:5). An individual whose actions are divorced from those of a group squanders his potential and ultimately fails to accomplish his divine obligations.

Because the effect of isolated individuals on the world is limited, G-d selected the nation Yisra'el, rather than individuals, as the primary means for His revelation in this world: "The heavens and earth were created solely through the merit of Yisra'el" (*VaY.R.* 36:4). Therefore, the Torah was given to Yisra'el only after they had united "*as one man with one heart*" (Rashi on Shemoth 19:2, citing *Mechilta*, ibid.).[30] Following the sin of the golden calf, G-d reiterated this principle. Mosheh could not continue as G-d's mediator — in spite of his personal blamelessness — because his fitness for conveying the Torah was dependent not on his personal greatness but on the national greatness of Yisra'el: "Said R. Elazar: The Holy One, Blessed be He said to Mosheh, 'Mosheh! *Go down* from your greatness. Did I grant you greatness other than for the sake of Yisra'el? Now, Yisra'el has sinned; Why should you have greatness?' " (*Berachoth* 32a).[31] Shemu'el's explanation of "*benei maron*" as "the troops of the house of David" expresses this concept. The ascent to Beith Maron can be scaled only singly, but wars are waged communally.

This vision of community does not preclude individual distinctions.[32] Each individual should recognize his uniqueness and importance. But as a special limb of the communal body, his individuality is only truly significant if he integrates it into the organic whole of the nation Yisra'el. This relation is implied in the metaphor cited above from Rashi: "*as one man with one heart.*" Similarly, Shemu'el's vision of man builds on Reish Lakish's individualistic perspective and adds to it the importance of national integration. "The troops of the house of David" were a differentiated society of experts: cavalry, archers, and infantry all functioning in their proper roles. In such a community, each member contributes his own special skills; another specialist compensates for his weaknesses. An army's greatness is expressed in its unity as it marches in formation into battle. Each individual has his own special task, but he must march in step with his fellow soldiers.

A more careful analysis of the Gemara in *Makkoth* 23b cited earlier also reveals this need for communal integration. The Gemara states that one sanctifies each of his 248 organs by performing the 248 positive *mitzvoth*. This statement is perplexing, since no individual is obligated to observe all 248 commandments: some apply only to priests, others only to kings, and others only to judges. Does this mean that no one can sanctify all of his organs because no one can fulfill all 248 *mitzvoth*? Mabit resolves this difficulty by referring to the concept of *arvuth* (collective responsibility): one must aid others in their divine obligations even if personally exempt from those specific obligations.[33] The obligation of *arvuth* binds one to the nation Yisra'el; one becomes responsible even for *mitzvoth* addressed to kings and priests.[34] In this way, every Jew *is* obligated to perform 248 *mitzvoth*. Only through this communal vision can one sanctify all of one's organs and truly actualize one's complete potential.

Rambam regards this sense of community as a fundamental principle of the Torah: "It is improper for one to say, 'Since I shall not sin, if another will sin, of what [interest] to me is [his relationship] with G-d?' This is *a negation of the Torah*" (*Sefer HaMitzvoth, Aseh* 205). Torah is meant to awaken group consciousness.

Now, the peculiarities of the verse cited by our *mishnah* can be understood: "He Who formed [them, sees] their hearts together and understands *to where* all their actions [reach]" (Tehillim 33:15). Man's task is to perfect both himself and the nation Yisra'el. Therefore, G-d's focus must expand beyond the individual. Only by judging the individual as part of society — "their hearts together" — can G-d properly assess his impact. The seemingly superfluous "אל" — "*to where* all their actions [reach]" — expresses this perspective. G-d judges the consequences of man's actions for society and the world — to where they reach — not just their impact on the individual himself. The peculiarities of the verse allude to the theme of community found in the mishnah.

With this perspective in mind, one will prepare for the judgment of Rosh HaShanah by attempting to aid one's community achieve growth and completion. One will seek to determine the weaknesses of his society and to discover how he can mitigate them. The cogency of R. Yisra'el Salanter's advice now becomes apparent: "In preparation for Rosh HaShanah's judgment, make yourself a person whom the community requires."[35]

The Dangers of a Communal Vision

Shemu'el's interpretation of man's role explains our mishnah's form and style convincingly. Why then, we ask once more, did Chazal refrain from a more explicit statement in the mishnah and employ the ambiguous term "benei maron" instead? Once again, the evident response is that Chazal were wary of the inability of the masses to distinguish between goals and means. Unfortunately, the axiom that the full development of individual potential is a prerequisite of national service is often forgotten. From the Mishnaic period through our modern age, our rabbis and teachers have sensed a recurrent need to redress this error.[36] While the goal is certainly to assist the community, one who has yet to realize his own individual potential will have little of true consequence to contribute to this goal. A successful army is composed of specialists who first develop their own individual skills and then integrate their strengths to form a greater whole.

To avoid unintentionally abetting this error, the Mishnah chose not to express the goal of communal development explicitly. The Gemara likewise only alludes to this third, final level. The depth of the concept was left as a hint for later rabbis to reveal slowly, only to those students "who are pure of mind and well learned in the ways of investigative analysis."[37] Only such students will properly recognize all three facets of man. For most individuals this multiple perspective is too complex. Simpler approximations will prove more beneficial to them in their quest for growth.

6. CONCLUSION

The *mishnah* that we have studied contains within it a synopsis of the task that awaits each individual in preparation for Rosh HaShanah. Ultimately, to stand judgment, we must clarify our role and determine our level of readiness. To do so, we must first recognize our common obligations as human beings and as Jews. This remains the foundation upon which we must build. From there we must proceed to discern our own unique characteristics and aptitudes. To be fully human, we must recognize these as the basis of personal expression through which each individual fulfills the mission for which he was created. Finally, we must appreciate that the uniqueness of every individual, once fully actualized, can be truly significant only when integrated into the multifaceted *kelal*. It is with this recognition that we ready ourselves for Rosh HaShanah, the day of judgment.

NOTES

1. See Tehillim 33:15. See also *Rosh HaShanah* 18a, where this verse is explained in the manner suggested in this translation.

2. See Gra on Mishlei 25:11. This text is usually understood as a reference to the written Torah. Maharal, however, expands its scope to include Talmudic Aggadah. See *Be'er HaGolah, Be'er* 5 (p. 88).

   Ed. note: See also the preface of *Moreh HaNevochim*, where Rambam explicitly expounds this verse in reference to Aggadah.

3. See Gra on Mishlei 16:16 and 25:11. The metaphors of gold and silver are not incidental. Silver provides man with a currency of exchange through which he can procure his *daily needs*. Gold is too valuable to employ for daily transactions; it *defines value* and is used only for major investments. Similarly, the external understanding of an Aggadah is like silver: it inspires man, enabling him to meet a *basic need* for initial understanding. The deeper meaning, like gold, *gives value* to man's existence. (See also *Michtav MeEliyahu*, IV, 252.)

4. See also Gra on Mishlei 1:6.

5. Secrecy is required to prevent perversion of the Torah by unrefined minds. "R. Shimon b. Chalafta and R. Chaggai in the name of R. Shemu'el b. Nachman [said]: ... When the students are small, conceal from them [esoteric] words of Torah; [once] they have grown ... reveal to them the depths of Torah" (*Yer. Avodah Zarah* 2:7 [11a]).

   The negative consequences of unintegrated knowledge were vividly portrayed in the response of the masses to the teachings of Antigenos of Socho. He taught, "Do not be as servants who minister to the master in order to receive a reward; instead, be as servants who minister to the master not in order to receive a reward" (*Avoth* 1:3). While his intent was to inspire people to serve G-d altruistically, through pure love, this sublime goal was too abstract for the masses to understand. Consequently, the message was corrupted by some into a heretical belief that negated reward and punishment. Eventually, the heretical sects of Tzedukim and Baithusim arose, expounding this belief. Chazal criticized Antigenos for expressing so profound a concept so openly. Rambam concludes, "One does not teach the young and ... ignorant [to serve G-d altruistically, through pure love] ... until their abstract understanding increases and they become exceedingly wise. Then one reveals this wisdom to them little by little, and accustoms them to this matter gradually, until they grasp it and understand it and serve Him through love" (*Yad Hil. Teshuvah* 10:5).

6. Part of the beauty of Hebrew is its precision of expression. Synonyms are not interchangeable, but a family of terms each of which has its own specific connotation. *Amar, dibber, higgid, sipper,* and *tzivvah* all denote the verbal expression of ideas, but each has a distinct connotation. R. Avraham b. HaGra (see *Perush HaTefillah*) notes that *amar, dibber, sipper,* and *tzivvah* all refer to relatively explicit speech; *higgid* describes expression through subtle hints.

Chazal selected the term "Aggadah" (from the root of *higgid*) for their philo-
sophical statements, because it implies such subtle expression. See also *Nefesh
HaChayyim* 1:13 for additional sources that discuss this implication of the term
"Aggadah."

7. Many commentators have grappled with this Aggadah and the three disparate explanations offered by the Gemara for the term *"benei maron"* (see text,
below). These are obviously predicated upon different approaches to Aggadah.
For example, *"UNthanneh Tokef"* (quoted in the text, above) expresses Rashi's
understanding of the Mishnaic metaphor. See also *Chiddushei Aggadoth* (Maharsha)
on *Rosh HaShanah* ibid., *"Derashath Moharach"* (R. Chayyim Volozhiner), and
Kochevei Or (R. Yizchak Peterberg), *Ma'amar* 4, for other classic approaches to
this Talmudic passage. This essay is predicated upon the approach of Maharal. See *Chiddushei Aggadoth* (Maharal) on *Rosh HaShanah* ibid.

8. Maharal's eminence in esoteric literature establishes the significance of his
commentary. In *Be'er HaGolah, Be'er* 5 (p. 86), Maharal notes that many
concepts that are only implicitly suggested in Aggadah are expounded
explicitly in Kabbalistic sources. While Maharal does not generally employ
esoteric language, his content is often culled from more hidden sources.
Indeed, R. Yitzchak Hutner (*Sefer HaZikaron LeVa'al Pachad Yitzchak*, p. 76)
comments that Maharal's words are always laden with deeper meaning. It is
for this reason that Maharal's thoughts must be studied in depth and with
due care.

9. See Ran on *Rosh HaShanah* 17a.

10. See *Shabbath* 77b and *Machshevoth Charutz* (R. Tzadok HaKohen), ch. 7 (p. 44)

11. See *Makkoth* 23b.

12. See *Michtav MeEliyahu*, III, 353.

13. In *Be'er HaGolah, Be'er* 1 (p. 20), Maharal establishes the general framework
for this mode of analysis. For examples of this approach in the commentaries
of Maharal, see *Gur Aryeh* on BeReshith 4:8; *Derech HaChayyim* on *Avoth* 4:22;
Chiddushei Aggadoth on Babba Kamma 30a; and *Gevuroth HaShem*, ch. 9 (p. 59).

14. For examples of this approach in the commentaries of Maharal, see *Gur
Aryeh* on BeReshith 21:9; *Chiddushei Aggadoth* on Nedarim 41a, ד"ה בלא נר,
and on *Sotah* 11b, ד"ה ותרא אותו כי טוב וכו'; and *Nethivoth Olam*, "Nethiv HaKa'as,"
ch. 2 (p. 238).

15. See com. of Maharal, here: "The *targum* is ... according to the simple meaning." More detailed consideration of this principle is beyond the scope of this
essay. See for example *Rosh HaShanah* 30b and *Babba Metzi'a* 20a.

16. Regarding the role of Targum for common folk, see Rashi on *Megillah*
25a, ד"ה ועונין יהא שמיה הגדול מבורך; Tosafoth on *Berachoth* 3a, ד"ה ומעשה עגל;
and *Tifereth Yisra'el* (Maharal), ch. 65 (p. 196).

17. This principle is suggested by the observation of Rashi (on BeReshith 43:3),
R. Eliyahu Mizrachi (ibid. 40:10), and *Gur Aryeh* (ibid. 20:14), that the Targum

provides the "concept (עניין) and not the words." The Targum analyzes words based only on their context and is not concerned with analyzing the deeper nuances of connotation and syntax.

18. See also *Yad Hil. Sanhedrin* 12:3; *Derech HaChayyim* on *Avoth* 3:2; and *Pachad Yitzchak* (R. Yitzchak Hutner), "*Shavu'oth*," *Ma'amar* 21.

19. This important foundation is axiomatic in Judaism. See, for example, *Sifrei* on Devarim 32:2, *Sh.R.* 40:3, and *BeM.R.* 21:2.

20. See *Sanhedrin* 32b.

21. It should be emphasized that, although each man is judged on an individualized scale, G-d's judgment is not subjective. G-d's judgment is objective: that everyone actualize his potential. Of course, since each man's potential is distinct, this judgment is necessarily individual.

22. See *Sefath Emeth* on *Noach* (5631) and *Pachad Yitzchak* (R. Yitzchak Hutner), "*Shavu'oth*," *Ma'amar* 17.

23. See *Da'ath Chochmah UMusar*, II, 173.

24. It should be noted that the method of determination of one's own special potential in Torah appears to be rooted in an essential disagreement. According to R. Yisra'el Me'ir of Radin (see *Shem Olam*, I, "*Sha'ar Chezkath HaTorah*," ch. 13), one's "portion" in Torah is the subject that one naturally enjoys and is drawn to study. R. Tzadok HaKohen (see *Tzidkath HaTzaddik*, ch. 49) contends that the area that one finds most difficult to understand and actualize is one's special "portion." A more extensive analysis of this dispute is beyond the scope of this essay.

25. See *Torath Chovoth HaLevavoth* 4:3, Gra on Mishlei 22:6 and 16:4, and *Ha'amek Davar* on BeMidbar 15:41.

26. See *Torath Chovoth HaLevavoth* 3:3.

27. See *Nefesh HaChayyim* 1:12,14.

28. See *Shevu'oth* 39a, *Dev.R.* 11:3, *Tan. Nitzavim*:2, Tosafoth on *Shabbath* 4a, ד"ה וכי אומרים וכו', *Torath Chovoth HaLevavoth* 8:3 (Cheshbon 22) and 10:6, *Derech HaChayyim* on *Avoth* 2:2, and *Mishnah Berurah* 306:56.

29. See *Sifra* on VaYikra 26:8; *Zevachim* 41b; *Tan. Nitzavim*:1; *Derech HaChayyim* on *Avoth* 2:4; *Chiddushei Aggadoth* (Maharal) on *Sotah* 13b, ד"ה מפני שהנהיג עצמו ברבנות וכו'; and *Tomer Devorah, ch. 1*, ד"ה לשארית נחלתו וכו'.

30. Maharal emphasizes this idea repeatedly. See *Derech HaChayyim* on *Avoth* 4:12 and 6:7, ד"ה הל"א שיהיה אוהב; *Derush al HaTorah*, pp. 26-27; *Gevuroth HaShem*, ch. 38 (pp. 142-143); and *Nethivoth Olam*, "*Nethiv HaAvodah*," ch. 7 (p. 98).

31. This translation is in accordance with *Haghoth HaBach* on *Berachoth* ibid.

32. See *Pachad Yitzchak* (R. Yitzchak Hutner), "*Shavu'oth*," *Ma'amar* 21.

33. See *Kiryat Sefer*, Introduction, ch. 7.

34. See *Shevu'oth* 39a, *VaY.R.* 4:6, and *Tomer Devorah* loc. cit.

35. See *Alei Shor*, II, 424.

36. See *Yer. Pesachim* 3:7 (21b-22a), *Chazon Ish* 4:16, and *Sefer HaZikaron LeVa'al Pachad Yitzchak*, p. 107. See also the advice of R. Yisra'el Me'ir of Radin to his son regarding communal responsibility (quoted in *Kol Kithvei Chafetz Chayyim HaShalem*, III, "*Dugma MiDarchei Avi z.tz.l.,*" *p. 19*).

37. It should be emphasized that, in spite of the dangers inherent in recognition of this highest level, such recognition is important because it gives man direction, clarity, and inspiration. (See *Michtav MeEliyahu*, III, 174.)

UNMASKING AVRAHAM'S SLAVE:
A Midrashic Analysis of Eli'ezer

Chaim Eisen

1. INTRODUCTION

Unquestionably one of the most pivotal, but mysterious, personalities in Sefer BeReshith is Eli'ezer, slave of our forefather Avraham. He is identified by Chazal[1] as the anonymous "elder of [Avraham's] household who rules over all that is his" (BeReshith 24:2), who bridges between the first two generations of patriarchs and the future by finding an appropriate wife for Yitzchak and bringing her back to Eretz Yisra'el. And yet, the same individual is described in the same verse and throughout the adjacent narrative in the Torah as a mere "slave." He is apparently the only member of Avraham's illustrious household to whom the Torah refers by name (ibid. 15:2). But the context of this apparent reference to Eli'ezer is disqualification: "This one will not be your heir" (ibid. 15:4); moreover, since the Midrash considers the possibility that this reference to "Eli'ezer" may not be a name at all but a descriptive label for Lot,[2] even this mention is contested. The man who faithfully insures the perpetuation of Avraham's

RABBI EISEN, formerly of the faculty of the Yeshivat Hakotel, has lectured extensively in *machsheveth Yisra'el* and *parshanuth HaMikra* at post-secondary institutions in Israel. He teaches at Yeshivat Ohr Yerushalayim and at the OU-NCSY Israel Center, and he is an editor of *Jewish Thought*.

spiritual mission into its third generation remains himself un-perpetuated: He is cloaked in anonymity in the Torah, never identified by name and never mentioned again in the Bible. Yet it is in reference to Eli'ezer that Chazal teach us that "the chatter of slaves of the patriarchs is preferable to the teaching of the children" (BeR.R. 60:8).[3] Clearly, if we are to learn so much from Eli'ezer's chatter, we must elucidate his identity, by reading between the lines of the Torah in the footsteps of Chazal.

Ostensibly, Chazal preserve and even enhance the ambiguity of the Torah's treatment of Eli'ezer. On the one hand, Eli'ezer is portrayed as a *talmid chacham* (a Torah scholar) of the stature of Avraham.[4] He is described as a *tzaddik* (righteous),[5] who controls his passions as well as does Avraham himself.[6] He is listed as one of nine people in all of human history who merited entry into Gan Eden while still alive.[7] But on the other hand, his level of spiritual sensitivity is likened to that of a donkey.[8] He is described with suspicion as an unreliable, degenerate, and accursed slave.[9] Furthermore, he is cast not only as the faithful, righteous servant entrusted with matching Yitzchak and Rivkah (see above),[1] but in several other roles as well, including Kena'an, the accursed son of Cham,[10] and Og, the giant king of Bashan, who attempted to annihilate the nation of Yisra'el and was ultimately slain by Mosheh.[11] Nonetheless, the recognition that all these sources reflect a single Source in the Torah's brief description[12] impels us to dig beneath the divergent references, to seek a coherent picture of the man entrusted with perpetuating the spiritual legacy of our forefather Avraham.

2. ELI'EZER THE SLAVE

Slavery — The Curse of Kena'an

In all accounts, Eli'ezer's career in Avraham's household is that of a slave. In the narrative in which he appears most prom-inently — procuring a wife for Yitzchak — he is principally identified (thirteen times) as "slave" and never once mentioned by name, as if he were nothing more than an anonymous exten-sion of his master. Even his own introduction is anonymous: "He said, 'I am Avraham's slave' " (BeReshith 24:34).[13] Only in Chazal (see above)[1] is this anonymous slave identified as Eli'ezer. The implication is self-evident that Eli'ezer's enslavement is an essential component of his identity, an obvious parallel with Kena'an, the only man explicitly designated in the Torah to "be utterly enslaved" (ibid. 9:25-27). Hence, presumably, the Midrashic inference that Kena'an is Eli'ezer.

The concept of slavery is an anathema to us, with the implied oppression of one human being by another. The Mishnah teaches us, "Man was created singly ... so that no one may say to his fellow, 'My father is greater than your father' " (*Mish. Sanhedrin* 4:5).[14] Yet the Torah not only sanctions slavery but even mandates its perpetuation: "You shall bequeath them [Kena'ani slaves] to your children after you to inherit as a possession and have them serve you forever" (VaYikra 25:46). The Talmud understands this to be a commandment of the Torah: "Said R. Yehudah: Anyone who frees his slave violates a positive commandment, as it is said, '*Have them serve you forever*' " (*Berachoth* 47b).[15] Moreover, slavery was legitimized and even ordained in the Torah much earlier, by Noach, father of all postdiluvian mankind: "Noach awoke from his intoxication and knew what his smallest son had done to him. He said, 'Kena'an is accursed; he shall be utterly enslaved to his brothers' " (BeReshith 9:24-25).

It seems unthinkable to imagine anyone callously cursing his own grandson, in particular Noach, described as "a righteous man, faultless in his generation, walking with G-d" (BeReshith 6:9), who uniquely in his generation "found favor in G-d's eyes" (ibid. 6:8) to merit salvation when the rest of mankind perished in its iniquity. Consider that Noach was a prophet, functioning at a spiritual level that is unfathomable by even the greatest among us today. But careful reading of the Torah indicates that it was not Noach who cursed Kena'an. Noach pronounces no verdict that "Kena'an *shall be* accursed." What he asserts is a characterization: "Kena'an *is* accursed."[16] The enslavement of Kena'an that ensues should be understood as all punishments ordained by the Torah: "measure for measure."[17] Punishment in the Torah is not an arbitrary act of excoriation but a direct consequence of the offensive behavior.[18] Thus the punishment can be not only expiatory but rehabilitative as well. If we are to understand the implications of slavery for Kena'an and Eli'ezer, we must explore its antecedents in the "accursed" behavior of Kena'an and his father, Cham.

**"Cham, father of Kena'an, saw
his father [Noach] exposed [when he was intoxicated],
and he recounted it to his two brothers outside."**

(BeReshith 9:22)

In the Torah itself, the conduct of Cham and Kena'an is described tersely in this single verse. It is noteworthy that the Torah employs "ויגד" ("he recounted it"), instead of the ordinary "ויאמר" ("he said"). "ויגד" is distinct in its implication of storytelling or the elaborate recounting of a tale.[19] Similarly, we refer to the recounting of the Exodus at the Seder with the same root — "הגדה" — inasmuch as "anyone who elaborates in recounting the story of the Exodus from Mitzrayim is praiseworthy" (*Haggadah Shel Pesach*, "*Maggid*"). Cham did not merely "say" to his brothers what he saw; he reveled in an elaborate, graphic description. The Midrash comments, "He went out and recounted it to his two brothers in the market as a mockery of his father" (*Pir.DeR.E.* 23).[20] Cham's reaction to his elderly father's disgrace is public mockery. One wonders what conscience, what value system, could enable a son to disgrace his father so callously.

Perhaps herein lies the key to understanding Cham. Cham is a nihilist who has voided his conscience. Not only does he have no value system, he denies the legitimacy of values. No morals restrain him from publicly mocking his father's disgrace. Furthermore, inasmuch as Noach is the spiritual leader of the world, the paragon of righteousness and a prophet of G-d, Cham revels in his father's disgrace as symbolic of the disgrace of all that is sacred in life. His mockery of his father is a mockery of spirituality and righteousness in general, a vindication of profanity and repudiation of holiness. In this light, Chazal assert that Cham engaged in coitus in the ark despite a prohibition on such behavior.[21] Only a man utterly devoid of conscience could so blithely ignore G-d's command while the rest of mankind was destroyed for its iniquity.

Although no other offense is specified, the Torah tells us also that "Noach awoke from his intoxication and knew what his smallest son *had done* to him" (BeReshith 9:24), implying that some unmentioned act was perpetrated against Noach.[22] The Talmud records the opinions of Rav and Shemu'el, identifying this act as either castration or sodomy.[23] Clearly both opinions are consistent with Cham's character. According to the former opinion, Cham's rationale for his deed is articulated in the Midrash: "The first man [Adam] had two sons, and one arose and killed his fellow. This [Noach] has three, and he wishes to have four!" (*BeR.R.* 36:5, Rashi on BeReshith 9:25). One notes Cham's dehumanizing reference to his father as "זה" ("this"). Such form is certainly consistent with the logic of Cham's argument, which is clearly unacceptable to anyone who regards life per se as sacred and begetting children as a divine gift. Cham defends his outrage against Noach with a transparent rationalization of his own selfishness that essentially reduces his own father to an impersonal "*this*" and life in general to a utilitarian commodity of no intrinsic value.

This perspective is plainly echoed in the latter opinion that Cham committed sodomy, whether his intention was deliberately to profane the spirituality that his father personified or merely to use his intoxicated father as a utilitarian means to his own sensual gratification. Moreover, it is noteworthy that Cham is continually implicated in sexually indecent behavior. As one of the three cardinal sins, such behavior appears to represent unmitigated materialism — in the literal sense, regarding physical matter as the only reality — and, as such, the ultimate negation of spirituality and of its realization through Torah.[24] Again, this is certainly consistent with the portrait of Cham implied in the Torah and detailed by Chazal.

The reference here to Cham as "father of Kena'an" is perhaps to be understood similarly,[25] since Kena'an's descendents figure continually in the Torah as the paradigm of moral bankruptcy.[26] In addition, the Torah's reference to Kena'an — ostensibly superfluous — seems to implicate Kena'an in the deed.[27] Thus surmises R. Nechemyah in the Midrash, "Kena'an saw and recounted it to Cham" (*BeR.R.* 36:7, Rashi on BeReshith 9:22).[28] Given the turpitude of Kena'an's descendents,[29] such a conclusion is natural. Furthermore, it is noteworthy that Kena'an himself is nevertheless not explicitly identified in the Torah as perpetrator of the act for which he is accursed. Perhaps his utter lack of values and

conscience deprives him of even a minimally autonomous identity. As nothing more than an extension of his equally bankrupt
father, he does not even warrant mention as an independent
entity.

**"He said, 'Kena'an is accursed;
he shall be utterly enslaved, to his brothers.' "**

(BeReshith 9:25)

In light of the foregoing analysis, Noach's characterization of
Kena'an as "accursed" is understandable. Through their dis-
graceful conduct, Cham and Kena'an have flaunted their nihilistic denial of all spiritual value and true meaning in life. Such
an attitude will inevitably yield a nation indoctrinated in depravity and is, in principle, accursed.[16] Likewise, the Talmud describes
the legacy of Kena'an to his offspring: "Kena'an commanded his
children concerning five matters: love one another, love robbery,
love debauchery, hate your masters, and do not speak truth"
(*Pesachim* 113b). Rashi (ibid.) notes that this need not imply a
literal command but characterizes the typical behavior of the
nation as if it were literally commanded. In essence, such conduct
is the accursed legacy of Kena'an.[30]

It appears that the enslavement of Kena'an is a direct consequence of this "accursed" legacy. His inability to find meaning in
life has deprived him of the essential autonomy upon which
freedom is predicated. By reducing life to a utilitarian commodity
of no intrinsic value (see above), he has transformed himself into
a commodity. In principle, he lacks a basic moral commitment
that is prerequisite to any quest for true liberation. For Kena'an
and his descendents, the Talmud concludes, "A slave prefers a
dissolute life [of unbridled lust and licentiousness over free-
dom]" (*Kethubboth* 11a, *Gittin* 13a). Thus, according to one opinion in Chazal, freeing a Kena'ani slave is not regarded Halachically
as even beneficial to him: "It is disadvantageous for a slave to
leave his master's authority for freedom" (*Gittin* 11b and 12b,
Kiddushin 23a). Slavery, then, is Kena'an's reality, not mere punishment.[31]

Furthermore, it is obviously not incidental that "עבד" ("slave")
is from the same root as "עבודה" ("service"). "עבודה" is used to

connote not only servitude but any devotional service, as in " עבודת ה' " ("service of G-d," a reference to the sacrificial service in the Beith HaMikdash or, more broadly, to the prayer service or to *mitzvoth* in general). In principle, "עבודה" implies dedicating oneself to something that transcends oneself. (Hence, perhaps, the proximity of the root "עבד" [~ serve] to the root "אבד" [~ lose]. True service entails by definition "losing" oneself as the focal point of one's existence.) Kena'an has shown himself incapable of recognizing any spiritual meaning in life; he does not countenance any transcendent reality toward which his life is dedicated. So he is provided with a framework designated to teach him this concept. Since the abstract notion of devotional "עבודה" is alien to him, he is introduced to it on the most concrete level possible: as an "עבד," through slavery. He will learn devotion to something beyond himself by subordination as a slave serving his master.

Moreover, if Kena'an's incapacity to discover meaning in his life has deprived him of an autonomous identity, slavery will at least restore to him a vicarious identity as an extension of his master. Indeed, such is the Halachic status of a Kena'ani slave: "If a slave acquires possessions, to whomever the slave belongs [his master] the possessions belong" (*Megillah* 16a, *Sanhedrin* 91a and 105a).[32] Legally, he is an extension of his master. And for Kena'an's edification, he will be principally enslaved to Shem and Yefeth.[33] For just as Cham and Kena'an displayed their lack of values in reacting as they did to Noach's exposure, so did Shem and Yefeth affirm their values in their reaction.[34] Particularly through servitude to masters who regard themselves as subordinate to transcendent values, Kena'an, too, may begin to discover meaning in his life and to devote himself to it. Given Kena'an's intrinsically accursed condition, his enslavement is principally a boon for Kena'an himself.[35]

It should be noted that, under normal circumstances, Kena'an is still deemed incapable of actually transcending his status as slave. Hence the Torah's mandate to "have them serve you forever" (VaYikra 25:46), understood by Chazal to dictate that "anyone who frees his slave violates a positive commandment" (*Berachoth* 47b).[15] Kena'an remains continuously in need of slavery as the means for his ongoing rehabilitation. Nevertheless, certain contingencies mandate his liberation. The Midrash comments:

> Said the Holy One Blessed be He, "Inasmuch as [Kena'an] is sold
> into slavery, he will be released with the *eye* that saw ['Cham, father
> of Kena'an, *saw* his father exposed ...' (ibid. 9:22)] and the *mouth* that
> recounted it ['... and he *recounted it* to his two brothers outside'
> (ibid.)]. It is just that he should be released to freedom with the [loss
> of his] tooth and eye." As it is written, "And if a person smites his
> slave's eye [or his maid-servant's eye and blinds it], he shall send
> him free in payment for his eye" (Shemoth 21:26). And it is written,
> "And if he fells his slave's tooth or his maid-servant's tooth, he shall
> send him free [in payment for his tooth]" (ibid. 21:27).
>
> (*Tan. Noach*:13, *BeR.R.* 36:5)

It seems unclear why such loss of the organs that were explicitly
involved in the sin of Cham and Kena'an should justify their
descendents' release from slavery. In particular, the liberation
does not have the Halachic status of compensatory damages and
does not function as reimbursement for the slave's debilitation.
The Halachic status of the release is that of *kenas*, a fine levied by
the Torah on the master as punishment for his recklessness.[36] Of
what relevance is this fine to the sin of Cham and Kena'an? If we
recall, however, that punishment in the Torah is intended to be
not only expiatory but also rehabilitative and that the enslavement of Kena'an is intended for his own edification, the connection is evident. If Kena'an's sin is manifest principally in his eyes
and mouth, then his enslavement is intended to reform these
organs. If, instead, his master destroys them, that master indicates his incompetence in executing the task for which his slave
was entrusted to him. Consequently, his right to the slave is
forfeit.

Similarly, while Chazal derive from the verse "have them
serve you forever" (VaYikra 25:46), that "anyone who frees his
slave violates a positive commandment," also derived from the
same verse are the principles: "they are given for service but not
to be shamed" (*Niddah* 47a, *Yad Hil. Avadim* 9:8) and "you may
derive only service from them" (*Sifra* on VaYikra ibid.).[37] Slavery
is a responsibility for the master no less than for the slave.
Specifically with this comprehension of slavery, we can attempt
to understand the subordination of Kena'an and the consummate slave, Eli'ezer.

"Kena'an is Eli'ezer"

The Midrashic identification of Eli'ezer as Kena'an (who was nine generations his senior) seems astounding. One might object that such an identification would grant unusual longevity (over four hundred years) to a particularly unsavory character. While such a life-span was not extraordinary during this period, and was matched or exceeded by contemporaries of Kena'an (e.g., Arpachshad, Shelach, and Ever), we should emphasize that our concern here is not to establish biological or historical truths from the Midrash. Rambam considers such an approach, "believing [Midrash and Aggadah] as literal without attributing to them any hidden meaning," as indicative of those "who have not learned wisdom and are far from understanding" (*Introduction to Perek Chelek*, ch. 2). He lauds the few who "recognize clearly the greatness of the Sages ... whose words have both revealed and concealed components ... who speak in riddles and parables as this is the way of great scholars" (ibid.).[38] Indeed, regarding Midrashic identifications of this sort, Maharal[39] suggests that they may be understood as familial, one character descended from — but not necessarily identical with — the other.[40] Zekukin DeNura[41] proposes that one character should be understood as an incarnation of the other. Similarly, our concern is to elucidate the ethical and ideological truths to which Chazal allude in identifying the slave Eli'ezer as Kena'an, progenitor of slavery.

Perhaps it is Eli'ezer's status as anonymous slave in the narrative in which he figures so prominently that impelled Chazal to identify him as Kena'an. Eli'ezer, like Kena'an, appears to lack even a minimal measure of autonomy. He is only "Avraham's slave," by even his own admission. According to one opinion in the Midrash, he is mentioned by name but once in the Torah (BeReshith 15:2); according to the alternate opinion, he is mentioned not even once at all.[2] Once his role as Avraham's slave is complete, neither he nor his descendents are ever mentioned in the Bible again — in dramatic contrast to Avraham's household, whose perpetuation he personally guarantees. His anonymity as a slave suggests the curse of Kena'an. The Midrash comments:

> "*The slave said to him [Avraham]*" (BeReshith 24:5) — To this Scripture refers: "*Kena'an possesses balances of deceit, loving to cheat*" (Hoshea

12:8). "*Kena'an*" refers to Eli'ezer. "*Possesses balances of deceit*" [means] that he was considering [lit. balancing] whether his daughter was suitable or not [to marry Yitzchak]. "*Loving to cheat*" (לעשק אהב) [means] to cheat the beloved (לעשק אהוב) of the world, Yitzchak. [Eli'ezer said, " '*Perhaps [the prospective bride] will be unwilling'* (BeReshith ibid.), and I will give him my daughter." [Avraham] said to him, "You are accursed and my son is blessed, and the accursed are incompatible with the blessed."

(BeR.R. 59:9)[42]

While the Midrash's pronouncement seems harsh, it is essentially a characterization of Kena'an's legacy, which defines the slave condition as we have seen. And particularly in the context of the Midrash — guaranteeing the continuation of Avraham's spiritual mission — Eli'ezer is manifestly accursed: Unlike Avraham, Eli'ezer remains without perpetuation in the Bible.

It is relevant in this context to consider another appearance of Eli'ezer in the Midrash, at the *akeidah* (the binding of Yitzchak):

> Avraham arose early in the morning and took Yishma'el and Eli'ezer and Yitzchak his son.... A contest erupted between Eli'ezer and Yishma'el [regarding the inheritance of Avraham upon Yitzchak's apparently imminent death].... Eli'ezer responded to Yishma'el, saying to him, "[Avraham] already banished you like a divorced wife sent away to the wilderness. But I am his slave, serving his household day and night, and I am the heir of Avraham." And the Holy Spirit responded, saying to them, "Neither one nor the other will inherit."
>
> On the third day, they reached Tzofim [from which the Temple Mount is visible].[43] Upon reaching Tzofim, [Avraham] saw the glory of G-d's presence manifest upon the mountain, as it is said, "*On the third day, Avraham looked up and saw the place from afar*" (BeReshith 22:4). What did he see? He saw a pillar of fire [stretching] from earth to heaven. He said to Yitzchak his son, "My son, do you see anything on one of these mountains?" [Yitzchak] responded, "Yes." [Avraham] said to him, "What do you see?" [Yitzchak] responded, "I see a pillar of fire manifest [stretching] from earth to heaven." And Avraham understood that the youth was accepted for the offering.
>
> He said to Yishma'el and Eli'ezer, "Do you see anything on one of these mountains?" They responded, "No." He considered them like donkeys and said to them, "You remain here with the donkey." He said to them, "Just as the donkey sees nothing, so you see

nothing," as it is said, "*Avraham said to his youths, 'You remain here with the donkey'*" (ibid. 22:5): *a nation that resembles a donkey.*

(*Pir.DeR.E.* 31)[44]

Eli'ezer remains limited by the spiritual myopia that character- izes Kena'an's legacy. Just as Kena'an denied spirituality, so is Eli'ezer blind to a vision of G-d's presence — the presence of spirituality — in this world. He sees as does a donkey ("חמור"), an obvious allusion to an utterly materialistic ("חומר") perspec- tive.

Moreover, the Midrash here alludes not only to Eli'ezer's spiritual barrenness, but his consequent impotence as well. The quarrel between Eli'ezer and Yishma'el over the inheritance of Avraham is obviously more than a financial squabble. They argue over the identity of the spiritual heir of Avraham, charged with conveying his spiritual mission onward. And G-d disquali- fies them both, as He does explicitly in the Torah.[45] The Talmud, deriving from "you remain here with the donkey" that the de- scendents of Kena'an are "a nation that resembles a donkey," concludes from this principle that "all agree that a [Kena'ani] slave has no [legally recognized] descent" (*Yevamoth* 62a).[46] This essential humanness was rejected by Kena'an, by reducing life to a utilitarian commodity devoid of any abiding, intrinsic value (see above). Indeed, Eli'ezer has no descent and no continuation. R. S.R. Hirsch, in his commentary on BeReshith 3:14, notes the relationship between the root "ארר" (~ cursed) and the root "ערר" (~ desolate, barren). Conversely, the root "ברך" (~ blessed) may be related to the root "פרח" (~ blooming, flourishing).[47] Yitzchak, son of Avraham, is "ברוך" ("blessed"): Not only is he a biological progenitor of the nation of Yisra'el, but also the spiri- tual fountainhead of a new way to serving G-d.[48] Spiritually, Eli'ezer is not only "ארור" ("accursed") but "ערירי" ("childless"); he has no future. He appears in the Torah as the ultimate spiritual cul-de-sac.

In light of Eli'ezer's background, we can readily appreciate Avraham's suspicious attitude toward him. The Talmud relates that, on the third day following their circumcision, "Avraham sent Eli'ezer outside [to look for guests]. He went out and found none. [Avraham] said, 'I do not believe you.' As it is said, 'There is no faithfulness in slaves' " (*Babba Metzi'a* 86b). Similarly, upon Eli'ezer's successful return with Rivkah, we are told by the Midrash, "Avraham said to Yitzchak, 'My son, this slave is suspect [to violate] all transgressions, and he possesses deceit' " (*Pir.DeR.E.* 16, *Yal.Sh.* BeReshith:109). The Midrash proceeds to detail Avraham's concerns that Eli'ezer may have raped Rivkah on the way. A consistent picture seems to emerge of Eli'ezer as a typical faithless slave, true to the legacy of Kena'an.

Clearly we can comprehend in a similar light variant Midrashic traditions regarding Eli'ezer that identify him not as Kena'an himself, but as Nimrod's son[49] or grandson.[50] Other sources describe Eli'ezer as Nimrod's slave.[51] Nimrod, son of Kush, was Cham's grandson and Kena'an's nephew.[52] He seems to represent the epitome of Cham's rejection of all spiritual values. Even his name is understood by Chazal to suggest this denial: "Why was he called 'Nimrod' (נמרוד)? Because he incited the entire world to rebel (המריד) against [G-d]" (*Eruvin* 53a).[53] Nimrod is depicted as institutionalizing idolatry[54] and initiating the tower of Bavel,[55] the ultimate architectural project to rebel against G-d. So deliberate was his willful rejection of G-d[56] that he was prepared to kill Avraham for daring to oppose him.[57] Thus, the Midrash repeatedly portrays Nimrod as the pre-eminent adversary of Avraham,[58] who is the exemplar of righteousness and a sanctified life. Understandably, the Midrash characterizes him in terms of his grandfather's legacy: "Nimrod is a slave, son of a slave, because all of the descendents of Cham are slaves" (*Pir.DeR.E.* 24). While Eli'ezer functions as Avraham's slave, he hails from a lineage that represents the antithesis of Avraham's values and strives to destroy him. Whether from Kena'an or Nimrod's household, he seems to represent the quintessential faithless, accursed slave.

Such a picture of Eli'ezer, however, is far from complete. The Talmud and Midrash clearly indicate that in all cases in which Avraham suspected Eli'ezer of impropriety, his suspicions were unjustified. Furthermore, such a picture contrasts shockingly with the singular faithfulness of Eli'ezer in procuring a wife for Yitzchak and thus insuring the continuation of Avraham's legacy into its third generation. In fact, any understanding of Eli'ezer must confront not only his enslavement to Avraham but also the effect that having such a master has upon him, culminating in Eli'ezer's pivotal role in perpetuating Avraham's spiritual mission.

3. THE FAITHFUL SERVANT

The Development of Eli'ezer

Chazal provide us with several significant indications of Eli'ezer's dynamic growth during the period of his enslavement. Perhaps most explicitly, the Midrash comments:

> "He said [to Eli'ezer], 'Come in, O blessed of G-d'" (BeReshith 24:31) —
> ... Said R. Yosei b. Dosa: Kena'an is Eli'ezer, but *by serving the righteous [Avraham] faithfully, he left the category of "accursed" for the category of "blessed."*
>
> (BeR.R. 60:7)[59]

Commenting on the Midrash, *Yefeh To'ar* (ibid.) specifies the means of Eli'ezer's growth: "Subjection to great people is the essence of freedom and liberty." We recall the rehabilitative effect that slavery is intended to have on Kena'an and his descendents: He is to learn devotion to something beyond himself by subordination as a slave serving his master. Particularly through servitude to masters who regard themselves as subordinate to transcendent values, it is hoped that Kena'an, too, may learn to discover meaning in his life and to devote himself to it.

Apparently, Eli'ezer recognizes this potentially constructive role in slavery. Chazal emphasize that Eli'ezer, confronting the reality of his enslavement, does not even attempt to conceal it:

> Said Rava to Rabbah b. Mari: Whence comes the popular saying, "A shameful matter regarding you, you should take the initiative to state"?
> He responded: As it is written, "He said, 'I am Avraham's slave'" (BeReshith 24:34).
>
> (Babba Kamma 92b)[60]

In light of this recognition, cites the Midrash:

> "A wise slave" (Mishlei 17:2) — This is Eli'ezer. What is his wisdom? He said, "Since I am already accursed [with eternal enslavement (Rashi)], what if a Kushi or a Barbar should come and subjugate me?

> It would be better for me to be subjugated in this household [of Avraham] and not in another household."
>
> (*BeR.R.* 60:2, *Yal.Sh.* BeReshith:107)

Sefath Emeth (on *Chayyei Sarah* [5639]) comments on the Midrash, "What wisdom is [manifest] here that Scripture should praise him? ... [It is] that he did not consider seeking a way to escape from enslavement but only to discover [the path to] his own rehabilitation in the enslavement itself." Eli'ezer feels attracted to Avraham, in recognition of both his own innate curse and Avraham's spiritual greatness. The slave senses that, while slavery is his irrevocable destiny, in Avraham's household lies the key to his rehabilitation.

It is perhaps to this wisdom that Chazal allude in another bizarre reference to Eli'ezer, in contention with the perverted legal system of Sedom. Chazal graphically recount the deliberate perversity of Sedom's judges and citizens and the misery and suffering they inflicted on their hapless victims. In this context, three confrontations are cited involving Eli'ezer slave of Avraham as the potential victim. In all three, he emerges victorious after shrewdly outwitting the people of Sedom by using their techniques to his own advantage:

> When one person would wound his fellow, they [the "judges" of Sedom] would say [to the victim], "Pay [the assailant] his wages for phlebotomizing you." ... Eli'ezer slave of Avraham happened [to come] there. They wounded him. He came before the judge. [The judge] said to him, "Pay [the assailant] his wages for phlebotomizing you." [Eli'ezer] took a stone and wounded the judge. [The judge] said, "What is this!" [Eli'ezer] said to him, "The wages that accrue to me from you give to this one [my assailant], and my money remains as it was [with me]....
>
> (*Sanhedrin* 109b, *Yal.Sh.* BeReshith:70)

The other two confrontations (see ibid.) are of a similar style. Ostensibly, these appearances of Eli'ezer overcoming the people of Sedom are not only extraneous but inappropriate to the portrayal of Sedom as a city of victimizers. Of what value are such examples in indicting Sedom? Consider, however, the roots of Sedom: "The *Kena'ani* borders [extended] from Tzidon toward Gerar until Azzah, and toward *Sedom* and Amorah and Admah and

Tzvoyim until Lasha" (BeReshith 10:19). Sedom, descended from Kena'an, represented the epitome of Kena'an's bankruptcy: a society that institutionalized immorality and wickedness, as emphasized in the Torah61 and detailed by Chazal (see above). Perhaps the most damning indictment of Sedom lies in the comparison of its citizens with another Kena'ani who, having mastered their methods, exploits them to vindicate justice. Eli'ezer hails from the same stock as Sedom. He too begins his career as an accursed descendent of Kena'an; he innately knows Sedom's techniques. But *"by serving the righteous [Avraham] faithfully, he left the category of 'accursed' for the category of 'blessed'* " (*BeR.R.* 60:7).[59] His success is the ultimate indictment of Sedom's premeditated failure. Chazal may, however, be implying still more in Eli'ezer's conflict with Sedom. Eli'ezer's own development is the result of his resolution of a similar conflict that occurred within himself between the "accursed Kena'ani" and the "slave of Avraham." In describing his confrontation with Sedom, Chazal are presenting a recapitulation of the inner conflict through which, in his wisdom, Eli'ezer "slave of Avraham" emerged victorious as a member of Avraham's blessed household.

The Midrash records an analogous confrontation between Eli'ezer and Lavan:

> *"When [Lavan] saw the nose-ring"* (BeReshith 24:30) — He immediately went to kill [Eli'ezer]. [Eli'ezer] perceived that he was running to [do him] evil, mentioned the [Ineffable] Name, and set the camels over the fountain in the air, with himself standing over the camels in the air. When [Lavan] saw this, he realized that [Eli'ezer] was righteous and said, *"Come in, O blessed of G-d"* (ibid. 24:31), thinking that [Eli'ezer] was Avraham because his facial features resembled [Avraham's].
>
> (*Mid. Avkir, Yal.Sh.* BeReshith:109)[62]

Again Chazal depict Eli'ezer overcoming his degenerate and deceitful adversary. Recall that the Midrash[63] ascribes to Eli'ezer the reference, "Kena'an possesses balances of *deceit*" (Hoshea 12:8), the same vice that so characterized deceitful Lavan. Perhaps, through his conflict with Lavan as well, the Midrash is alluding to the *inner* conflict, *within* Eli'ezer, through which he overcame his roots in deceit that threatened his destruction. In this context, the immediate continuation of the Midrash is most appropriate: "Kena'an is Eli'ezer, but *by serving the righteous [Avraham] faithfully, he left the category of 'accursed' for the category of 'blessed' "* (ibid.). The conflict just presented hints at the conflict that was resolved through this transformation. And significantly, Eli'ezer's success is associated with his emulation of Avraham; they even look alike. It would appear that Eli'ezer's enslavement has accomplished its ultimate purpose. Eli'ezer has overcome the curse of Kena'an by learning devotion to something beyond himself through subordination as a slave. Particularly by serving Avraham, Eli'ezer has learned from his master the meaning of values and devotion to them. Moreover, while his Kena'ani incapacity to discover meaning in life had deprived him of an autonomous identity, slavery has restored to him a vicarious identity as an extension of Avraham himself.

Eli'ezer the Righteous Scholar

The success of Eli'ezer's rehabilitation may be inferred from the Torah, inasmuch as he is singly entrusted with choosing the second matriarch of Yisra'el and insuring the perpetuation of Avraham's spiritual venture. The extent of this success, however, is to be principally deduced from the Midrash, where Eli'ezer is depicted as a paragon of righteousness:

> *"The righteous eats to satisfy his spirit"* (Mishlei 13:25) — This refers to Eli'ezer, who said to Rivkah, "Let me please sip a little water [from your pitcher]" (BeReshith 24:17): one swallow.
> *"But the stomach of the wicked will be lacking"* (Mishlei ibid.) — This refers to Esav, who said to Ya'akov, "Glut me please [from this red red stuff]" (BeReshith 25:30). Said R. Yitzchak b. R. Zeira: Esav widened his mouth like a camel and said, "I will open my mouth, and you fill it."
>
> (BeM.R. 21:20)[64]

The verse cited, "The righteous eats to satisfy his spirit, but the stomach of the wicked will be lacking," is divided here into its two clauses. In the context of the Midrash,[64] these clauses are ascribed respectively to three pairs: Eli'ezer versus Esav (quoted above), Ruth the Mo'aviyyah versus idol worshipers, and Chizkiyyah king of Yehudah versus the kings of East and West.

The first clause is also ascribed to G-d Himself. An obvious common denominator of Eli'ezer, Ruth, and King Chizkiyyah is that all three were raised in settings that were fraught with corruptive influences,[65] in spite of which they each earned the designation "righteous." In the context of the verse cited, this righteousness is evidently synonymous with self-restraint and refinement, necessarily imposed by the protagonists themselves in an environment that flouted such values. Such morally transcendent behavior is so G-dly as to hint, so to speak, at G-d Himself.

In addition, the Midrash (ibid.) obviously emphasizes the contrast between the two elements of each pair through their juxtaposition. Thus, Ruth the proselyte is juxtaposed with idol worshipers to emphasize through contradistinction her greatness in abandoning her idolatrous heritage and their hedonistic degeneracy in maintaining it. Similarly, the righteous King Chizkiyyah is juxtaposed with the vain gluttony of the kings of East and West.

While the intent of the Midrash in pairing Eli'ezer and Esav is less obvious, an essential theme is apparent here as well. Esav was the product of two generations of patriarchs, reared by Avraham and Yitzchak in a household of quintessential blessedness and sanctity. Yet, through his own volition, he became "the nation of [G-d's] curse" (Yeshayahu 34:5), "to be a desolation, a disgrace, a waste, and a curse" (Yirmeyahu 49:13), "a border of wickedness and the nation against whom G-d's indignation is directed forever" (Malachi 1:4). Eli'ezer hailed from the line of Cham and Kena'an, a stock of perversity and moral bankruptcy that is intrinsically accursed. But through his own efforts, "*by serving the righteous [Avraham] faithfully, he left the category of 'accursed' for the category of 'blessed'*" (BeR.R. 60:7).[59] Furthermore, in spite of Esav's primogeniture, his actions earned him the status of "*small* among the nations, exceedingly despised" (Ovadyah 1:2), voided of scholars and understanding (ibid. 1:8). Eli'ezer, through his righteousness and wisdom, overcame Noach's characterization of Cham — or Kena'an[66] — as "his *smallest* son" (BeReshith 9:24), that is, "unfit and disgraced" (BeR.R. 36:7).[67] Eli'ezer's juxtaposition with Esav emphasizes the extent of both his success and Esav's failure.

Indeed, the extent to which Eli'ezer appears to have succeeded in overcoming the curse of Kena'an is incredible. The

Talmud indicts even Avraham for insufficient recognition of Eli'ezer's greatness:

> Said R. Abbahu in the name of R. Elazar: Why was Avraham our forefather punished that his descendents were subjugated to Mitzrayim for two hundred ten years? [This is] because he subjected a Torah scholar to forced labor, as it is said, "*He prepared for battle his neophytes who had been born in his household*" (BeReshith 14:14)....
>
> "*Three hundred eighteen*" (ibid.) — Said R. Ami b. Abba: Eli'ezer is equivalent to all of them [combined]. Others say: This refers to Eli'ezer, by numerological allusion [since "אליעז"ר" ("Eli'ezer") in numerology is three hundred eighteen, i.e., no one accompanied Avraham into battle except Eli'ezer alone (Rashi)].
>
> (*Nedarim* 32a)

The Midrash elaborates further on Avraham's preparations for battle and on the spiritual greatness of Eli'ezer in singly, from among all the members of Avraham's household, accompanying him into the fray:

> "*He prepared* (וירק) [*them]*" (ibid.) — [This] teaches that [Avraham] depleted them (הוריקן) with his words. He said to them, " '*Whoever is fearful*' (Devarim 20:8) of iniquities [he committed] '*and faint-hearted*' (ibid.) from bad deeds that he perpetrated '*should go and return to his house and not demoralize [his brothers' heart as his own]*' (ibid.)." By saying that to them, he depleted them one by one and was left with Eli'ezer alone. Whence do you learn this? ["אליעז"ר" ("Eli'ezer") numerologically calculated is:] א=1, ל=30, י=10, ע=70, ז=7, ר=200, hence three hundred eighteen. Thus, what is written subsequently is: "*he pursued*" (ibid.), not: "they pursued" [because only one man (Eli'ezer) pursued].
>
> (*Tan. Lech*:13)[68]

Clearly, the Midrash emphasizes not Eli'ezer's physical prowess but his moral purity as the indispensable virtue that uniquely enables him to accompany Avraham in his miraculous victory of right over might. It is noteworthy that the Midrash perceives Eli'ezer as uniquely capable of escorting Avraham. Considering that "serving the righteous [Avraham] faithfully" (*BeR.R.* 60:7)[59] was the basis of Eli'ezer's spiritual rehabilitation, through which he functions as an extension of Avraham himself, this is readily understandable.[69] Moreover, inasmuch as this rehabilitative process essentially involved overcoming Kena'ani nihilism with Avraham's devotion to spirituality, Eli'ezer is uniquely accoutered for this battle of right versus might, having already fought a similar conflict within himself.

Equated with Avraham

The Talmud, it seems, far surpasses allusions to Eli'ezer as Avraham's extension or escort. In fact, it sets Eli'ezer on a par with the patriarchs themselves:

> Avraham our forefather was an elder occupied in study, as it is said, "Avraham was old (זָקֵן) [lit. elder, implying scholarship],[70] advanced in years" (BeReshith 24:1). Yitzchak our forefather was an elder occupied in study, as it is said, "Yitzchak had grown old (זָקֵן)" (ibid. 27:1). Ya'akov our forefather was an elder occupied in study, as it is said, "Yisra'el's eyes were heavy with old age (זֹקֶן)" (ibid. 48:10). Eli'ezer slave of Avraham was an elder occupied in study, as it is said, "Avraham said to his slave, elder (זְקַן) of his household" (ibid. 24:2).
>
> "Who rules over (הַמֹּשֵׁל) all that is his" (ibid.) — Said R. Eli'ezer: [This implies] that [Eli'ezer] has mastered (מוֹשֵׁל) the teaching of his master. "[He] is Damesek (דַּמֶּשֶׂק) Eli'ezer" (ibid. 15:2) — Said R. Elazar: [This implies] that [Eli'ezer] draws (דוֹלֶה) and gives to drink (מַשְׁקֶה) of the teaching of his master to others.
>
> *(Yoma 28b, Rashi on BeReshith 15:2)*

It is noteworthy that the Talmud specifically cites only four individuals from all of Jewish history as "elders occupied in study": the three patriarchs and Eli'ezer. The glorious legacy of Torah study that so typified the nation of Yisra'el throughout history is depicted as epitomized by these four. One wonders what would justify Eli'ezer's inclusion on so exclusive a list.

Furthermore, the Midrash evokes an even greater status for Eli'ezer, apparently equating him and Avraham:

> "Avraham said to his slave, elder (זְקַן) of his household" (BeReshith 24:2) — [Elder (זְקַן) implies] that the splendor of [Eli'ezer's] appearance (זִיו אִיקוֹנִין) resembled his [Avraham's].
> "Who rules over all that is his" (ibid.) — [This implies] that [Eli'ezer] ruled over his passions like him [Avraham].
>
> *(BeR.R. 59:8, Yal.Sh. BeReshith:106)*[71]

Similarly, the Midrash exegetically ascribes the same verse, "Who among you fears G-d" (Yeshayahu 50:10), alternately to Avraham and to Eli'ezer.[72] The Midrash even derives the same Halachic lesson from both the behavior of Avraham and the behavior of Eli'ezer.[73] Certainly such descriptions of Eli'ezer's righteousness are not mere hyperbole. What are Chazal implying by establishing such a parity between him and Avraham?

4. THE DIALECTIC OF ELI'EZER

The Paradoxical Portrayal

In order to resolve this difficulty, we must assess the compound identity of Eli'ezer that has coalesced thus far, with all its apparent contradictions. We recall that, while Eli'ezer is cast as accursed Kena'an, he has risen from this status to become the blessed slave of Avraham, personifying Avraham's spiritual mission and even functioning as an extension of Avraham himself. Through his own efforts, *"by serving the righteous [Avraham] faithfully, he left the category of 'accursed' for the category of 'blessed'"* (BeR.R. 60:7).[59] His association with Avraham has transformed him from a Kena'ani nihilist into a consummate scholar and a paragon of righteousness.

Yet, according to Chazal, Avraham still suspects Eli'ezer of both faithlessness and infidelity.[74] He labels him — apparently even after Eli'ezer's rehabilitation — as "accursed" (BeR.R. 59:9).[42] Moreover, the Midrash[63] regards Eli'ezer as subject of the verse, "Kena'an possesses balances of deceit, loving to cheat" (Hoshea 12:8). Ultimately he remains utterly materialistic, blind to the presence of spirituality in this world, characterized as "a nation that resembles a donkey" (Yevamoth 62a, Pir.DeR.E. 31).[44, 46] In the Torah, while Eli'ezer executes his mission with such faithfulness, he is still considered an anonymous slave lacking any autonomous identity. And although he insures the perpetuation of Avraham's household, he himself remains without continuation at all, never again even mentioned in the Bible: a spiritual impasse. How are all these diverse sources to be reconciled with one another?

It appears that the Midrash provides us with a significant key to elucidating Eli'ezer, with its cryptic comment that "his [Eli'ezer's] facial features resembled [Avraham's]" *(BeR.R. 60:7, Yal.Sh. BeReshith:109).*[75] This seems incompatible with the principle of the uniqueness of every human being.[76] In particular, we regard a person's face as a reflection of that person's innermost self. "פָּנִים" ("face") is from the same root as "פְּנִים" ("interior"). Chazal assert, "Just as their faces do not resemble one another, so their minds do not resemble one another" *(Yer. Berachoth 9:1 [57a]).*[77] Perhaps the Midrash is emphasizing not simply Eli'ezer's exceptional lack of a unique face but his singular lack of an independent identity: He is, both internally and externally, a reflection of his master. His role as extension of Avraham is not incidental but fundamental; it characterizes his very essence.

A Reflection of Avraham

This is, of course, compatible with the Torah's recurrent references to Eli'ezer as Avraham's anonymous slave, as if that were a quintessential description of him. Furthermore, as we have seen, this is consistent with the character of Kena'an, whose utter lack of values and conscience deprives him of an autonomous identity. Finally, we recall the intended goal of Kena'an's enslavement. He is to learn devotion to something beyond himself through subordination as a slave serving his master. Particularly through servitude to masters who regard themselves as subordinate to transcendent values, it is hoped that Kena'an too will begin to discover meaning in his life and to devote himself to it. Thus, while Kena'an's nature has deprived him of an autonomous identity, slavery may restore to him a vicarious identity as an extension of his master. Therein lies Eli'ezer's prodigious, but limited, success: He has followed the prescription of slavery through to its ultimate conclusion.

We must bear in mind that the curse of Kena'an is a characterization of Kena'an's essence.[16] "Anyone who frees his slave violates a positive commandment" *(Berachoth 47b),*[15] because under normal circumstances, Kena'an is still deemed incapable of actually transcending his status as slave, continuously in need of slavery as the means for his ongoing rehabilitation. It is specifically within these constraints that Eli'ezer can function. Only *"by serving the righteous [Avraham] faithfully,*" has Eli'ezer "*left the category of 'accursed' for the category of 'blessed'*" (*BeR.R.* 60:7).[59] He is "blessed" solely to the extent that he is an extension of Avraham.

This principle is fundamental to understanding Eli'ezer as Chazal portray him. By confronting his own innate curse and Avraham's spiritual greatness, he extricates himself from the status of "accursed Kena'ani" to "slave of Avraham." But he does so specifically *as* the "slave of Avraham," through imitation of Avraham's spirituality. Eli'ezer learns self-restraint and refinement[78] only by mimicking his master. He becomes a righteous scholar of sufficient moral purity to singly accompany Avraham in his miraculous victory,[79] because he apes Avraham so adroitly that the latter's impeccable behavior becomes his own. He is included with the patriarchs in the Talmud's exclusive list of pre-eminent "elders occupied in study" (*Yoma* 28b), because a list that evaluates Avraham's external behavior, as opposed to his inner self, must in principle include Eli'ezer (as Avraham's copy) since his external behavior is identical.

"The Teaching of His Master"

It is noteworthy that the Talmud emphasizes not only the faithfulness of Eli'ezer's scholarship but also its conspicuous lack of originality. Eli'ezer's Torah is not his own:

> Said R. Eli'ezer: ... [Eli'ezer] has mastered the teaching *of his master*....
> Said R. Elazar: ... [Eli'ezer] draws and gives to drink of the teaching *of his master* to others.
>
> (*Yoma* 28b)

Eli'ezer's Torah remains exclusively "the teaching *of his master.*" Significantly, by contrast, Avraham "*from his own self* learned the Torah" (*BeR.R.* 95:3, *Tan. VaYiggash*:11).[80] The Midrash specifically emphasizes the innovative novelty of Avraham's Torah learning that has, so to speak, a divine character:

> R. Pinchas said in the name of R. Shemu'el: Even the new name that the Holy One Blessed be He will, in the future, call Yerushalayim ... Avraham knew. R. Berechyah and R. Chiyyah and the rabbis there in the name of R. Yehudah said: There is not a single day upon which the Holy One Blessed be He does not innovate a *halachah* in

the heavenly court.... Even those *halachoth* Avraham knew.

(BeR.R. 49:2, *Yal.Sh.* Iyyov:921)

Such originality is predicated on an internalization of Torah that remains alien to Eli'ezer.

It should be emphasized that this originality is not at all extraneous to true study of Torah. Chazal assert, to the contrary, that "it is inconceivable for a house of study to be without novel innovation" *(Chagigah* 3a).[81] True study of Torah, that pervades the being of the student, is necessarily predicated upon such personal involvement:

> Said Rava: A person should always learn Torah regarding a subject that *his heart* desires [to learn]. As it is said, "*His* desire is in the Torah of G-d" (Tehillim 1:2). And said Rava: Initially, [the Torah] is ascribed to the Holy One Blessed be He, and ultimately it is ascribed *to him* [the person engaged in study (Rashi)]. As it is said, "His desire is in the Torah of G-d, and *his* [the student's] Torah he articulates day and night" (ibid.).
>
> *(Avodah Zarah* 19a, *Yal.Sh.* Tehillim:614)

Eli'ezer's Torah is never ascribed to him; it is always "the teaching *of his master.*" Throughout, he is only the distributor of Torah that is not essentially his. Recall the Halachic status of a Kena'ani slave as an extension of his master: "If a slave acquires possessions, to whomever the slave belongs [his master] the possessions belong" *(Megillah* 16a, *Sanhedrin* 91a and 105a).[32] Even Eli'ezer's spiritual possessions are not truly his own; in reality, his Torah belongs to Avraham. His Kena'ani incapacity to acquire an autonomous identity renders him even spiritually an extension of Avraham. While he is superficially an "elder occupied in study" *(Yoma* 28b) on a par with Avraham, his Torah remains specifically Avraham's and external to himself. As a truly anonymous extension of his master, he functions like a chameleon, faithfully displaying Avraham's colors. And he has the wisdom to apprehend that "it would be better for me to be subjugated in this household [of Avraham] and not in another household" *(BeR.R.* 60:2, *Yal.Sh.* BeReshith:107), since presumably in another household he would with equal deftness display the perverse colors of another master.

Superficial Spirituality — The Curse of Eli'ezer

In this light, we can readily appreciate Avraham's error in having "subjected a Torah scholar to forced labor" (*Nedarim* 32a). Avraham, assessing Eli'ezer's internalization of Torah, never considered him a Torah scholar. While Avraham comprehended "that [Eli'ezer] ruled over his passions like him" (*BeR.R.* 59:8, *Yal.Sh.* BeReshith:106), he realized also that this righteousness was only to be "*like him*" and was essentially no more than a superficial reflection. He consequently suspects Eli'ezer every time the latter is not in his presence, since Eli'ezer has no autonomous righteousness upon which to rely and can only be expected to reflect his master. Thus the magnitude of Avraham's suspicions is proportional to Eli'ezer's distance from him. When Eli'ezer is sent outside to look for guests, he is suspect for faithlessness;[82] when he is sent to Charan, he is suspect for rape.[83] In principle, Avraham concludes regarding Eli'ezer that "this slave is suspect [to violate] all transgressions, and he possesses deceit" (*Pir.DeR.E.* 16). In spite of his external righteousness, his essential nature remains suggestive of deceitful, nihilistic Kena'an; his faithfulness has the constancy of a reflection.

It is understandable in this context that, in spite of a seemingly prodigious spiritual level, Eli'ezer is likened to a donkey and characterized as "a nation that resembles a donkey" (*Yevamoth* 62a, *Pir.DeR.E.* 31).[44, 46] He remains blind to a vision of G-d's presence — the presence of spirituality — in this world; his concept of spirituality — aping Avraham — is but a superficial veneer on materialism. Note that the context of this characterization is as Avraham and Yitzchak part from Eli'ezer and Yishma'el within sight of the Temple Mount, on their way to the *akeidah* (the binding of Yitzchak). The sacrifice of an only, beloved son by his father, as an expression of their mutual, perfect devotion to fulfill G-d's bidding, can be understood only by one who also embodies such devotion; otherwise it will be apprehended as either an abomination or authorization of wanton manslaughter. Inasmuch as Eli'ezer's spirituality is only a superficial reflection of such devotion, his participation, even passively, in the *akeidah* would be not only inappropriate but potentially dangerous as well.[84] In spite of his righteousness and scholarship, he sees as does a donkey ("חמור"), limited by an intrinsically materialistic ("חומר") perspective.[85]

Eli'ezer is, therefore, inherently "accursed" (*BeR.R.* 59:9).[42] Recall that the root "ארר" (~ cursed), as related to the root "ערר" (~ desolate, barren), implies Eli'ezer's lack of a future (see above). In a spiritual sense, he is not only "ארור" ("accursed") but also "ערירי" ("childless"): He has no continuation in the Bible. It is an empirical verity of genetics that only intrinsic qualities can be perpetuated; extrinsic characteristics are not transmitted. Inasmuch as Eli'ezer's spirituality is merely a superficial reflection with no internalized content, in principle it cannot be perpetuated. Significantly, Avraham characterizes Eli'ezer as "accursed" in the Midrash[63] specifically when Eli'ezer proposes that Yitzchak marry his daughter. As Eli'ezer's spirituality is never internalized, it cannot possibly have a continuation; spiritually, he is by definition childless. In considering his spiritual future as derivative of his current *internal* spiritual level, all his righteousness and scholarship are irrelevant to the ultimate assessment that he is "accursed."

This is perhaps implied by context in the single possible reference[86] to Eli'ezer by name in the Bible:

> Avram said, "G-d O L-rd, what will you give me as I am childless, and the steward of my household is Damesek Eli'ezer?"
> Avram said, "After all, to me you have given no seed, and here a member of my household is my heir."
> And lo, the word of G-d came to him: "This one will not be your heir, but one who issues from your loins will be your heir."
> (BeReshith 15:2-4)

The Midrash comments on the last verse, "utterly accursed; he will not inherit Avraham" (*BeR.R.* 44:11,[87] *Yal.Sh.* BeReshith:76). Clearly, the context throughout is inheritance: determining the heir of Avraham. Obviously, Avraham's principal concern is spiritual: to insure the perpetuation of his theological legacy.[88] He contends that, if he remains childless, all of G-d's promises to him will amount to naught, since his spiritual undertaking will follow him to the grave. It is specifically in the context of Avraham's childlessness that Eli'ezer's name is mentioned. Given Eli'ezer's spiritual sterility, his appearance in Avraham's plea is understandable. Promises are valueless, Avraham asserts, if his mission has no future, if his only heir is the spiritually barren and accursed Eli'ezer.

Furthermore, it is significant that only in this context does Eli'ezer's name appear in the Torah. The problem with Eli'ezer does not relate to the anonymous "slave of Avraham," the righteous extension of his master. The problem arises with respect to the intrinsic Eli'ezer; it is manifest when considering Eli'ezer per se, *by name*. From this perspective, we recognize that he has internalized nothing, and essentially he remains spiritually barren and accursed Kena'an.

It is nevertheless ostensibly surprising that specifically this mention of "*Damesek* (דמשק) Eli'ezer" is understood by the Talmud to imply "that [Eli'ezer] draws (דולה) and gives to drink (משקה) of the teaching of his master to others" (*Yoma* 28b). By now, however, this description is comprehensible even in its context, since it essentially characterizes the very dialectic upon which any understanding of Eli'ezer is predicated. He is a righteous extension of Avraham, an "elder occupied in study" who "rules over his passions like him" and distributes "the teaching of his master" far and wide. But the teaching remains "*of his master*"; Eli'ezer within remains Kena'an, accursed and barren. He has become "blessed," but only to a degree. True to the legacy of Kena'an, it is *only* "by serving the righteous [Avraham] faithfully," and *only to that extent*, that Eli'ezer "left the category of 'accursed' for the category of 'blessed' " (*BeR.R.* 60:7).[59]

Avraham emphasizes that, even with a potential heir like the righteous scholar Eli'ezer, he will still remain without a perpetuator of *his spiritual legacy*. A superficial reflection cannot function as a spiritual heir. In that sense, Eli'ezer is "utterly accursed; he will not inherit Avraham" (*BeR.R.* 44:11, *Yal.Sh.* BeReshith:76). Ultimately, he remains vacuous and sterile, lacking both identity and perpetuation. The verdict inevitably remains: "*This one will not be your heir*" (BeReshith 15:4). After Eli'ezer's return to Eretz Yisra'el with Rivkah, having faithfully and successfully insured the perpetuation of Avraham's spiritual undertaking through Yitzchak, the Torah concludes, "The slave related to Yitzchak all of the matters that he had done" (BeReshith 24:66). He is not even called a man, and he is never mentioned in the Bible again. Having completed his role as anonymous extension of his master, Eli'ezer disappears from the stage, forever.[89]

5. CONCLUSION — THE CHATTER OF SLAVES

Through our Midrashic odyssey, a coherent image of Eli'ezer, slave of Avraham, has emerged from amid the myriad, disparate Midrashim that intimate his mysterious identity. What initially appeared as a plethora of inconsistent and contradictory sources is resolved, upon further investigation, as diverse components of one intricate, composite portrait with which Chazal provide us. Upon consideration, this emergent portrait of Eli'ezer seems depressingly bleak. It appears that the faithful servant was ultimately a failure, never internally illuminated by the spiritual effulgence of the illustrious household that he served. One wonders what real purpose was served by his belonging to that household and particularly by his presence being recorded in the Torah. Yet the Torah not only informs us of Eli'ezer's existence, but dedicates an inordinate segment of Sefer BeReshith to detailing his exploits. Regarding Eli'ezer, Chazal conclude, "The chatter of slaves of the patriarchs is preferable to the teaching of the children" (BeR.R. 60:8).[3] This preference seems incomprehensible. The "teaching of the children" has substance; the "chatter of slaves" is a mere echo.

In a sense, this preference seems didactic. As a polished reflection of his master, Eli'ezer can offer us a more faithful display of Avraham than can any other man, since Eli'ezer lacks an identity of his own to interfere. While the "chatter of slaves" is a mere echo, it echoes the master himself more rigorously than does the "teaching of the children." Moreover, through Eli'ezer's behavior, we can glimpse the image of Avraham on a more comprehensible, earthly level than that of the patriarch himself.[90] Of course, as we have seen, Eli'ezer's behavior is only a superficial display. But inasmuch as the Torah continuously emphasizes the pre-eminence of deed over creed, our concern is principally to learn the ways of Avraham in practice. These ways are faithfully exhibited by Eli'ezer, reflection of Avraham, purveyor of the teaching of his master.[91]

In a broader sense, Eli'ezer's chatter, faithfully echoing Avraham, is a testimony to perseverance and dedication, of both himself and his master. Avraham, devoted to his universal mission to infuse spirituality into every aspect and every level of life, refuses to surrender to the apparent incorrigibility of Eli'ezer that is rooted in the curse of Kena'an. With dogged steadfastness, he actualizes his dedication to permeating his slave as well with G-dliness. And indeed, nothing is left of external Eli'ezer that is not touched by the sanctity of his master: To the extent that Eli'ezer exists, he has become an echo of Avraham. Similarly, Eli'ezer himself, undaunted by his roots in so accursed a stock, confronts his reality without despairing of rehabilitation, and emerges, at least externally, as Avraham's faithful servant. While Eli'ezer himself has no future in this world, to that extent he is a shareholder in the future of Avraham, the legacy of us all. Even if "Kena'an is Eli'ezer," nevertheless *by serving the righteous [Avraham] faithfully, he left the category of 'accursed' for the category of 'blessed'"* (*BeR.R.* 60:7).[59] To that extent, Eli'ezer, even as an ultimate failure, has succeeded and can teach us of his success.

NOTES

1. See *Yoma* 28b, *Ta'anith* 4a, *Sanhedrin* 95a, *Chullin* 95b, *Tar. Yonathan* on BeReshith 24:2, and numerous Midrashic references.

2. See *BeR.R.* 44:9, 11 (and *Mathnoth Kehunah*, ibid.) and *Yal.Sh.* BeReshith:76.

3. See also *Yal.Sh.* BeReshith:109 and Rashi on BeReshith 24:42.

4. See *Yoma* 28b and *Nedarim* 32a.

5. See *BeM.R.* 21:20, *Tan. Pinchas:*13, and *Yal.Sh.* BeReshith:109.

6. See *BeR.R.* 59:8 and *Yal.Sh.* BeReshith:106.

7. See *Derech Eretz Z.* 1 and *Yal.Sh.* BeReshith:76, 109.

8. See *VaY.R.* 20:2, *Koh.R.* 9:7, *Pir.DeR.E.* 31, and *Yal.Sh.* BeReshith:98-100.

9. See *Babba Metzi'a* 86b, *BeR.R.* 44:11 and 59:9, *Pir.DeR.E.* 16, and *Yal.Sh.* BeReshith:76, 107, 109 and Hoshea:528.

10. See *BeR.R.* 59:9 and 60:7, *VaY.R.* 17:5, and *Yal.Sh.* ibid.

11. See *Sofrim* 21:9, *T.DeV.Eli.Z.* 24, *Pir.DeR.E.* 16, and *Yal.Sh.* BeReshith:109 and BeMidbar:765.

12. Implied here is the principle that "these and those are the words of the Living G-d" (*Gittin* 6b, *Eruvin* 13b). See also *Michtav MeEliyahu*, III, 353-354 (and II, 68), for a more detailed exposition on this subject.

13. See *Ha'amek Davar*, ibid.

14. See also *Sanhedrin* 38a and *Tos. Sanhedrin* 8:3.

15. See also *Sotah* 3b and *Gittin* 38b. It should be noted that this injunction is

enumerated as one of the six hundred thirteen commandments of the Torah. See *Sefer HaMitzvoth* (Rambam), *Aseh* 235, and *Chinuch, Mitzvah* 332. Moreover, both *Mishneh Torah* and *Shulchan Aruch* quote the Gemara as basis for the Halachic conclusion that one who frees a Kena'ani slave "violates a positive commandment." See *Yad Hil. Avadim* 9:6 and *Yoreh Dei'ah* 267:79.

16. See R. S.R. Hirsch on BeReshith 9:25-27. Regarding Kena'an's innately accursed nature, see also *Chiddushei Aggadoth* (Maharal) on *Sanhedrin* 108b, ד"ה וישלח את העורב וכו', and *Be'er HaGolah, Be'er* 5 (p. 103); *Ha'amek Davar*, ibid. 9:24; and *Sefath Emeth* on *Chayyei Sarah* (5649).

17. This principle is axiomatic in Judaism and cited repeatedly by Chazal. See for example *Shabbath* 105b, *Megillah* 12b, *Nedarim* 32a, *Sotah* 8b, *Sanhedrin* 90a, *Kallah Rabbathi* 1, *BeR.R.* 9:11, *BeM.R.* 10:2, and *Yal.Sh.* Devarim:940 (on Devarim 31).

18. This principle is articulated or suggested in numerous statements by Chazal, regarding both reward and punishment. Its broader implications are beyond the scope of our discussion here. See for example *Eruvin* 19a; *Yoma* 38b-39a; *Sukkah* 52b; *Ta'anith* 11a; *Chagigah* 16a; *Mish. Sotah* 1:7-9; *Sotah* 3b, 8b-9b, 11a, and 42a; *Babba Bathra* 16a; *Sanhedrin* 103a; *Avodah Zarah* 2a and 5a; *Avoth* 2:7 and 4:2, 11; *Avoth DeRabbi Nathan* 30:4; *Kallah Rabbathi* 3, *BeR.R.* 22:6, 41:7, and 50:8; *Sh.R.* 7:4 and 40:1; *Koh.R.* 3:9; and *Tan. VaYera*:12; and see commentaries loc. cit.

19. See also R. Ovadyah Seforno, R. S.R. Hirsch, and *Ha'amek Davar*, ibid.

20. See also the Midrash cited by *Da'ath Zekenim MiBa'alei HaTosafoth* on BeReshith 9:25: "Cham saw and recounted the story to his brothers in a mocking and disrespectful manner, revealing the matter in the market." In addition, see *Tar. Yonathan* and *Tar. Onkelos*, ibid., who also translate "outside" as "in the market."

21. See *Sanhedrin* 108b (and *Chiddushei Aggadoth* [Maharal], ibid., ד"ה וישלח את העורב וכו'), *Yer. Ta'anith* 1:6 (7a), *BeR.R.* 36:7, and *Tan. Noach*:12.

22. See also *Gur Aryeh*, ibid. 9:22, and *Be'er HaGolah, Be'er* 5 (p. 103).

23. See *Sanhedrin* 70a and Rashi on BeReshith 9:22. See also *BeR.R.* 36:7, *Tan. Noach*:15, *Pir.DeR.E.* 23, and *Yal.Sh.* BeReshith:61.

    The deeper implications of these opinions are beyond the scope of our discussion. Maharal discusses them at length (see *Chiddushei Aggadoth* on *Sanhedrin* 70a, ד"ה חד אמר סרסו וכו', and *Be'er HaGolah, Be'er* 5 (pp. 103-104).

24. Regarding the inherent association of Cham with sexual indecency, see especially *Chiddushei Aggadoth* (Maharal) on *Sanhedrin* 70a, ד"ה חד אמר סרסו וכו', and *Be'er HaGolah, Be'er* 5 (p. 103). Regarding the symbolism of such behavior as the ultimate debasement of man and the quintessential negation of Torah, see ibid. and particularly *Derech HaChayyim* on *Avoth* 1:2. See also n. 30, below.

25. See R. S.R. Hirsch on BeReshith 9:18, 22. See also *Chiddushei Aggadoth* (Maha-

ral) on *Sanhedrin* 70a, 'ד"ה חד אמר סרסו וכו, and *Be'er HaGolah, Be'er* 5 (p. 103).

26. See BeReshith 27:46 and 28:8; VaYikra 18:3, 24-29 and 20:23; and Devarim 8:20, 9:4-5, 12:2, 29-31, and 18:9-14.

27. See R. Ovadyah Seforno and *Ha'amek Davar* on BeReshith 9:22.

28. See also *Tan. Noach*:15, *Pir.DeR.E.* 23, *Yal.Sh.* BeReshith:61, and the Midrash cited by *Da'ath Zekenim MiBa'alei HaTosafoth* on BeReshith 9:25.

29. See also *Sifrei* on Devarim 12:30 and *Sh.HaSh.R.* 4:8 (3).

30. See also *Chiddushei Aggadoth* (Maharsha), ibid., who offers an analogous assessment of Kena'an's "commands."

    In addition, Maharal (see n. 24, above) notes a correspondence between the three pillars upon which the world stands — "Torah, service, and active loving-kindness" (*Avoth* 1:2) — and the three cardinal sins (respectively) — sexual immorality, idolatry, and murder (see *Sanhedrin* 74a). While the deeper implications of this correspondence are beyond the scope of this discussion, one notes an additional correspondence between these and the three central components of Kena'an's legacy (respectively): "*love debauchery*," "*hate your masters*," and "*love robbery*." Kena'an's initial "command" to his progeny, "*love one another*," guarantees a united front in these nihilistic directives. The final "command," "*do not speak truth*," epitomizes the ideology expressed in all the foregoing, utterly antithetical to G-d Whose seal is Truth (see *Shabbath* 55a, *Yoma* 69b, *Sanhedrin* 64a, *Yer. Sanhedrin* 1:1 [1b], *BeR.R.* 8:5 and 81:2, *Dev.R.* 1:10, *Sh.HaSh.R.* 1:9 [1], and *Yal.Sh.* Tehillim:834).

31. See also R. S.R. Hirsch on BeReshith 9:25, 27 and *Ha'amek Davar* on BeReshith 9:25, who discuss Kena'an's innate tendency toward slavery. See also *Sefath Emeth* on *Chayyei Sarah* (5649), who relates the ameliorative role of slavery for Kena'an to the opinion (see text) that freeing a Kena'ani slave is not regarded Halachically as even beneficial to him.

32. See also *Tan. Lech*:8 and *Yal.Sh.* Yeshayahu:473. In addition, see *Pesachim* 88b, *Kiddushin* 23b, and *Yal.Sh.* Koheleth:968.

33. See BeReshith 9:25-27 and R. S.R. Hirsch, ibid. 9:27.

34. Both Shem and Yefeth demonstrated their values and consequent filial responsibility in covering Noach (see BeReshith 9:23). See also *Chiddushei Aggadoth* (Maharal) on *Sanhedrin* 70a, 'ד"ה חד אמר סרסור וכו, and R. S.R. Hirsch on BeReshith 9:27, regarding the roles of Noach's three sons as archetypes and the contrast between the roles of Shem and Yefeth and the role of Cham.

    It should be noted that, while Shem and Yefeth both participated in covering Noach, the Torah implies that each had a distinct role. Significantly, the Torah commences its description of their conduct by employing the singular form, "ויקח שם" ("Shem took"), in lieu of a plural reference ("ויקחו") to both Shem and Yefeth acted on Shem's initiative. (See BeR.R. 36:6, *Tan. Noach*:15, Yal.Sh. BeReshith:61, and Rashi on BeReshith ibid.) Shem, progenitor of Hellenistic culture (see BeReshith 10:2, *Megillah* 9b, and *Yal.Sh.*

BeReshith:61), reacted to the aesthetic offense in his father's disgrace. (See *Gur Aryeh* on BeReshith 9:23, R. S.R. Hirsch on BeReshith 9:27, *HaTorah VeHaMitzvah* (Malbim) on BeReshith 9:23, and *Ha'amek Davar* on BeReshith 9:23, 26-27.) Shem asserted values of G-dliness and spirituality, while Yefeth asserted values of aesthetics and social etiquette.

Regardless of this distinction, however, the motives of both represent civilizing forces with respect to Kena'an, that may ultimately be harnessed to tame the nihilistic beast within him through his enslavement to Shem and Yefeth.

35. See especially R. S.R. Hirsch, ibid.: "It will be the salvation of Kena'an that the approach that is antithetical to his should dominate... Thus, Kena'an too will merit fulfilling his divine mission." (R. Hirsch [ibid.] presents a far more extensive thesis to detail the respective roles of Yefeth and Shem — and Kena'an's subordination to them — in realizing this goal.) See also *Sefath Emeth* on *Chayyei Sarah* (5649): "By being enslaved to one who is blessed, [Kena'an] will be able to rehabilitate his soul."

36. See *Babba Kamma* 74b and *Yad Hil. Avadim* 5:17.

37. See also R. S.R. Hirsch and *HaTorah VeHaMitzvah* (Malbim) on VaYikra ibid.

38. Rambam's assertion is echoed in all classic commentaries on the Midrash and Aggadah. See also, for example, the introduction to *Moreh HaNevochim*, *Ma'amar al Odoth Derashoth Chazal* (R. Avraham b. Rambam), the introduction of Rashba to his commentary on Aggadah (cited in *Ein Ya'akov* on *Berachoth* 6a), the introduction of *Ein Ya'akov*, the introduction of *Chiddushei Aggadoth* (Maharsha), *Kelalei HaMidrash* and *Darchei HaAggadoth VeHaDerashoth* (R. Yeshayahu Horowitz), *Ma'amar al Aggadoth Chazal* (Ramchal), the introduction of *Yefeh To'ar* on *Midrash Rabbah*, the introduction of *Etz Yosef* on *Ein Ya'akov*, and *Mevo HaAggadoth* (Maharatz Chayyoth).

39. See *Gur Aryeh* on BeReshith 14:13.

40. See also a similar approach employed by R. Eliyahu Mizrachi and *Gur Aryeh* on BeReshith 38:24, Maharzu on *BeR.R.* 85:10, and *Torah Temimah* on BeMidbar 22:5, n. 2.

41. See com. on *Sanhedrin* 105a, also cited by *Etz Yosef*, ibid.

42. See also *Yal. Sh.* BeReshith:107 and Hoshea:528, and Rashi on BeReshith 24:39.

43. See *Mo'ed Katan* 26a and *Makkoth* 24b.

44. See also *VaY.R.* 20:2, *Koh.R.* 9:7, and *Yal.Sh.* BeReshith:98-100. In addition, see *BeR.R.* 56:2 and *Tan. VaYera*:23, where Avraham's youths are not identified.

45. See BeReshith 15:4 and 17:20-21, 21:12.

46. See Rashi on *Yevamoth* ibid., ד"ה שבו לכם פה, who relates "you remain here with the donkey" to Eli'ezer slave of Avraham. See also *Da'ath Zekenim MiBa'alei HaTosafoth* on BeReshith 22:5.

47. Note the initial usage of ברך in the Torah (BeReshith 1:22,28) as a blessing to "be fruitful and multiply." See also R. S.R. Hirsch on BeReshith 3:14.

48. The pre-eminent *middah* (attribute) of Avraham is *chesed* (active loving-kind-ness). Briefly stated, this implies that the portal of Avraham's relationship with G-d is *chesed*, the channel through which Avraham approaches G-d and through which G-d is revealed to Avraham. Avraham seeks G-d as the prime Giver: the ultimate Author of all *chesed* manifest in the world. And indeed, thus is G-d revealed to Avraham: "Give... *chesed* to Avraham" (Michah 7:20). See also *BeR.R.* 60:2 and *Yal.Sh.* BeReshith:72.

In contrast, the *middah* of Yitzchak is *gevurah* (overwhelming awe). While Avraham's approach to serving G-d is primarily through *active* loving-kind-ness, Yitzchak seeks G-d principally through *muted* awe and *passive* transcen-dence of this world. See BeReshith 31:42,53 and Ramban, ibid. 31:42 and 46:1. See also *Shabbath* 89b (and *Netzach Yisra'el* [Maharal], ch. 13), *Sifra* on VaYikra 26:42, and *VaY.R.* 36:5.

The unique *middoth* that epitomize each of the three patriarchs and their individual innovativeness in each forging a new way to serving G-d are suggested in numerous Midrashim and are axiomatic in classic Jewish thought. Obviously, an extensive discussion of these subjects is beyond the scope of this essay. See, for example, *Semachoth* 1:14, *Berachoth* 16b (and *Iyyei HaYam*, ד"ה אין קורין אבות אלא לשלשה כו' [cited in *Chiddushei Ge'onim* on *Ein Ya'akov* ibid.], and *Etz Yosef*, ibid., ד"ה אלא עד הכא חשיבי כו'), *Chiddushei Aggadoth* (Maharal) on *Babba Metzi'a* 85b, ד"ה אליהו הוי שכיח וכו', and *Etz Yosef* and *Dover Shalom* on "*Shemoneh Esreh*," ד"ה א-לקי אברהם וכו'. See also the responsum of Rashba cited by *Tefillah LeDavid* (Addereth), n.5, ד"ה בעבור אבותינו שבטחו בך (quoted in *Olath Re'iyyah*, II, 393), *Teshuvoth Panim Me'iroth* 1:39, and *Tifereth Yisra'el* (Maharal), ch.20.

49. See. *Tar. Yonathan* on BeReshith 14:14.

50. See *Mid. Talpiyoth*.

51. See *Sofrim* 21:9, *Pir.DeR.E.* 16, and *Yal.Sh.* BeMidbar:765.

52. See BeReshith 10:6-8.

53. See also *Pesachim* 94b, *Chagigah* 13a, *BeR.R.* 42:4, *Tan. Acharei*:1, *Yal.Sh.* BeReshith:72, *Tar. Yerushalmi* on BeReshith 10:9, and Rashi on BeReshith 10:8-9 and on *Chullin* 89a, ד"ה נמרוד.

54. See *Tan. Lech*:12.

55. See *Chullin* 89a, *BeR.R.* 23:7 and 26:4, *Pir.DeR.E.* 24, *Yal.Sh.* BeReshith:62, and Rashi on BeReshith 10:8, 11 and on *Pesachim* 94b, ד"ה שהמריד.

56. See *Sifra* on VaYikra 26:14, *Tar. Yonathan* on BeReshith 10:8-9, and the sources cited in nn. 53-55, above.

57. See *Eruvin* 53a, *Pesachim* 118a, *BeR.R.* 38:13 and 42:4, *Tan. Lech*:2, 6, *Yal.Sh.* BeReshith:62, 72, and *Tar. Yonathan* and Rashi on BeReshith 14:1.

58. See for example *BeR.R.* 44:7 and 59:5; *VaY.R.* 27:5 and 28:4; *Koh.R.* 2:14, 2:26, 3:15, and 4:13; *Tan. Lech*:12, *Acharei*:1, and *Emor*:9; *Mid. Tehillim* 24:8; and *Yal.Sh.* BeReshith:76, Yeshayahu:449, and Tehillim:697.

59. See also *VaY.R.* 17:5 and *Yal.Sh.* BeReshith:109.

60. See also *BeR.R.* 60:9 and *Yal.Sh.* BeReshith:109.

61. See BeReshith 13:13, 18:20-21, and 19:4-13.

62. See also *BeR.R.* 60:7.

63. See *BeR.R.* 59:9 and the sources cited in n.42, above.

64. See also *Tan. Pinchas*:13, *Mid. Mishlei* 13:25, and *Yal.Sh.* BeReshith:109 and Mishlei:950.

65. Eli'ezer's roots have already been discussed extensively.

Ruth hailed from Mo'av (see Ruth 1:4), where according to Chazal she was a royal princess (see *Nazir* 23b, *Sotah* 47a, *Sanhedrin* 105b, *Horayoth* 10b, *Ru.R.* 2:9, and *Yal.Sh.* Shofetim:42 and Ruth:600). Mo'av appears in the Torah and the Midrash as the embodiment of licentiousness: a nation whose heritage is incest and whose confrontation with Yisra'el is predicated upon seduction to immorality and idolatry. (See BeReshith 19:33-37; BeMidbar 25:1-3; *Sifrei* on Devarim 33:2; *BeR.R.* 51:10; *BeM.R.* 20:23; *Ru.R.* 5:14; *Tan. Balak*:17; and *Yal.Sh.* BeReshith:86, BeMidbar:771, Devarim:951, and Yirmeyahu:331.) Mo'av, together with Ammon, becomes the paradigm of depravity, the nation to be shunned for all eternity (see Devarim 23:4-7 and *Sifrei*, ibid. 23:7). Ruth's conversion to Judaism and particularly her exceptional modesty (see *Shabbath* 113b, *Ru.R.* 4:9, *Tan. BeHar*:3, and *Yal.Sh.* Ruth:601) contrast vividly with her quintessentially corrupt origins.

King Chizkiyyah was the son of Achaz, one of the only kings of Yehudah who is implicated in idol worship (see Melachim II 16 and Divrei HaYamim II 28). "He went in the ways of the kings of Yisra'el and also cast idols for the Be'alim. He... burned his children in fire according to the abominations of the heathen nations... He sacrificed to the gods of Darmesek... He shut the doors of the house of G-d, and he made for himself altars in every corner in Yerushalayim. And in each and every city of Yehudah he made private altars to burn incense to other gods" (Divrei HaYamim II 28:2-3, 23-25). Given such an environment, the Midrash understandably characterizes King Chizkiyyah as "pure from amid impure" (*BeM.R.* 19:1 and *Tan. Chukkath*:3 on Iyyov 14:4) and asserts that "through himself he came to a recognition of the Holy One Blessed be He" (*BeM.R.* 14:2). See also *VaY.R.* 36:3.

66. See R. Avraham b. Ezra, R. Ovadyah Seforno, and *HaTorah VeHaMitzvah* (Malbim) on BeReshith 9:24.

67. See also *Yal.Sh.* BeReshith:61 and Rashi on BeReshith ibid.

68. See also *BeR.R.* 43:2 (and Maharzu, ibid.) and *Yal.Sh.* BeReshith:73. In addition, see *BeR.R.* 44:9, *VaY.R.* 28:4, *BeM.R.* 18:21, *Pir.DeR.E.* 27, *Mid. Tehillim* 110:4, *Yal.Sh.* BeReshith:76, and *Tar. Yonathan* and Rashi on BeReshith 14:14, that cite the numerological equivalence.

69. See also *Gur Aryeh, Keli Yakar*, and *Torah Temimah* on BeReshith 14:14.

70. See Ritva (cited in *Ein Ya'akov*) and *Chiddushei Aggadoth* (Maharsha), ibid. See

also VaYikra 19:32 and com., ibid. In addition, see *Kiddushin* 32b and *Sifra* on VaYikra ibid.

71. See also *BeR.R.* 60:7 and *Yal.Sh.* BeReshith:109. In addition, see R. S.R. Hirsch on BeReshith 24:2, 27.

72. See *BeR.R.* 60:1 and *Yal.Sh.* BeReshith:107 and Yeshayahu:473.

73. Compare *BeR.R.* 59:8 and *Yal.Sh.* BeReshith:102 with *BeR.R* 60:6 and *Yal. Sh.* BeReshith:109.

74. See *Babba Metzi'a* 86b, *Pir.DeR.E.* 16, and *Yal.Sh.* BeReshith:109 (cited above).

75. See also *BeR.R.* 59:8 and *Yal.Sh.* BeReshith:106 (cited above).

76. See *Mish. Sanhedrin* 4:5, *Sanhedrin* 38a, and *Tos. Sanhedrin* 8:3.

77. See also *BeM.R.* 21:2 and *Tan. Pinchas:*10. In addition, see *Berachoth* 58a and *Tos. Berachoth* 6:5.

78. See *BeM.R.* 21:20 and the sources cited in n.64, above.

79. See *Nedarim* 32a, *Tan. Lech:*13, and the sources cited in n.64, above.

80. See also *BeR.R.* 61:1, *Mid. Tehillim* 1:13 and 16:7, *Avoth DeRabbi Nathan* 33:1, and *Yal.Sh.* BeReshith:109 and Tehillim:614, 667.

81. See also *Yer. Chagigah* 1:1 (1a), *Yer. Sotah* 3:4 (14b), *Tos. Sotah* 7:6, and *BeM.R.* 14:4. In addition, see *Avoth DeRabbi Nathan* 18:2 (*Nuschath HaGra*, ibid., n.1) and *Mechilta* on Shemoth 13:2.

82. See *Babba Metzi'a* 86b (cited above). It is noteworthy that, while Eli'ezer *did* look for guests (and fine none), Avraham (upon going to look himself) beholds G-d's presence at the door. Evidently, Eli'ezer was incapable of relating to so spiritual an experience. To that extent, Eli'ezer *is* faithless, and Avraham's characterization of him with the maxim that "there is no faithfulness in slaves" is valid.

    Similarly, Maharal (in *Chiddushei Aggadoth*, ibid., ד"ה לית הימנותא בעבדי), relates this characterization, that "there is no faithfulness in slaves," to the assessment of Eli'ezer as "a nation that resembles a donkey" (see nn. 44 and 46, above). Inasmuch as Eli'ezer is limited to an utterly materialistic ("חומר") perspective (see text, above), he cannot possibly relate to truth ("faithfulness") in its ultimate sense as a transcendent absolute.

    See also n.83, below.

83. See *Pir. DeR.E.* 16 and *Yal.Sh.* BeReshith:109 (cited above). Significantly, these Midrashim also specify that Eli'ezer's return to Chevron was miraculously accelerated "so that the slave would not be alone with Rivkah at night," implying at least some basis for Avraham's suspicions, had special divine intervention not been forthcoming.

    Furthermore, the implication of Eli'ezer in such sexually indecent behavior is strikingly reminiscent of the legacy of Cham (see text, above).

    See also n.82, above.

84. See also R. S.R. Hirsch, *HaTorah VeHaMitzvah* (Malbim), and *Meshech*

Chochmah on BeReshith 22:5.

85. In contrast, it should be noted that Maharal analyzes Avraham's relationship with the donkey in the context of the *akeidah* as symbolic of Avraham's transcendence with respect to materialism. (See *Derech HaChayyim* on *Avoth* 5:19 and *Chiddushei Aggadoth* on *Nedarim* 32a, 'וכו בתורה שהורייקן ה"ד.)

86. As indicated above, even this reference is contested, since the Midrash considers the possibility that "Eli'ezer" may in fact not be a name at all but a descriptive label for Lot. (See n. 2, above.) While Chazal (see n. 1, above) identify Eli'ezer as the anonymous "elder of [Avraham's] household who rules over all that is his" (BeReshith 24:2), his name is not mentioned at all in the ensuing narrative. Moreover, while *Targum Yonathan* identifies this "elder of [Avraham's] household" as Eli'ezer, neither *Targum Onkelos* nor *Targum Yerushalmi* state such an association. In any case, Eli'ezer is mentioned nowhere else in the Bible.

87. See *Mathnoth Kehunah*, ibid.

88. See also *Ha'amek Davar* on BeReshith 15:3.

89. Unquestionably, Eli'ezer's disappearance is one of the central enigmas surrounding him. While limitations of space preclude a more extensive treatment of this subject in the current essay, a brief overview of some of the issues involved is provided below. (*Ed. note*: A far more detailed analysis of this subject, from which this overview is abridged, will be furnished by the author upon request.)

Chazal provide the necessary conclusion to Eli'ezer's career in two alternate, uncanny directions. Perhaps the stranger of these epilogues is the identification of Eli'ezer as Og, the malevolent giant king of Bashan (see n. 11, above):

> "The elder of Avraham's household" was his slave Eliezer. Whence was he his slave? When [Avraham] left Ur Kasdim, all the great men of the generation arose and gave him gifts. And Nimrod arose and signed his slave Eli'ezer over to Avraham. And when [Eli'ezer] bestowed kindness upon Yitzchak [Avraham's] son [by bringing him Rivkah, Avraham] released him to freedom. And the Holy One Blessed be He rewarded him in this world, in order that there be no reward for the wicked in the world to come, and established him as a king, and he is Og, king of Bashan.
>
> (*Pir.DeR.E.* 16, *Yal. Sh.* BeReshith:109)

It is ostensibly unclear what motivated Chazal to fuse two such thematically — and chronologically — disparate characters. Apparently, a proper understanding of Eli'ezer requires investigating the character of Og as well.

In light of such investigation, however, the identification of Avraham's slave as Og seems particularly odd, since in numerous Midrashim Og appears as the paradigmatic adversary of Avraham and his heirs. (See *BeR.R.* 42:8 and *Dev.R.* 1:25 regarding his confrontation with Avraham. See *BeR.R.* 53:10, *Dev.R.* 1:25, and *Yal.Sh.* BeReshith:94 and Devarim:810 regarding his confrontations with the other patriarchs. See also *Niddah* 61a; *BeM.R.* 19:32, *Tan. Chukkath*:25; *Yal.Sh.* BeReshith:72, BeMidbar:765, and Tehillim:884, *Tar. Yonathan* on BeReshith 14:13, on BeMidbar 21:34; and Rashi on BeReshith 14:13, on BeMidbar 21:34, and on Devarim 1:4 and 3:2, 11.) Upon investigation, it becomes clear that the conflict of Og with Avraham — and subsequently with Yitzchak and Ya'akov and (explicitly) the nation of Yisra'el en masse — intimates his struggle to supplant Avraham's spiritual values and mission with his own. Any endeavor to comprehend Og, then, must focus on what Og represents.

While the Torah refers only briefly to Og's size (see Devarim 3:11), Chazal describe his incredible physical proportions at great length. (See Berachoth 54b; *Niddah* 24b; *Sofrim* 21:9; *Dev.R.* 1:24; *T.DeV.Eli.Z.* 24; *Yal.Sh.* BeMidbar:765, Devarim:810, and Tehillim:884; and *Tar. Yonathan* on BeMidbar 21:35.) He is — literally — physical in the extreme. It appears that Og, as the ultimately overblown giant, represents the ultimate egocentric perspective. His vast size implies a disproportionate significance accorded to himself in particular and man in general. Og is self-centered in the extreme: For himself, he is the final barometer of all meaning, and he acknowledges the existence of nothing beyond the sphere of man. (Regarding the quasi-divine, symbolic role embodied by Og, pre-eminent adversary of Yisra'el, see also Rashba on *Berachoth* 54b, 'ד"ה עקר טורא וכו; *Derash Mosheh*, ibid., 'ד"ה אבן שבקש עוג וכו, and on *Niddah* 24b, 'ד"ה תניא אבא שאול אומר וכו [both cited in *Chiddushei Ge'onim* on *Ein Ya'akov*]; *Gur Aryeh* on BeReshith 14:13 and *Chiddushei Aggadoth* [Maharal] on *Niddah* 24b, 'ד"ה קובר מתים הייתי וכו, and on *Niddah* 61a, ד"ה שמא תעמוד לו זכותו של צדיק; and *Chiddushei Aggadoth* [Maharsha] on *Berachoth* 54b, 'ד"ה אבן שבקש עוג וכו, and on *Niddah* 24b, (.'ד"ה קובר מתים וכו.)

Thus, Og indeed represents the antithesis of Avraham's mission to proclaim the immanence of G-dliness and spirituality in the world. Avraham's entire life is the ultimate negation of the closed, self-centered circle with which Og circumscribes all worldly existence. Og's struggle with Avraham, and subsequently with Yitzchak, Ya'akov, and the nation of Yisra'el as a whole, is an inevitable ideological conflict regarding the destiny of the world. At every critical stage in the spiritual metamorphosis of Yisra'el into the nation of G-d, Og necessarily emerges as principal adversary, intent upon annihilating Yisra'el and supplanting its mission with his own. For Yisra'el to emerge with its unique identity as the nation of G-d, each stage with its Og must be confronted. Ultimately, for the nation of Yisra'el to enter the Land of Yisra'el and truly realize its spiritual destiny, Og and all that he represents must be destroyed. Ultimately, Og and Yisra'el, mutually exclusive, cannot coexist.

We have clearly encountered the spiritually vacuous attitude of Og before; one senses a kinship between Og's egocentricity and Eli'ezer's equally barren Kena'ani nihilism. Kena'an completely lacked values and ideals and degraded man as a utilitarian commodity. Og is *obsessed* with man as the *only* value and inflates himself in particular into an overblown giant. But neither sees man created in the image of the divine; both agree on the utter absence of transcendent spirituality manifest in this world. The substance of the two ideologies is identical, regardless of distinctions in basis and form. The conclusion of Chazal, then, is a reflection of this essential reality: *"He [Eli'ezer] is Og, king of Bashan" (Pir.DeR.E.* 16, *Yal. Sh.* BeReshith:109).

Significantly, in the biography of Og, like that of Kena'an, slavery figures prominently, although as a self-imposed condition: offering himself as slave to Noach and his sons (see *Pir.DeR.E.* 23). Inasmuch as Og's essential problem is his obsession with himself, this is not surprising. One who regards any man, including himself, as the supreme value can readily submit to domination by a greater man.

Since Og is man-centered, he will orient himself with respect to any great man, whether saint or scoundrel. He initially presents himself to Noach and his sons, as they are the sole survivors of humanity. Subsequently, according to the Midrash, he was enslaved to Nimrod (see n. 51, above). This is certainly consistent with Og's anthropocentric obsession, since Nimrod is specifically described in the Torah as the innovator of extraordinary might in the world (see BeReshith 10:8-9) and is the first man in history to whom the Torah ascribes kingship (see ibid. 10:10). Chazal amplify this description of worldly greatness, describing Nimrod as one of ten kings in all of history, and the first king after G-d Himself, who ruled over the entire world (see *Pir.DeR.E.* 11 and *Tar. Sheni* on Ester 1:1). Og subordinates himself to this human greatness. When Avraham emerges from Ur Kasdim victorious over Nimrod's idolatrous ideology, however, Og's allegiance is naturally transferred to him, as "the man greatest among the giants" (Yehoshua 14:15; see the sources cited in n. 51, above).

Clearly the domination of Og can potentially have a rehabilitative effect on his spiritual barrenness, analogous to the desired impact of slavery on equally barren Kena'an. Og's egocentric obsession subordinates him, by transference, to all human greatness. If, then, his master regards himself as subordinate to transcendent values, Og too may orient himself toward those values out of reverence for his master. This then is Avraham's challenge in educating Eli'ezer — né Og — an educational process graphically described by Chazal (see *Sofrim* 21:9 and *Yal.Sh.* BeMidbar:765). While a more detailed analysis of this process is beyond the scope of the current discussion, we can observe its conclusion. Avraham endeavors to orient Eli'ezer toward Avraham's spiritual mission as an extension of Eli'ezer's own egocentricity. Eli'ezer is constrained to function *as* Avraham so that his self-centered dedication to himself will include Avraham's mission; he is to personally insure the perpetuation of Avraham's legacy by himself finding Yitzchak's wife. Apparently, Avraham's strategy is successful: Eli'ezer functions faithfully as Avraham himself. As we have seen, he becomes so faithful a spiritual reflection of his master on every external level that, throughout the entire narrative that ensues, he is never once even mentioned by his own name.

Paradoxically, we thus confront once again Eli'ezer's failure. Externally,

Eli'ezer becomes the embodiment of Avraham's mission. And yet, when his task is concluded, in his last appearance in the Torah, he is still merely "the slave" (BeReshith 24:66). He is faithful only to the extent that he is an anonymous slave; within, his identity has remained unchanged. The righteousness of Avraham that he so faithfully embodied was merely egotistic dedication to his assignment. When his task is over, the mission reverts to Avraham, and Eli'ezer remains the same overblown giant Og that he was, devoid of all values beyond himself. Thus, at this point, Avraham releases Eli'ezer (see *Pir.DeR.E.* 16 and *Yal.Sh.* BeReshith:109). Having done his utmost to reform Eli'ezer already, perhaps Avraham realizes that, as any master who fells his slave's eye or tooth (see above), there is nothing more that he can accomplish. On the one hand, Eli'ezer's *external* conduct is more than impeccable; it provides the nation of Yisra'el with its second matriarch, remaining for all eternity one of the pillars upon which the very existence of Yisra'el is predicated. On the other hand, *internally* Eli'ezer remains beyond even Avraham's reach. If the primary purpose of slavery is to rehabilitate the slave, nothing is to be achieved by further subjugation of Eli'ezer. After his tenure as Avraham's "faithful" slave is over, he remains overblown, egocentric Og, the antithesis of Avraham and his heirs, spurner of all transcendent spirituality and meaning in life. "Eli'ezer," the faithful servant of Avraham, disappears entirely.

Recall, however that the fate of Eli'ezer as Og is but one of two alternate conclusions offered in the Midrash for Eli'ezer's life. Especially in light of the foregoing, the alternate conclusion is particularly significant:

> Nine [individuals] entered Gan Eden while alive, and these are they: Chanoch son of Yered and Eliyahu and Mashiach and *Eli'ezer slave of Avraham...*

> (*Derech Eretz Z.* 1, *Yal.Sh.* BeReshith:76, 109)

Considering the perspective on Eli'ezer that we have already seen conveyed throughout Chazal, his inclusion on so extraordinary a list seems incomprehensible, especially since Avraham himself is not granted such accolades. Yet is appears that the Talmud posits specifically this fate for Eli'ezer (see *Babba Bathra* 58a and Rashi, ibid., ד"ה אשכחיה לאליעזר). *Bayith HaGadol* (on *Pir.DeR.E.* 16) notes the blatant inconsistency between Eli'ezer's fate as Og and his entry while alive into Gan Eden, but he provides no resolution of the contradiction between these divergent Midrashic traditions. Of course, it would be naive to imagine that such disparate conclusions can be reconciled with one another. Nevertheless, with the realization that both traditions are predicated upon the same description of Eli'ezer in the Torah and the same essential philosophical truths of Jewish tradition, it seems unacceptable to treat this contradiction as mere incoherence (see n. 12, above). We therefore feel impelled to understand this approach to Eli'ezer as well, how it relates to all the foregoing, and exactly how it differs. Obviously such understanding must be predicated on consideration of the role of Gan

Eden in general and, in particular, its significance here.

While an extended analysis of Gan Eden is obviously beyond the scope of our discussion here, it is significant that Gan Eden represents both the prologue and epilogue of human existence in this world. The first man was brought there upon his creation (see BeReshith 2:15) prior to his banishment (see ibid. 3:23-24), and the souls of all mankind are described as existing there prior to birth (see *Tan. Pekudei*:3). Ultimately, men, if meritorious, return there immediately after their demise. (See *Berachoth* 16b and 28b; *Yoma* 87a; *Kethubboth* 77b; *Avoth* 5:20; *Temurah* 16a; *BeR.R.* 65:22; *Sh.R.* 2:2; *Mid. Tehillim* 11:6,7; and *Yal.Sh.* BeReshith:20, 115, Shemu'el:123, and Melachim:252. See also *Sha'ar HaGemul* [Ramban], ch.8, and *Ma'amar HaIkkarim* [Ramchal], "BaGan Eden VeGeihinom.") Existence in this world is framed parenthetically by Gan Eden. To understand what Gan Eden signifies, we must compare it to the nature of existence in this world.

This world is pre-eminently an inconstant, dynamic world of becoming, not a static world of being. "In this world, one who is small can become great, and one who is great can become small" (*Ru.R.* 3:1, 2). (See also *Yal.Sh.* Yechezkel:362 and Koheleth:979 [on Koheleth 9]. In addition, see *Shabbath* 151b, *Avoth* 4:16, *Sh.R.* 31:14, *VaY.R.* 34:3, *Koh.R.* 1:13 and 3:10, *Tan. Mattoth*:6, *Mid. Mishlei* 6:6, and *Yal.Sh.* Devarim:898.) Man in this world is identified as "moving ones," in contradistinction to the angels, who are characterized as "the standing ones" (Zecharyah 3:7; see commentaries, ibid.). Chazal repeatedly emphasize that specifically this world is the realm of dynamic spiritual growth through Torah and *mitzvoth*. "A person should always occupy himself in Torah and *mitzvoth* before he dies, for once he dies he is suspended from the Torah and the *mitzvoth*, and for the Holy One Blessed be He there is no profit in him" (*Shabbath* 30a). (See also *Shabbath* 151b and *Niddah* 61b. In addition, see *Shabbath* 153a; *Eruvin* 22a and 65a; *Pesachim* 50a; *Yoma* 39a; *Mo'ed Katan* 28a; *Kethubboth* 77b; *Babba Bathra* 10b; *Avodah Zarah* 3a and 4b; *Avoth* 4:16; *Ru.R.* 3:3; *Koh.R.* 1:15 [1] and 9:10 [1]; *Pir.DeR.E.* 43; *Mid. Mishlei* 6:6; and *Yal.Sh.* Yeshayahu:454, Yirmeyahu:297, and Koheleth:967). Indeed, in terms of the greatness of such creative growth, Chazal assert that nothing beyond this world can compare to it. "An hour of repentance and good deeds in this world is better than all existence in the world to come" (*Avoth* 4:17; see also *VaY.R.* 3:1 and *Koh.R.* 4:6). While the grandeur of the world to come lies in the attainment of perfection, the hallmark of this world is human creativity.

The distinction of this world as the domain of creativity is accentuated by contrast to the condition of man in Gan Eden prior to eating of the tree of knowing good and evil. Adam's principal achievement, as recorded in the Torah and vastly amplified in the Midrash, lay in naming all cattle, birds, and beasts (see BeReshith 2:19-20 and com., ibid.). Naming all creatures involves comprehending the nature of the creation; it is a *perceptive*, not *creative*, act. Indeed, Chazal continually describe Adam in Gan Eden as specifically a perceptive being. (See for example *Sanhedrin* 59b, *Avoth DeRabbi Nathan* 1:8, *VaY.R.* 20:2, *BeM.R.* 11:3, *Sh.HaSh.R.* 3:6 [5], *Koh.R.* 7:13 and 8:1 [2], *Tan.*

*Acharei:*2, and *Yal.Sh.* Tehillim:795.) Significantly, it is only after Adam's sin that the innovation of fire, paradigm of human creativity, is explicitly as-cribed to him, when, at nightfall, "the Holy One Blessed be He gave abstract understanding to Adam, a reflection of the heavenly model [G-d's creativity]" (*Pesachim* 54a; see also *Yer. Berachoth* 8:5 [54a] and *BeR.R.* 11:2). Similarly, in classic Jewish thought, man's level prior to eating of the tree of knowing good and evil (the nature of which is beyond the scope of our discussion here) is portrayed as one of passive intellectual *perception* of absolutes; only subse-quent to Adam's sin (and his banishment from Gan Eden) does his interaction with reality become one of human *creation.* (This profound subject is discussed in numerous sources, including *HaKozari* 1:95, *Moreh HaNevochim* 1:1-2, Ramban on BeReshith 2:9, and *Nefesh HaChayyim* 1:6, הגה"ה ד"ה והענין כי קודם החטא [and *Ruach Chayyim* on *Avoth* 3:3]. See also *Michtav MeEliyahu,* II, 137-149.)

It is noteworthy that, according to the Midrash, the snake's seduction of man to sin, and man's consequent banishment from Gan Eden to this world, hinged explicitly upon the theme of creativity. "'*You will be like G-d*' (BeReshith 3:5) — Just as He does, creating worlds ... so you will be able to *create worlds*" (*Pir.DeR.E.* 13). (See also *BeR.R.* 19:4; *Dev.R.* 5:10; *Tan. BeReshith:*8, *Tazria:*9, and *Metzora:*2; *Mid. Tehillim* 1:9; *Yal.Sh.* BeReshith:27 and Tehillim:613; and Rashi on BeReshith ibid.). In spite of the crime in this seduction, Chazal inform us that the snake "spoke the truth" (*Pirka DeRabbeinu HaKadosh,* cited by Ramban on BeReshith 2:9). This is consistent with Rashi's commentary (on BeReshith 2:25 and on Yeshayahu 5:7), that the transformation in man consequent to eating of the tree of knowing good and evil was the acquisition of the *yetzer hara,* the so-called drive to evil (see also *Zohar,* I, 35-36). Chazal repeatedly empha-size that specifically upon the *yetzer hara* all human creativity is predicated. "Were it no for the *yetzer hara* no one would build a house or marry or procreate or deal in business" (*BeR.R.* 9:7). (See also *Koh.R.* 3:11 [3], *Mid. Tehillim* 9:1, and *Yal.Sh.* BeReshith:16 and Tehillim:643. In addition, see *Yoma* 69b, *Sanhedrin* 64a, *Avoth DeRabbi Nathan* 16:3, and *Tan. BeReshith:*7.) In prin-ciple, it is the assertion of autonomy upon which, for better (see *Mish. Berachoth* 9:5, *Yer. Sotah* 5:5 [25b], *Avoth DeRabbi Nathan* 16:3, and *Tan. BeReshith:*7) or for worse, life on the level of this world is predicated. While the *yetzer hara* is innate in man in this dynamic world of human creativity, it was not so in Gan Eden. Likewise, inasmuch as Gan Eden is a percep-tive, but not creative, realm, the *yetzer hara* — this worldly creativity — must be purged on both an individual and universal level as a prerequisite of the return to that realm of perfection. (See *Sukkah* 52a; *Babba Bathra* 58a; *BeR.R.* 48:11 and 89:1; *Sh.R.* 41:7 and 46:4; *BeM.R.* 15:16; *Tan. Noach:*19, *VaYikra:*6, *BeHa'alothcha:*10, and *Ekev:*11; *Avoth DeRabbi Nathan* 16:3; and *Yal.Sh.* Iyyov:915.)

On an individual level, the *yetzer hara* is obviously purged through death, ordinarily an indispensable prerequisite of man's return to Gan Eden. If, according to Chazal, this prerequisite is waived for Eli'ezer, we may conclude that his *yetzer hara* is functionally insignificant even while he is alive: Even in this world, he is not a creative, autonomous human being. The portrayal of Eli'ezer in the Torah and Midrash as an anonymous slave who functions as an extension of Avraham but lacks any autonomous identity is certainly consistent with this conclusion. From this perspective, we would assess Eli'ezer's inner self not as evil or even as materialistic, but as literally nonexistent. Eli'ezer, the paradigmatic slave, has inherited from Kena'an his vacuous and barren interior. He lacks not only autonomous values; he lacks even the most minimal measure of inner autonomy. He is so internally vacant that he has nothing that needs to be purged through death prior to leaving this world. Even after successfully fulfilling Avraham's mission, he is still characterized by the Torah as Avraham's anonymous slave; he is not even identified as a man. Eli'ezer has no *yetzer hara* for death to purge. He requires no death to leave a world to which, in any case, he does not really belong. Ultimately desolate and impotent, he lacks both identity and posterity.

Essentially, whether his fate is to fall as Og, the overblown giant antithesis of Yisra'el, or to enter Gan Eden while yet "alive" (since, in essence, he never truly lived), the fundamental truth remains undisputed that Eli'ezer is a failure in this world. The verdict inevitably remains: "*This one will not be your heir*" (BeReshith 15:4).

90. See also *Meshech Chochmah* on BeReshith 24:52 and *Sefath Emeth* on *Chayyei Sarah* (5641). In this context, both *Meshech Chochmah* and *Sefath Emeth* explain not only the Midrash regarding the "chatter of slaves" but also the Gemara's characterization specifically of Eli'ezer as the one who "draws and gives to drink of the teaching of his master to others" (*Yoma* 28b, see above).

91. It is interesting to note that, according to one opinion, it is specifically from the conduct of Eli'ezer, not Avraham, that we learn the Halachic structure of blessings. See *Rokeach*, ch.363, on BeReshith 24:27 and *Torah Temimah* on BeReshith ibid.

A few words
from happy Atlas owners.

*Our enthusiastic members tell us
how much they like the National Geographic
Picture Atlas of OUR WORLD...*

◆◆◆◆◆◆◆◆◆◆◆◆◆◆◆◆◆◆◆◆◆◆◆◆◆◆◆◆◆◆◆◆◆

"We use OUR WORLD nearly every night just before our boys go to bed. The boys, my husband, and myself find this very enjoyable and educational."

Byron, Michigan

"I especially like the pictures, the maps of the specific areas, and the in-depth profiles of each country."

Lethbridge, Alberta

"My grandnephew preferred looking at it instead of an airplane kit he had picked out for his birthday!"

Newington, Connecticut

☐ **National Geographic Society**   ⊕ Recycled Paper

SUKKOTH AND CHANUKKAH:
Common Threads from Common Themes

Gershon Kitzis

1. INTRODUCTION

While we regard the holidays of the Jewish year as occasions that possess great religious and philosophical significance, we usually view these holidays as autonomous from one another. Particularly, one expects to find little common ground between the Torah-ordained festival of Sukkoth, which serves as a remembrance for the Exodus from Mitzrayim, and the holiday of Chanukkah, innovated rabbinically to commemorate the miraculous victory of Judaism over Hellenism over one thousand years later. Yet the Midrash suggests a direct association between Sukkoth and Chanukkah, as if a cause and effect relationship exists between them:

> Said the Holy One Blesses be He: You [Greeks] thought to uproot the seven lights [of the *menorah* in the Beith HaMikdash] and the eight day of the [Sukkoth] festival! Behold, I shall bring upon you eight days [of Chanukkah] and seven[1] sons of Chashmona'im who will eradicate you from the world.
>
> *(Midrash Chanukkah, Beith HaMidrash I, 134a)*

RABBI KITZIS lectures in Midrash and *machsheveth Yisra'el* at Michlalah - Jerusalem College for Women and serves as consultant at the Israel Institute for Talmudic Publications. He has published extensively in the various fields of Judaic studies.

Obviously the Midrash presumes a thematic relationship between the two holidays that it juxtaposes.

To fully appreciate what the Midrash intends, further investigation of both Sukkoth and Chanukkah as they appear in
classic sources is necessary. In fact, the relationship between
Sukkoth and Chanukkah is suggested in a wide variety of sources.
References to the connection between these holidays may be
found in historical documentation, Biblical and Midrashic allusions, Talmudic parallels, and teachings of the Chasidic masters.
Likewise, this connection is manifest in various communal customs. In the following, some of these sources will be outlined, as
the basis for implied philosophical links between the two festivals.

2. HISTORICAL DOCUMENTATION

Sefer Chashmona'im relates that, in the year of the Chanukkah
miracle, during the holiday of Sukkoth, the Jews were compelled
to flee their homes in the wake of religious persecution and seek
refuge in the mountains. Consequently, they were unable to
dwell in *sukkoth* or celebrate Shemini Atzereth. Therefore, following their victory, "They celebrated a holiday of G-d for eight days
as in the festival of Sukkoth. They then recalled the recent days
during the festival of Sukkoth when they were in mountains and
caves, straying in the wilderness like beasts of the field" (*Sefer
Chashmona'im* II 10:9-10). On Chanukkah that year, when they
came to express their thanksgiving and praise to G-d for the
miracles and wonders that had been bestowed upon them, "They
took leaf-covered branches and wicker baskets *and also palm
branches [lulavim]* and sang songs of praise and thanksgiving to
G-d" (ibid. 10:10).

The eight days of the Chanukkah miracle were regarded as
compensation for the eight days of the Sukkoth festival that had
been violated earlier that year. One clearly senses an echo of this
attitude in the Midrash quoted above. To express this feeling
tangibly, the victorious Jews even brought *lulav* branches —
mementos of the four species brought on Sukkoth — with them
to the Beith HaMikdash. Not surprisingly, they even referred to
Chanukkah as "the Sukkoth festival of the month of Kislev" (ibid.
9:22). Their agony over the desecrated Sukkoth holiday was

transformed into the rejoicing of Chanukkah; the shame of their flight from their own homes was supplanted by the joy of victory in the rededication of their national home, the Beith HaMikdash. The correspondence of eight days in each holiday was seen as a clear indication from above that Chanukkah had been given to them in compensation for Sukkoth that year.[2]

While the historical roots of Chanukkah provide the most explicit link between it and Sukkoth, the connection between the essential themes of the two holidays is far deeper. In the general sense of *chanukkah* as dedication, even the dedication of the first sanctuary of the nation of Yisra'el over one thousand years earlier in the wilderness is associated with Sukkoth. Following the sin of the golden calf, Mosheh descended from Sinai on Yom Kippur with tidings of forgiveness for the nation of Yisra'el. The following day, he immediately began the construction of G-d's sanctuary as he had been commanded. The construction of the sanctuary thus began immediately prior to Sukkoth. This historic association is expressed in Halachah as well, designating the day following Yom Kippur as the day upon which we are enjoined to commence construction of the *sukkah*. It is noteworthy that, according to the Midrash, "on the twenty-fifth of Kislev [Chanukkah] the construction of the sanctuary was completed, and the Holy One Blessed be He postponed its dedication until the month of Nisan" (*Yal.Sh.* Melachim:184). The construction period of the sanctuary then literally joins between Sukkoth and Chanukkah at its two ends.

This association between Sukkoth and *chanukkah* — in its general sense as dedication — is expressed in the first Beith HaMikdash as well. According to Jewish tradition, the original *chanukkath HaBayith* (the dedication of the first Beith HaMikdash) also coincided with Sukkoth:

> Shelomoh made at that time the feast, and all Yisra'el with him ... seven days and seven days — fourteen days. On the eighth day, he sent the nation away....
>
> (Melachim I 8:65-66)

The Gemara deduces that the dedication of the first Beith Ha-Mikdash began prior to Yom Kippur. When the Sages of that time concluded that the dedication should take Halachic precedence over the fast of Yom Kippur,[3] the solemnity of Yom Kippur was superseded that year by feasting and rejoicing. Instead of postponing the festivities until after Yom Kippur and Sukkoth, the *chanukkath HaBayith* specifically culminated on Sukkoth and Shemini Atzereth.

Even more emphatically, in the construction and dedication of the second Beith HaMikdash, the association of Sukkoth and Chanukkah is again highlighted:

> *In the seventh month, on the twenty-first day of the month,* the word of G-d came by Chaggai the prophet: ... Now be strong Zerubbavel, says G-d, and be strong Yehoshua son of Yehotzadak, the *kohen gadol,* and be strong all the people of the land, says G-d, and work; for I am with you, says the G-d of Hosts.... I shall fill this house with glory.... Greater will be the glory of this latter house than that of the former, said the G-d of Hosts; and in this place I shall give peace, says the G-d of Hosts.
>
> (Chaggai 2:1, 4)

On the seventh day of Sukkoth (Hoshana Rabbah), Chaggai exhorts the nation of Yisra'el, newly restored to its land, to complete the restoration of the Beith HaMikdash. The encouragement and the reinforcement to build are expressed on Sukkoth. But the completion of the task, the dedication of the reconstructed Beith HaMikdash, are the domain of Chanukkah:

> Take heed from this day and onward: *from the twenty-fourth day of the ninth month,* from the day upon which the sanctuary of G-d is founded, take heed.
>
> (ibid. 2:18)

On *erev* Chanukkah, the construction was completed. The following day, the twenty-fifth of Kislev, the Beith HaMikdash was dedicated, and the Beith HaMikdash service began.[4] While the realization took place on Chanukkah, the impetus and aspirations have their origin in Sukkoth.

Given this chronology for the dedication of the second Beith HaMikdash, we can comprehend the enormity of the outrage deliberately perpetrated by the Greeks and the greatness of the Chanukkah miracle:

> On the fifteenth day of Kislev ... [the Greeks] built an abomination

on the altar, while in the surrounding cities of Yehudah they built private altars, and brought sacrifices in the doorways of the houses and in the squares, and rent and burnt any Torah scrolls that they found.... And on the twenty-fifth day of the month [of Kislev], they offered sacrifices on the private altar....

(Sefer Makkabbim I, p. 102)

Ten days prior to the twenty-fifth of Kislev, the Greeks commenced construction of the abomination on the altar, in preparation for the twenty-fifth of Kislev, when a sacrifice would be offered on that abomination. Why were they so eager to sacrifice specifically on that day, choosing it as the climax? Recognizing the significance of the twenty-fifth of Kislev as the day upon which the Beith HaMikdash service began, we may surmise that this day was sustained in the national consciousness as a great holiday: the holiday of the Beith HaMikdash. No doubt the Greeks were also aware of this and deliberately intended to desecrate the Beith HaMikdash specifically on this day, correctly assuming that so doing would be infinitely more offensive to the Jews than the choice of any other day.

From this perspective, we begin to appreciate the magnitude of the miracle that G-d wrought for Yisra'el in restoring its national pride and purifying the Beith HaMikdash on the self-same day, the twenty-fifth of Kislev, upon which the nation had been so degraded and the Beith HaMikdash so defiled. As in the days of Chaggai, the twenty-fifth of Kislev was again designated as the day of dedication for the renewed Beith HaMikdash: a dedication whose roots extend backwards to Sukkoth.

3. ALLUSION IN THE TORAH

On a far more subtle level, the relationship between the themes of Sukkoth and Chanukkah is rooted in the Torah. While there is of course no explicit reference to Chanukkah in the Torah, it is significant that, immediately following the laws pertaining to Sukkoth, the Torah discusses the preparation of pure olive oil for the *menorah*:

> You shall dwell in *sukkoth* seven days;
> everyone included in Yisra'el must dwell in *sukkoth*.

Thus, future generations will know
that I had the nation of Yisra'el dwell in *sukkoth*
when I brought them out of the land of Mitzrayim.
I am G-d your L-rd.
Mosheh spoke of the appointed festivals of G-d
to the nation of Yisra'el.
G-d spoke to Mosheh:
Command the nation of Yisra'el to bring you pure olive oil, beaten,
for the light; to keep the lamp burning continually.

(VaYikra 23:42 - 24:2)

Considering the centrality of the *menorah* in the miracle of Chanukkah (and in the *mitzvah* of Chanukkah lights), mention of the *menorah* immediately after a list of all the holidays (ibid. 23:4-44) may readily be perceived as an allusion to Chanukkah.[5] It is noteworthy that this allusion comes on the heels of the laws of Sukkoth.

Significantly, according to *Rokeach*, this juxtaposition has Halachic ramifications. The proximity of the mandate "to keep the lamp burning continually" to the laws of Sukkoth implies the *halachah* that the celebration of *simchath beith hasho'evah* (the joyous procession to and from the well from which water was drawn for libation in the Beith HaMikdash on Sukkoth) is accompanied by lights. Indeed, the Mishnah relates: "There was not a courtyard in Yerushalayim that was not illuminated by the light of *beith hasho'evah*" (*Mish. Sukkah* 5:3)

4. PARALLELS IN THE TALMUD

It is interesting to note that one of the motifs that appear in the Talmud regarding Sukkoth appears derived from *chanukkah*, in its broader sense as a reference to the dedication of the Beith HaMikdash. In the Talmud, "*chag*," used as a generic term (without specifying a particular holiday, as in "*chag HaPesach*"), refers exclusively to Sukkoth.[6] In the Bible, "*chag*" appears in the context of the dedication of the Beith HaMikdash: "Shelomoh made at that time the *chag*" (Melachim I 8:65). The common reference to both Sukkoth and the *chanukkath HaBayith* with the word "*chag*" is surely due both to the coincident timing of Shelomoh's *chanukkath HaBayith* with Sukkoth (see above) and to the extraordinary number of sacrifices that were brought on both these occasions (since "chag," in its original sense, denotes sacrifice).[7] Its dual usage nevertheless suggests an additional link between the festival of Sukkoth and Chanukkah, which commemorates the rededication of the Beith HaMikdash and its sacrificial service.

In addition, various themes in the Talmud are expressed in the context of both Sukkoth and Chanukkah. The first rule of the Mishnah in *masecheth Sukkah* is: "A *sukkah* that is higher than twenty cubits is invalid" (ibid. 1:1). This ruling is expressed practically verbatim regarding the Chanukkah lights as well, with explicit reference to Sukkoth: "A Chanukkah light that is placed higher than twenty cubits is invalid *as in the case with a* sukkah ..." (*Shabbath* 22a).

Furthermore, Sukkoth and Chanukkah are explicitly associated in another domain of Halachah. The Mishnah states:

> From Shavu'oth *until Sukkoth,* one may bring [bikkurim (first fruits)] and recite [mikra bikkurim (see Devarim 26:3, 5-10)]. From Sukkoth *until Chanukkah,* one may bring [bikkurim] but not recite [mikra bikkurim].

> (Mish. Bikkurim 1:6)

Sukkoth and Chanukkah are both perceived as pivotal dates in the ascent to Yerushalayim with the first fruits.

Moreover, in several domains of Halachah, a direct linkage between Sukkoth and Chanukkah is manifest. These are the only two festivals whose duration is eight full days. Furthermore, on both holidays the full "Hallel" is recited for the entire eight days of the *chag.*

Besides such obvious parallels, certain motifs of both holidays suggest a connection between them. Of special significance is "hiddur," the mandate to adorn and beautify the *mitzvoth.* While this concept applies to all *mitzvoth,* the Torah relates it particularly to Sukkoth: "You shall take for yourself fruit of the *hadar* (הדר tree" (VaYikra 23:40). Likewise, in listing examples of adornments of *mitzvoth,* Chazal specifically commence with the examples of "a comely *sukkah* and a comely *lulav*" (*Shabbath* 133b). And in describing "how beloved the *mitzvoth* are by [Yisra'el]" (*Sukkah* 41b), the *mitzvah* chosen as an illustration is the *mitzvah* of *lulav.* The concept of *hiddur* is correspondingly emphasized in

Chanukkah as well, in the singular concepts of *"mehadrin"* and *"mehadrin min hamehadrin"* (*Shabbath* 21b). Over the generations these terms acquired various borrowed meanings. In their original sense, however, they are unique to Chanukkah and express the essence of *hiddur* as it impinges on the focal point of the holiday, the lights of Chanukkah:

> The *mitzvah* of Chanukkah is [to light] one lamp for each man and his household. And the *"mehadrin"* [light] one lamp for each and every member [of the household]. And the *"mehadrin min hamehadrin"* [light multiple lamps]: according to Beith Shammai, in descending order, and according to Beith Hillel, in ascending order.
>
> (*Shabbath* 21b)

It is in this context of *hiddur*, as expressed in the *"mehadrin"* and *"mehadrin min hamehadrin,"* that perhaps the most explicit Talmudic link between Sukkoth and Chanukkah is established. The Gemara (ibid.) concludes that Beith Shammai's opinion is based upon a correspondence between the lights of Chanukkah and *parei hachag* (the seventy bulls offered as sacrifices during Sukkoth). Just as the number of bulls sacrificed diminishes each day, from thirteen on the first day to seven on the seventh day,[8] so too (according to Beith Shammai) one should kindle the lights of Chanukkah in descending order, from eight on the first day to one on the eighth day. The assumed relationship between Sukkoth and Chanukkah is regarded by the Gemara as significant enough to justify the manner of fulfillment of the central *mitzvah* of Chanukkah.

Finally, just as *masecheth Sukkah* begins with a rule that pertains to Chanukkah, it concludes with an episode that is permeated with the themes of Chanukkah:

> Our rabbis have taught: There was an incident concerning Miryam daughter of Bilgah who apostatized and proceeded to marry one of the officers of the Greek kings. When the Greeks entered the sanctuary [in the days of Mattithyahu son of Yochanan (Rashi)], she kicked with her sandal upon the altar and said, "Wolf! Wolf! How much longer will you consume the money of Yisra'el and not stand up for them in their time of distress?"

The Sages heard the matter [after the house of Chashmonai achieved supremacy (Rashi)]....

(*Sukkah* 56b)

In its beginning and end, *masecheth Sukkah* alludes to Chanukkah, the holiday linked in so many ways to Sukkoth and imbued with the *hadar* that illuminates both festivals.

5. CHASIDIC TEACHINGS AND CUSTOMS

R. Chayyim Elazar Shapira of Munkatch notes that the closing words of *masecheth Sukkah* are "fortunate is the righteous and fortunate is his neighbor" (*Sukkah* 56b). He comments, "And who is the neighbor of Sukkoth? We conclude that the reference is to Chanukkah!" (*Divrei Torah* 8:71). Particularly in light of the perspective we have already gleaned from considering sources in *masecheth Sukkah* (above), his observation is especially germane. The effulgence of Sukkoth illuminates Chanukkah as well.

In addition, Chasidic tradition extends the association between Sukkoth and Chanukkah much further back, to the days of the patriarchs:

> According to the tradition in our possession, [Ya'akov our forefather was interred in the cave of Machpelah] in Kislev during Chanukkah.[9] Ya'akov "drew his feet back onto the bed [and expired]" (BeReshith 49:33) on the first day of Sukkoth, according to the tradition in our possession[10] ... and the seventy days of mourning (ibid. 50:3) then conclude on Chanukkah.
>
> (*Benei Yissachar*, "Kislev," *Ma'amar* 1)

Ya'akov expired on Sukkoth, but he was buried on Chanukkah. Here as well, Chanukkah is depicted as the culmination of Sukkoth.

As an extension of this theme on a more cryptic note, Chasidic tradition links Chanukkah with the days of judgment — including Sukkoth — in the month of Tishrei. The Gemara states: "Those who are wholly righteous are inscribed and sealed immediately [on Rosh HaShanah] for life.... *[Judgment regarding] those who are intermediate is suspended from Rosh HaShanah until Yom Kippur*" (*Rosh HaShanah* 16b). According to *Zohar* (ibid., I, 220), judgment is suspended until Hoshana Rabbah. Another version[11] defers judgment until Shemini Atzereth. But according to Chasidic tradition,[12] this deadline was extended by the righteous until the last day of Chanukkah. Thus, R. Aharon of Zitomir relates, "The spiritual abundance and illuminations that the Holy One Blessed be He bestows upon Yisra'el begin [annually] on Chanukkah, since the final judgment *from Hoshana Rabbah* extends *until Chanukkah*" (*Toledoth Aharon*, "Chanukkah").

Furthermore, the relationship between Sukkoth and Chanukkah is expressed in practice as well, and various customs have been noted that clearly articulate this connection. There are those who tangibly express an element of Chanukkah on Sukkoth:

> There is a custom to hang as an ornament in the *sukkah* a flask of olive oil that is designated for the Chanukkah lights.
>
> (*Michtam LeDavid* [R. D.Z. Lezer], p. 116)

Likewise, there is a practice that explicitly invokes Sukkoth in the kindling of the Chanukkah light:

> It is a good custom of the wholehearted ... to keep this canvas [wrapping in which the *ethrog* is kept during Sukkoth] and twist from it wicks for the Chanukkah lights.
>
> (*Mo'ed LeChol Chai* [R. Chayyim Palagi])

In addition, R. Chayyim Halbershtam of Sanz, the renowned Chasidic master and *posek*, emphasized graphically the linkage between Sukkoth and Pesach. He "had the practice to study the themes of Chanukkah on *motza'ei* Simchath Torah in *Siddur shel Mishnath Chasidim*" (*Darchei Chayyim*, quoted in *Otzar HaChayyim*, "*Minhagei Sanz,*" *p. 306*).

Finally, R. Alter Me'ir of Gur provides us with a tale that is particularly apropos of our discussion:

> A certain villager visited R. Yitzchak Me'ir of Gur, the celebrated *Chiddushei HaRim*, on one of the days of Chanukkah. After the rabbi completed the kindling of the [Chanukkah lights ... the villager approached him in dismay and asked, "Why did the rabbi not place the *lulav* and *ethrog* opposite the Chanukkah lights?" Said the rabbi to him, "From where do you derive this mandate?" The villager responded, "Isn't it written explicitly in *masecheth Shabbath* that one kindles the lights 'כנגד פָּרֵי החג'?" The villager erred, reading the Gemara's statement, "כנגד פָּרֵי החג," as "*opposite the fruit* of Sukkoth,"

namely the *lulav* and *ethrog*. He was therefore amazed that the rabbi neglected to fulfill the Gemara's dictate...

(*"Shemonath Yemei Chanukkah"*)

Of course, the Gemara actually means *"in correspondence with"* the *bulls* of Sukkoth," referring to the seventy bulls offered as sacrifices during Sukkoth (see the opinion of Beith Shammai on *Shabbath* 21b, cited above). But in light of what we have seen reiterated continually in the sources above, R. Alter Me'ir aptly concludes, "Subconsciously, the villager sensed that the *lulav* and *ethrog do* have a relationship with Chanukkah as well, and naively he inserted this feeling into the words of Chazal in *masecheth Shabbath.*"

6. CONCLUSIONS

From various perspectives, we have demonstrated the linkage that binds Chanukkah with Sukkoth. The connections between the two holidays are expressed in a broad range of subjects and themes. They are most explicitly manifest in the historical dimension, Chanukkah being initially regarded as a direct compensation for Sukkoth. In a more sublime sense, one notes an association of themes in the dedication of the sanctuary and of the first and the second Battei Mikdash. Still more subtly, this relation finds expression in the Torah, albeit by allusion. Amplifying this implied bond, we find numerous statements by Chazal and later scholars, in the realms of both Halachah and Aggadah, and in both exoteric and esoteric domains. Finally, the nation of Yisra'el, if not composed of the prophets and scholars themselves, is at least composed of their descendants. Innately sensitive to the implicit connection between Sukkoth and Chanukkah, the nation developed various customs that articulated this relationship in practice.

Utilizing these sources as raw materials provides much food for thought regarding the essential nature of both festivals, a subject of inquiry to which a wide range of fundamental questions in Judaism relate. These include, for example, defining the proper relationship between nature and supernatural miracles, between the private domain and the national domain, between the minimal fulfillment of a *mitzvah* and its *hiddur* (adornment), and between the nations of the world and Yisra'el. Understanding the association between Sukkoth and Chanukkah may be expected to shed much light on these general issues as well.

On the one hand, Sukkoth serves as the basis for Chanukkah. We have already noted multiple examples in which Chanukkah provides the ultimate realization of the concepts introduced by Sukkoth. Similarly, among the general issues cited above, Sukkoth represents the original, more basic, aspect of the dichotomy: the natural as opposed to the supernatural, the private domain of the individual rather than of the nation, the initial mandate of *hiddur mitzvah*, and the initial confrontation between Yisra'el and the nations of the world. Chanukkah represents the fruition of these issues: the natural transcended by a supernatural miracle (the flask of oil), the private domain illuminated by the Chanukkah lights as a reflection of the national dimension (the *menorah* in the Beith HaMikdash), the fulfillment of the *mitzvah* in the ultimate *hiddur* as "*mehadrin min hamehadrin*," and the victory of Judaism in its confrontation with Hellenism.

On the other hand, Chanukkah serves also as the basis for Sukkoth. The final confrontation between Yisra'el and the nations of the world is designated for Sukkoth, the holiday of ingathering. In the end, that time is appointed for the ingathering of all the nations to Yerushalayim, as expressed in the prophecy of Zecharyah, read as the *haftarah* on the first day of Sukkoth: "All who remain from among the nations that came against Yerushalayim will ascend from year to year to bow down to the King G-d of Hosts and to celebrate the Sukkoth holiday" (Zecharyah 14:16). The seventy bulls offered as sacrifices on Sukkoth correspond to the seventy nations of the world. The order of sacrifice — diminishing each day — suggests their eventual decline[8] and ultimate transformation through doing battle with Yerushalayim and being vanquished by G-d Himself (ibid. 14:1-11). Chanukkah, commemorating the miraculous victory of Judaism over Hellenism and the heathen forces of assimilation, is the definitive preparatory phase for the conclusive ideological victory on Sukkoth of the values of Judaism over all its adversaries. Through the bond between Sukkoth and Chanukkah, this final goal is achieved: "Then, G-d will be King over the entire world; on that day, G-d will be One and His name One" (ibid. 14:9).

NOTES

1. The actual number of Mattityahu's sons relates to broader issues in the historical background of Chanukkah and is beyond the scope of this essay.

2. See also *Kuntres Or HaGanuz* (R. David HaKohen), p. 25

3. See *Mo'ed Katan* 9a, *Shabbath* 30a, and commentaries on Melachim ibid.

4. See also *Mor UKtzi'ah* (R. Ya'akov Emdin) that explains this verse in Chaggai as a reference to the completion of the Beith HaMikdash.

5. Note also that, in the aftermath of *chanukkath hamizbeach* (the dedication of the altar), the Torah continues:

> G-d spoke to Mosheh:
> *Speak to Aharon, and say to him: When you light the lamps,*
> the seven lamps should illuminate the body of the *menorah....*
> G-d spoke to Mosheh:
> *Take the Leviyyim* from among the nation of Yisra'el, and purify them.
> (BeMidbar 8:1-6)

This juxtaposition may be construed as alluding that, in the future, a *chanukkah* (dedication) will again occur, through the agency of a *kohen gadol* (Yochanan) of the tribe of Levi. (See *Rokeach.*)

6. See, for example, *Mish. Rosh HaShanah* 1:2.

7. See Tehillim 118:27 and Radak, ibid.

8. See BeMidbar 29:12-32. It is noteworthy that the Gemara understands the seventy bulls of Sukkoth and their diminishing order to be symbolic of the seventy nations of the world — antithetical to Yisra'el — and their eventual decline (see *Sukkah* 55b). The ultimate victory over their ideology is expressed *seventy* days after Sukkoth, with the advent of Chanukkah.

9. It should be noted that much has been said regarding the relationship between the Chanukkah miracle and Ya'akov in particular, especially in esoteric works including traditions in the name of HaAri. A more extensive discussion of this subject is beyond the scope of this essay.

10. The expression, "the tradition in our possession," is well chosen here, because there is no apparent basis for this tradition in any written source known. Indeed, other traditions place the date of Ya'akov's interment on either the first or fourth day of Sukkoth. (See R. Menachem Tziyoni on *"VaYechi"* and *Dor Dor VeDoreshav* [R. Yosef Levenstein].)

11. See *Peri Etz Chayyim* (R. Chayyim Vital), *"Sha'ar HaLulav,"* ch. 4.

12. See *Sha'ar Bath Rabbim,* quoted in *Otzar HaChayyim, "Minhagei Sanz,"* p. 306. See also *Ta'amei HaMinhagim* (R. Avraham Yitzchak Shperling), p. 363, who cites many sources for this opinion.

IN DEFENSE OF SHA'UL:
The King and the Ba'alath-Ov

Moshe Ch. Sosevsky

The essay that follows is based upon the sources provided below:

And Shemu'el died,	ושמואל מת,
and all Yisra'el lamented him,	ויספדו־לו כל־ישראל,
and they buried him in Ramah,	ויקברהו ברמה,
within his city.	ובעירו;
And Sha'ul had abolished	ושאול הסיר
the necromancers and the oracles	האבות ואת־הידענים,
from the land.	מהארץ:
The Pelishtim gathered,	ויקבצו פלשתים,
and they came,	ויבאו,
and they encamped in Shunem.	ויחנו בשונם;
Sha'ul gathered all Yisra'el,	ויקבץ שאול את־כל־ישראל,
and they encamped in Gilboa.	ויחנו בגלבע:
Sha'ul saw the Pelishtim encampment,	וירא שאול את־מחנה פלשתים;
and he feared and trembled greatly.	וירא, ויחרד לבו, מאד:
Sha'ul inquired of G-d,	וישאל שאול בה',
and G-d did not answer him,	ולא ענהו ה',
neither by dreams, nor by the Urim,	גם בחלמות, גם באורים,
nor by the prophets.	גם בנביאם:

RABBI SOSEVSKY is Rosh Yeshivah of Yeshivat Ohr Yerushalayim and a lecturer in the Torah Umesorah teachers' seminars held annually in Israel. He is the author of the "Commentary Digest" in *The Book of Samuel 2*, part of the *Judaica Books of the Prophets* series (New York: Judaica Press, 1978), and is an editor of *Jewish Thought*.

Sha'ul said to his servants,
   "Seek for me a necromancer,
   and I shall go to her,
   and I shall inquire of her."
   His servants said to him,
   "Behold there is a necromancer,
   in Ein Dor."

Sha'ul disguised himself,
   and donned other garments,
   and he went with two men,
   and they came to the woman
   by night.
   He said,
   "Please divine for me
   through necromancy,
   and conjure up for me
   whomever I tell you."

The woman said,
   "Whom shall I conjure up for you?"
   He said,
   "Shemu'el conjure up for me."

(Shemu'el I 28:3-8, 11)

ויאמר שאול לעבדיו,
בקשו־לי אשת בעלת־אוב,
ואלכה אליה,
ואדרשה־בה;
ויאמרו עבדיו אליו,
הנה אשת בעלת־אוב,
בעין דור:

ויתחפש שאול,
וילבש בגדים אחרים,
וילך הוא, ושני אנשים עמו,
ויבאו אל־האשה,
לילה;
ויאמר,
קסמי־נא לי
באוב,
והעלי לי,
את אשר־אמר אליך:

ותאמר האשה,
את־מי אעלה־לך?
ויאמר,
את־שמואל העלי־לי:

Sha'ul died
   in the transgression
   that he committed against G-d,
   for not keeping the word of G-d,
   and also asking counsel
   of a necromancer
   and inquiring of her.

And he did not inquire of G-d;
   therefore He slew him.
   And He turned the kingdom
   to David son of Yishai.

(Divrei HaYamim I 10:13-14)

וימת שאול,
במעלו
אשר־מעל בה',
על־דבר ה' אשר לא־שמר;
וגם־לשאול
באוב,
לדרוש:

ולא־דרש בה',
וימיתהו;
ויסב את־המלוכה,
לדויד בן־ישי:

1. INTRODUCTION

"How have the mighty fallen!" (Shemu'el II 1:19). King Sha'ul was deemed just a few years earlier as "special in deeds" (Shemu'el I 8:9), and was introduced by the prophet Shemu'el to the assembled nation of Yisra'el with the accolade, "there is none like him in all the nation" (ibid. 10:24). The selfsame Sha'ul who had personally "abolished the necromancers and the oracles from the land" (ibid. 28:3) now trudges clandestinely and incognito to a necromancer in order to conjure up the prophet Shemu'el. Such behavior is in apparent contradiction with the Torah's prohibition of the various forms of divination and witchcraft.[1] King Sha'ul, who had lived at so high a level of sanctity that he applied to his daily meals the stringent laws of purity that are demanded of sacrificial feasts (*Mid. Tehillim* 7:2), now enters the shadowy world of the necromancer, whose powers derive from the forces of impurity.[2] Furthermore, through this agency of impurity Sha'ul seeks to conjure up none other than the holy prophet Shemu'el, who is deemed comparable to Mosheh and Aharon:[3] a prophet raised from birth as *nazir*[4] and initiated — by his prophetess mother Channah — into a life of holiness and selfless dedication to G-d and the nation of Yisra'el at the tender age of two.

It seems inconceivable to assume that the righteous King Sha'ul[5] in fact committed so blatant a transgression, violating in doing so his saintly guide and mentor, Shemu'el. Yet, how are we to rationalize Sha'ul's bizarre behavior, particularly since it appears to be in direct defiance of the Torah's general prohibition against necromancy and divination?

2. THE SINS OF THE EARLY GENERATIONS

The Talmud relates:

> It has been taught: All the outstanding individuals ["אשכולות," derived from the Talmud (ibid.) as an acronym for "איש שהכל בו," meaning "one who encompasses all"][6] who arose in Yisra'el from the days of Mosheh until the death of Yosef b. Yo'ezer of Tzereidah[7] possessed no blemish of sin.
>
> Henceforth, did they then possess the blemish of sin? Has it not been taught: There was an incident regarding a certain pious indi-

vidual who was groaning from heart pains. They asked the doctors, who said, "There is no remedy unless he sucks fresh milk every morning." They brought a goat and tied it to the feet of his bed, and he would suck milk from it. The following day, his colleagues came to visit him. Upon seeing the goat, they exclaimed, "There is an armed robber in his household [since it is impossible to watch goats carefully enough to prevent grazing in other people's fields (Rashi)], and we are coming to visit him?" They stopped and investigated and found no other sin for which he was accountable other than the goat. And he, too, at the time of his death said, "I know myself that I am accountable for no sin other than that of the goat, wherein I transgressed the ruling of my colleagues; for the Sages said: It is forbidden to raise goats and sheep in the Land of Yisra'el."

We have an established tradition that wherever it says, "an incident regarding a certain pious individual," it refers either to R. Yehudah b. Bava or R. Yehudah b. Ilai.[8] And these masters lived many generations after Yosef b. Yo'ezer of Tzereidah.

(Temurah 15b)*

Given the attitude of Chazal regarding the righteousness of the early generations, it is difficult to understand how we are to account for the numerous transgressions attributed by the Bible to the outstanding personalities such as King Sha'ul and King David. The Talmud and Midrash, in their assessments of these luminaries, seem to retain the basic premise that they did not sin outright. Any transgression attributed to them is therefore to be considered as due to either faulty Halachic judgment on their part or their failure to have attained the lofty moral level of behavior that ought to have been commensurate with their great spiritual stature. Hence, what appears in the Bible as an actual violation of the law is in reality either comprised of error or assessed according to superlegal — rather than legal — standards.

The transgressions ascribed to the sons of Shemu'el typify the latter category: sins described by the Bible as actual but understood by Chazal as expressing a far more subtle shortcoming. The Bible records that Shemu'el's sons "did not go in his ways and veered toward gain and took bribes and perverted justice" (Shemu'el 8:3). Nevertheless, Chazal comment, "Whoever says that the sons of Shemu'el sinned is but in error" (*Shabbath* 56a).

In the view of Chazal (ibid.), their "sin" was only that they did not go in the ways of their illustrious father, who "went year after year, and made the rounds of Beith-El and Gilgal and Mitzpah; and he served as judge for Yisra'el, in all these places" (ibid. 7:16). Instead, they were "judges in Be'er Sheva" (ibid. 8:2), and did not circulate in the Land of Yisra'el. The scribes and clerks that they hired ultimately succumbed to the temptations of the court bureaucracy that was established, and took bribes and graft.[9] Undoubtably, Shemu'el must have recognized that, by maintaining his circuit, he avoided the pitfalls of any bureaucratic establishment. His sons, while not personally corrupt, were not sufficiently sensitive to this problem and were therefore held accountable for having "perverted justice" because of the abuses of their appointees.

Similarly, the Talmud declares, "Whoever says that David sinned [in his relationship with Bath-Sheva, wife of Uriyyah the Chitti][10] is but in error" (*Shabbath* 56a). The Talmud explains that "anyone who went out in the wars of the house of David wrote a divorce contract for his wife [to take effect retroactively when the husband failed to return from battle, thus eliminating the legal problems of *agunah*, a married woman whose husband cannot be located]"[11] (*Kethubboth* 9b). Yet King David, in taking Bath-Sheva, who was still emotionally attached to Uriyyah, is considered accountable in the Bible as if she had still been legally married.

3. RABBEINU NISSIM ON THE NATURE OF BIBLICAL NARRATIVES

In light of Chazal's perspective regarding the wrongdoings of righteous individuals described in the Bible, the Biblical description itself seems incongruous and tantamount to slander. If the transgressions were indeed so subtle, why does the Bible mislead us by describing them as such flagrant outrages? In *Derashoth HaRan*, Rabbeinu Nissim[12] attempts to resolve this problem by offering the following solution:

> One must explain why the transgression concerning Bath-Sheva was written literally as if David had actually sinned, especially since

it is the general nature of verses to cover up and hide such errors....
How then could the text have portrayed the incident of Bath-Sheva
and Uriyyah in a manner that would have us think that David had
committed a truly awesome transgression?

The resolution is, however, that both what is apparent to us (i.e.,
peshat) and what is hidden from us (i.e., *derash*) provide tremen-
dously significant lessons for the *ba'al teshuvah*. As our rabbis have
stated, "If an individual has sinned, one tells him to proceed to that
individual" (*Avodah Zarah* 5a) [i.e., to learn the lesson of *teshuvah*
from David, who himself transgressed and repented, and was for-
given].

Now, the text portrays David as having sinned grievously,
because the subtle transgression that the rabbis did in fact attribute
to him was reckoned [by the standard of the Bible] as tantamount
to someone else having transgressed all that appears suggested by
the literal text. In so doing, the text indicates to us that, should a
person commit even a grave sin, he can still be forgiven as was David
forgiven for his sin, however awesome the sin may appear in the
literal text, and even though — considering his exceptional righteousness — David was particularly liable to be punished....[13]

Nevertheless, our rabbis caution us based upon the true tradition [that they had received] that David did not in fact commit the
sin ascribed to him by the Bible, should the verse be read literally.
From this [dichotomy between the actual deed and the sin implied],
we can derive another valuable lesson: that a *ba'al teshuvah* ought
to continuously envision his sins as before him, like David, who —
although he did not actually sin — states nevertheless, "My sin is
before me always" (Tehillim 51:5).

(Derashoth HaRan, Derash 6)

Rabbeinu Nissim has provided us with a dual resolution of
our problem. First, since King David serves as the prototype *ba'al
teshuvah*, had the Bible described literally the actual, truly subtle
nature of his wrongdoing, the impression conveyed would have
been that atonement is possible for only minor infractions. The
lesson that — through repentance — even grave sins may be
forgiven would have been lost. This principle may be utilized
similarly to justify the Bible's description of the wrongdoings of
Shemu'el's sons (see above). They failed to repent and were
therefore not forgiven. Had the Bible described literally the ac-

tual, minute extent of their wrongdoings, the impression conveyed would have been of a vengeful and exacting G-d with implacable demands and excessively stern punishments for even minor misdeeds. By describing their deeds with commensurate severity given the exceptional standards expected from individuals of such great spiritual stature, an accurate impression of the nature of divine retribution emerges: G-d's punishments are always commensurate with the severity of the offense, given the standard of conduct that had been expected of the offender.

The second resolution provided by Rabbeinu Nissim derives from this perspective. In describing the deeds of righteous individuals with such severity, the Bible does not really mislead us, since the subtle misdeeds of such spiritually uplifted people are indeed fully tantamount to actual sins in ordinary individuals.

4. KING SHA'UL'S TRANSGRESSIONS

In contrast to the statements of Chazal regarding the deeds of King David and the sons of Shemu'el, we find no analogous Talmudic or Midrashic statement that "whoever says that King Sha'ul sinned is but in error." Indeed, the Bible seems to preclude such an assessment by explicitly emphasizing that "Sha'ul died in the transgression that he committed against G-d, for not keeping the word of G-d" (Divrei HaYamim I 10:13). Yet, in light of the examination of the relevant sources, it appears that the Talmud nevertheless suggests that King Sha'ul similarly never blatantly or defiantly disregarded G-d's will. His sins appear to have resulted from faulty Halachic judgment: the alternate basis outlined above to explain transgressions attributed to individuals of exceptionally great spiritual stature. This assessment is implied in a number of Talmudic references.

The Talmud offers the following comparison between King Sha'ul and King David:

> David's texts were revealed;[14] Sha'ul's texts were not revealed. Regarding David, whose texts were revealed, it is written, "Those who are in awe of You will see me and be happy" (Tehillim 119:74) [because his Halachic statements would accurately reflect that which is prohibited and permitted (Rashi)]. Regarding Sha'ul, whose texts were not revealed, it is written, "Wherever he turned, he did badly"

(Shemu'el I 14:47) [i.e., he did not merit rendering decisions in accord
with the Halachah (Rashi)].

(*Eruvin* 53a)

King Sha'ul's lack of divine Halachic guidance is similarly
suggested in the Aggadic interpretation of the verses describing
the nomination of David as Sha'ul's minstrel:

One of the attendants responded, saying,
"Behold, I saw a son of Yishai the Beith Lachmi,
who is adept at playing [music], and a mighty, valiant man and a
man of war,
and understanding in matters, and a comely man;
and G-d is with him."

(Shemu'el I 16:18)

Rav Yehudah said in the name of Rav: This entire verse was said by
Do'eg [according to the Talmud, the identity of "the attendant"
speaking (Rashi)] with only slanderous intent [to recount praises of
David so that Sha'ul would be envious of him and slay him (Rashi)]:

"*Who is adept at playing*" — [He is] knowledgeable in asking.
"*Mighty*" — [He is] knowledgeable in answering.
"*A man of war*" — [He is] knowledgeable in conducting himself in
the dialectical battles of Torah.
"*And understanding in matters*" — [He] understands matters deduced
from one another.
"*A comely man*" — [He] clarifies the face of Halachah [providing
proofs for his contentions (Rashi)].
"*And G-d is with him*" — Halachah is in accordance with his opinion
everywhere.[15]

In all of these, [Sha'ul] said to him, "My son Yehonathan is equivalent to him." When [Do'eg] said to him, "and G-d is with him"
[meaning that Halachah is in accordance with his opinion] — a
matter that was a deficiency in [Sha'ul] himself as well [for the
Halachah is not in accordance with Sha'ul, as noted in *Eruvin* 53a
(Rashi)] — he was dejected, and he became envious of him [David].

(*Sanhedrin* 93b)

It seems that, in the assessment of Chazal, King Sha'ul —
while unquestionably greatly learned and immensely G-d fear-
ing — apparently lacked both the dogged persistence and inspi-

rational guidance[16] upon which the capacity to derive Halachic-ally warranted conclusions is predicated.

We pay proceed to analyze King Sha'ul's visit to the necro-mancer in light of this conclusion. It appears that, to the degree that this act was at all sinful, he acted upon plausible deductions regarding the Halachic issues that relate to the Torah's prohibi-tion against necromancy and the various other forms of divina-tion and witchcraft.

5. THE TORAH'S PROHIBITION AGAINST NECROMANCY

After unsuccessfully attempting to invoke his spiritual powers to curse the nation of Yisra'el, the Gentile prophet, Bil'am son of Be'or, proceeds to laud the unique relationship between G-d and the nation of Yisra'el by emphasizing the absence of divination in their midst:

> For there is no divination in Ya'akov, nor enchantment in Yisra'el.
> For in due time, it shall be told to Ya'akov and to Yisra'el,
> what G-d has wrought.
>
> (BeMidbar 23:23)

In his commentary, Rashi suggests two alternate interpreta-tions for this verse:

> *"For there is no divination in Ya'akov"* — [This means] that they are worthy of blessing, since there are no diviners and enchanters among them.
> *"For in due time, it shall be told to Ya'akov"* etc. — There will yet come a time like this in which [G-d's] love for them will be manifest to all...
>
> Another interpretation:
> *"It shall be told to Ya'akov"* — [This is] not the future tense, but rather the present tense: [meaning that] they have no need for diviners and enchanters, because whenever it is necessary that it be told to Ya'akov and to Yisra'el what the Holy One Blessed be He has wrought and what are His decrees above, they do not divine and enchant. Instead, the decree of the Omnipresent One is told to them by their prophets, or the Urim VeThummim recount it to them.
>
> (ibid.)

In light of the latter interpretation, we may then ask: what is to be done if the prophets do not notify, and the Urim VeThummim do not respond? Is it possible to assume that, under such circumstances, one may be permitted to inquire through alternate channels that are otherwise forbidden? Let us remember the circumstances confronting King Sha'ul at this fateful juncture:

> Sha'ul saw the Pelishtim encampment,
> and he feared and trembled greatly.
> Sha'ul inquired of G-d, and G-d did not answer him,
> neither by dreams, nor by the Urim, nor by the prophets.
> Sha'ul said to his servants, "Seek for me a necromancer,
> and I shall go to her, and I shall inquire of her."
>
> (Shemu'el I 28:5-7)

With the Pelishtim encamped at Shunem and ready to attack, and King Sha'ul unsure of his capability to lead Yisra'el to victory, he first inquires of G-d through all legitimate channels.[17] Only after coming to the frightening realization that all these avenues of inquiry were sealed to him does Sha'ul seek a necromancer. The very juxtaposition of the verses seems suggestive of King Sha'ul's rationalization for his action: that G-d forbade the use of divination to learn of future events solely because He provided Yisra'el with pure and holy means — such as prophecy and the Urim VeThummim — to acquire such information. With such means rendered inaccessible and the nation of Yisra'el in such grave danger, would not Sha'ul then be permitted to seek other, less acceptable sources of information?

Indeed, considering the manner in which the Torah expresses the prohibition against the various forms of divination and witchcraft, it appears that such an argument possesses much credence:

> When you come to the Land, which G-d your L-rd is giving you:
> you shall not learn to do as the abominations of those nations.
> There shall not be found among you:
> one who passes his son and his daughter through fire,
> or enchants, or divines auspicious times, or divines by omens,
> or practices witchcraft,
> or charms, or consults necromancers or wizards, or inquires of the dead.
> For doing any of these is an abomination to G-d,

and because of these abominations, G-d your L-rd
is driving them out before you.
You shall be wholehearted with G-d your L-rd.
For these nations, with you are possessing,
hearken to diviners and enchanters;
but as for you, G-d your L-rd has not given you such.
A prophet from your midst, from among your brethren like me,
G-d your L-rd will set up for you;
you shall hearken to him.

(Devarim 18:9-15)

Rashi explains:

> *"You shall be wholehearted with G-d your L-rd."* — Go with Him whole-
> heartedly, and depend upon Him, and do not investigate the future.
> Instead, accept whatever befalls you wholeheartedly. Then you will
> be with Him and of His portion.

> *"G-d your L-rd has not given you such"* — [He has not permitted you]
> to hearken to diviners and enchanters, since He has caused the
> divine presence to rest upon the prophets and the Urim VeThummim.
> (Devarim 18:13-14)

Rashi relates the prohibitions against witchcraft and divination to the promise of prophecy in the same manner that, we may
infer, King Sha'ul surely connected them: *"You shall be wholehearted with G-d your L-rd"* and not seek to investigate the future
through divination, since this is the avenue employed by the
other nations that are not endowed with prophets and the Urim
VeThummim. *"G-d your L-rd has not given you such,"* outlawing all
forms of witchcraft and divination, because *"a prophet from your
midst ... G-d your L-rd will set up for you,"* and all necessary inquiries
may be directed to him.[18]

Based upon this conclusion — that if proper means are available for consultation then divination in its various forms is forbidden — King Sha'ul apparently proceeds to infer the inverse:
if all holy and pure means are no longer accessible, then divination is no longer forbidden. Only after all the legitimate modes
of inquiry fail does Sha'ul proceed to solicit the assistance of a
necromancer. While Sha'ul's assessment of the Halachah may
perhaps have been erroneous, we can readily empathize with

his error, given the immense duress under which he was constrained to act.

Even this attenuated indictment of King Sha'ul — as the victim of flawed Halachic deductions — may, however, be excessive. In the opinion of R. Naftali Tz.Y. Berlin, this perspective, associating the prohibition against divination with the accessibility of prophecy, should be carried to its ultimate conclusion in defense of King Sha'ul. In his Torah commentary (*Ha'amek Davar*), he argues that Sha'ul's solicitation of a necromancer may actually have been justified:

> According to our explanation of *"you shall be wholehearted"* — to continuously trust wholeheartedly [in G-d], what sort of wholehearted [trust] is it to inquire [even] of the prophet concerning future events? However, it must be understood that even though in an individual's conduct in his private life one should be wholehearted with G-d and not inquire concerning future events — as said by Bil'am, "For there is no divination in Ya'akov," etc. (BeMidbar 23:23) — nevertheless, in time of war, when there is no clear counsel, and life is endangered, it is proper to inquire [in order] to know. And this was the reason of the righteous King Sha'ul inquiring through necromancy. For the Torah explicitly said, "...as for you, G-d your L-rd has not give you such. A prophet from your midst [... G-d your L-rd will set up for you]," etc. This implies that, in the absence of a prophet or *efod* [the Urim VeThummim], Sha'ul is *mandated* to inquire through necromancy. And the fact that he was punished for this, as it is written, "[Sha'ul died in the transgression that he committed against G-d, for not keeping the word of G-d,] and also *asking counsel of a necromancer and inquiring of her*" (Divrei HaYamim I 10:13), is because he caused this [situation in which G-d did not respond to any legitimate inquiries]. For he should have repented and beseeched G-d to answer him through holy means.[19] But certainly he was mandated to know what to do.

> (*Ha'amek Davar* on Devarim 18:14)

Ha'amek Davar thus contends that, in the absence of other means, one may resort to divination and witchcraft for matters concerning the national welfare of Yisra'el. This argument, however, appears dangerously flawed. Are we to surmise that, "in the absence of a prophet of *efod*," we may today justify divination

in matters of great national import? Furthermore, are these generally undesirable avenues of inquiry to be regarded as sufficiently
reliable? Can one justify leading a nation into a perilous and potentially calamitous battle based upon their prognostications?[20]

It should be noted, however, that one of the many forms of
divination,[21] Sha'ul specifically selected necromancy.[22] Regarding this particular form of divination, Chazal comment:

> Three things were said concerning necromancy:
>
> 1) the one who conjures up [the deceased] sees him but does not
> hear his voice,
> 2) the one who inquires of him hears his voice but does not see him,
> and
> 3) all [others] present neither hear nor see.
>
> *(Tan. Emor:2)*

In choosing this specific avenue of inquiry, Sha'ul was undoubtably anticipating an exclusive audience with his mentor,
the prophet Shemu'el, whose reliability was beyond question.
Because Shemu'el was no longer alive, access to him would have
to derive from the impurity of necromancy. Nevertheless, the
word of G-d to be gained from His trusted prophet, Shemu'el, at so
critical a time for the nation of Yisra'el, could possibly warrant such
inquiry. It is perhaps only in such an exceptional situation that
Ha'amek Davar would seek to legitimize divination Halachically.[23]

The Midrash, in fact, suggests that Shemu'el proved more
forthright with Sha'ul after his death than he had ever been in
his lifetime:

> Shemu'el said to him [Sha'ul], "G-d has done to him [Sha'ul] as
> He spoke through me. G-d has torn the kingdom from your hand,
> and He has given it to your fellow, David" (Shemu'el I 28:17).
>
> [Sha'ul] said to him, "When you were with us, you said to me,
> 'He has given it to your fellow who is better than you,' and now you
> say, 'to your fellow, David.'"
>
> [Shemu'el] said to him, "When I was with you, I was in the world
> of falsity, and I would say to you words of falsity [i.e., not the
> complete truth].... But now I am in the world of truth; you will hear
> from me nothing but words of [absolute] truth."
>
> *(Tan. ibid.)*

6. CONCLUSION

In our defense of King Sha'ul, we have established that Sha'ul certainly did not act in deliberate defiance of the Torah. In inquiring of a necromancer, he may have possibly erred in deducing conclusions that, while inferred from the verses of the Torah, cannot provide an acceptable basis for proper Halachic decisions. Furthermore, according to *Ha'amek Davar*, Sha'ul's solicitation of a necromancer was actually Halachically warranted. His error was only in despairing too readily of successful inquiry through the legitimate avenues that might have become accessible to him through an intensified program of repentance and prayer. In either case, King Sha'ul remains to the very end "G-d's anointed" (Shemu'el II 1:14), essentially righteous, and fully committed to the ideals and values of the Torah.

NOTES

1. See Devarim 18:9-14.

2. See *Sanhedrin* 91a.

3. See Yirmeyahu 15:1 and Tehillim 99:6.

4. Part of Channah's vow regarding her unborn son, Shemu'el, is: "ומורה לא־יעלה על־ראשו" ("and no razor shall come upon his head" [Shemu'el I 1:11]). This translation follows the opinion of R. Nehorai (see *Mish. Nazir* 9:5), that Shemu'el was a *nazir*. It should, however, be noted that according to R. Yosei (see *Mish. Nazir* ibid.), the translation should read: "and no fear [of flesh and blood] shall come upon his head." *Tar. Yonathan* and Rashi (on Shemu'el, ibid.) accept R. Yosei's opinion, even though the Mishnah appears to favor R. Nehorai's position. Presumably, the rejection of R. Nehorai's explanation by *Tar. Yonathan* and Rashi results from the immense Halachic difficulties inherent in such a vow of *neziruth* taken by Channah on behalf of a child not yet conceived. See also *Mish. Nazir* 4:6, *Nazir* 28b-29 and Radak on Shemu'el, ibid.

5. See *Mo'ed Katan* 16b.

6. Rashi (ibid., ד"ה שהכל בו) interprets "encompasses to all" to include "Torah, fear of sin, and active loving-kindness." (Compare *Avoth* 1:2.)

7. Yosef b. Yo'ezer of Tzereidah, together with Yosei b. Yochanan of Yerushalayim, served as the first of the *zugoth*, the pairs of scholars who presided over the Sanhedrin in the early Mishnaic era beginning approximately 250 B.C.E.

8. R. Yehudah b. Bava lived in the third generation of Mishnaic sages (ca. 120 C.E.) and R. Yehudah b. Ilai lived in the fourth generation (ca 160 C.E.).

9. See *Shabbath* 56a: "ישבו בעריהם כדי להרבות שכר לחזניהן ולסופריהן" ("they remained in their cities in order to augment the gains of their clerks and their scribes"). It is noteworthy that Rashi (ibid., ד"ה בני שמואל חטאו) qualifies the statement, "Whoever says that the sons of Shemu'el sinned is but in error," as referring only to the sins of bribery and perversion of justice (implying that they did commit the lesser infractions attributed to them).

10. See Shemu'el II 11. Corresponding contentions are made by Chazal (see *Shabbath* 55b-56) regarding the righteousness and apparent sins of Re'uven son of Ya'akov, the sons of Eli the Kohen, King Shelomoh, and King Yoshiyyahu. It should be noted that in its insistence on the basic righteousness of these individuals, the Talmud does not rely merely on tradition, but equally on meticulous scrutiny of the relevant Biblical passages. Indeed, beyond the textual proofs cited in the Talmud in support of its contentions, various commentaries cite additional textual supports for Chazal's position. For example, regarding the relationship of King David and Bath-Sheva, see *Devar Shemu'el* (Malbim) on Shemu'el II 11 and *Me'or Einayim* (R. Yoshiyyahu b. Yosef Pinto) on *Shabbath* 56a. See also the author's essay in *The Book of Samuel 2, Judaica Books of the Prophets*, "Commentary Digest" on 11:4 (New York: Judaica Press, 1978).

11. See com. of Rashi and Tosafoth on *Shabbath* 56a and *Kethubboth* 9b. Rashi (on *Shabbath* 56a, ד"ה גט כריתות), and on *Kethubboth* 9b, ד"ה גט כריתות כתב לאשתו) explains that the divorce contract was written conditionally, to take effect retroactively in the case of death. In the Tosafoth (on *Shabbath* 56a, ד"ה כל היוצא וכו', and on *Kethubboth* 9b, ד"ה גט כריתות כתב לאשתו), R. Tam contends that the divorce contract was written unconditionally and granted outright, but secretively, so that outsiders would remain unsure of the woman's status and not solicit her prior to her husband's return from battle.

12. According to most authorities, *Derashoth HaRan* was written by R. Nissim b. Re'uven (ca. 1350 C.E.), a student of Rashba and the noted commentator on Rif's *Sefer HaHalachoth*. It is, however, attributed by some to Rabbeinu Nissim (ca. 1250 C.E.), a student of Ramban.

13. See *Yevamoth* 121b: "הקדוש ברוך הוא מדקדק עם סביביו כחוט השערה" ("The Holy One Blessed be He is exacting as a hairsbreadth with those [i.e., the righteous] who surround Him").

14. "גלי מסכתא" (here trans. "texts were revealed") is explained by Rashi (ibid., ד"ה דגלו מסכתא) as meaning either that King David taught others or that he labored at establishing the rationale of the Halachah. Both interpretations imply a dedication and persistence that were apparently deficient in King Sha'ul.

15. Midrashic interpretation of battle-related expressions as metaphors for the dialectical battles of Torah is a recurrent motif. See, for example, *Kiddushin* 30a. Here, this interpretation seems dictated by the context. Because Sha'ul's dejection (the reason for bringing a minstrel for him) was due to a spiritual

vacuum (see R. Yitzchak Abbarbanel and *Devar Shemu'el* [Malbim] on Shemu'el I 16:14), the Midrash concludes that David's nomination resulted from his immense spiritual stature rather than his military prowess.

16. See *Ha'amek Davar* on Devarim 33:12, where the view is articulated that King Sha'ul's lack of Halachic guidance emanated from a basically positive trait.

17. The Talmud relates King Sha'ul's unsuccessful inquiry of the Urim VeThummim to his complicity in the massacre of Nov, the city of Kohanim (see *Berachoth* 12b). Perhaps we may likewise partially relate Sha'ul's current inability to receive prophetic guidance to his failure to heed the words of the prophet Shemu'el twice previously (see Shemu'el I 13 and 15).

18. The connection between the prohibition against divination and the ready access that the nation of Yisra'el has to prophecy seems implied also in the Midrash (see *Tan. Emor*:2). See also *Ba'al HaTurim* on VaYikra 20:26-27.

19. Ostensibly, the contention in *Ha'amek Davar* that Sha'ul's sin consisted only of despairing too readily of legitimate avenues of inquiry seems unduly contrived. However, a careful reading of the relevant Biblical passages concerning King Sha'ul's sin lends credence to *Ha'amek Davar*'s claim. Divrei HaYamim I 10:13-14 states that Sha'ul was slain for "asking counsel of a necromancer and inquiring of her. And he *did not inquire of G-d*." But we read in Shemu'el I 28:6 that *"Sha'ul inquired of G-d*, and G-d did not answer him." The apparent contradiction is resolved by *Ha'amek Davar*'s assertion that, while Sha'ul *did* inquire of G-d, he despaired too readily, and an intensified program of prayer and repentance could have rendered accessible to him the pure and holy channels of prophecy or the Urim VeThummim. In that sense, he did *not* inquire of G-d, by consulting a necromancer in lieu of redoubling his efforts to solicit a response from G-d. (Compare R. Yitzchak Abbarbanel on Shemu'el I 28:7).

20. Regarding the fallibility of divination in its various forms, see Ramban, *Introduction to the Mishnah*, 2: "The enchanters and astrologers and the witches and the like recount imminent future events, but [while] they [may be] partially correct, they also necessarily partially falsify.... However, that they be accurate in every detail of their prognostications is impossible...." See also *Berachoth* 55a and *BeR.R.* 85:2.

In addition, see the opinion of the Ge'onim cited by Radak on Shemu'el I 28:24 that necromancy is "vanity and nothingness and falsehood and trickery," fraudulent in its claim to actually conjure up the dead. (See also R. Yitzchak Abbarbanel, ibid. 28:11, who cites their opinion as well.) Radak and R. Yitzchak Abbarbanel reject this opinion, arguing that the king — who together with the Sanhedrin was charged with ridding the nation of diviners and enchanters — was necessarily sufficiently knowledgeable concerning these matters not to be fooled by trickery and fraud. It is clear that the Talmud (see *Shabbath* 152b) and many Midrashim (see above) assume that necromancy is capable of actually conjuring up the dead.

21. See Devarim 18:10-11.

22. See Shemu'el I 28:7.

23. See *Ha'amek Davar*, ibid.: "And this was the reason of the righteous King Sha'ul inquiring *through necromancy*.... Sha'ul is mandated to inquire *through necromancy*." (Emphasis mine.)

UNDERSTANDING "AN EYE FOR AN EYE":
Where *Peshat* Contradicts Halachah

Yehudah Copperman

1. INTRODUCTION

Chazal were occupied primarily with the Midrash Halachah, deducing the Halachah through Midrashic expositions. Nevertheless, they taught us that "Scripture does not depart from its plain meaning" (*Shabbath* 63a, *Yevamoth* 11b and 24a). Ramban notes[1] that Chazal did *not* state that Scripture conveys *only* its plain meaning. However, recognizing the danger that Torah study would be confined to only its principal arena — Halachic expositions — Chazal warned us that even after we have completed studying the *halachoth* derived from the verse, we have still not completed studying the verse. For there are many dimensions to the words of the Torah, "like a hammer that shatters a rock [into many fragments]" (Yirmeyahu 23:29).[2] Even after we have exhausted all

RABBI COPPERMAN, the founder of the Michlalah - Jerusalem College for Women, is a noted writer and lecturer in various fields of Judaic studies. He is the author of *LiFshuto shel Mikra* (2nd ed., Yerushalayim: Haskel, 1981) and the editor of the annotated edition of *Meshech Chochmah* (Yerushalayim: Haskel, 1983).
"Understanding 'And Eye for and Eye'" was adapted (by Ch.Sh.E.) from *Lifshuto shel Mikra*, pp. 61-67.

the Halachic implications, we are still left with the *peshat* (the plain meaning). This, too, is Torah and demands study.

The question then arises, what Torah value does this study of *peshat* possess? If not for the Talmudic statement quoted above, we could have concluded that once we have completed learning the *halachoth* implied by the verse, nothing more remains to be learned from the text. Were we then asked, for example, why the Torah states, "And you shall cut off her palm" (Devarim 28:12), where monetary compensation is intended, we would respond that the manner in which the Torah is written relates to levels of study that are beyond our comprehension. These, of course, include the esoteric dimensions of Kabbalah that Ramban himself[3] warns us to avoid.[4] Similarly, the manner in which the Torah is written is also determined by additional considerations, such as that "the entire Torah is names of the Holy One Blessed be He,"[4] considerations that are completely understood only by the Creator Himself, Who dictated this Torah to Mosheh word by word and letter by letter.

Once Chazal have informed us that Scripture does not lose its plain meaning, however, we cannot content ourselves by directing the student to Kabbalistic disciplines; revealing esoteric names of G-d is certainly not the "plain meaning" of Scripture. So the question reasserts itself: What is one to do with the "plain meaning" of Scripture? More precisely, what did Chazal want us to extract from the text after having absorbed its Halachic and Midrashic implications? What function did Chazal ascribe to the *peshat* in instructing us that the verse does not lose its plain meaning while instructing us also that the Halachah does not accord with this meaning?

By delving deeply into the classic commentaries on the Torah, particularly those of the *acharonim* (later rabbinical authorities) who often grappled with this question, we discover that the plain meaning of Scripture is indeed not an empty matter. The *peshat* of Halachic statements in the Torah performs an especially important function as an integral component of G-d's Torah. In fact, broad dimensions of this Torah — both within and beyond the realm of Halachah — were entrusted specifically to the plain meaning, to teach a variety of lessons that might otherwise have remained concealed from us.

2. THE *PESHAT* REVEALING IDEAS BEHIND THE HALACHAH

Perhaps the best known example of *peshat* that appears irrelevant to the Halachah but nevertheless has implications for our understanding of the Halachah is the Torah law that demands "an eye for an eye" (Shemoth 21:24). Here, the plain meaning reveals not the actual law but what the law ought to be. This standpoint is particularly articulated in the commentary of R. Ovadyah Seforno:

> This [mandate of "an eye for an eye"] is appropriate according to strict justice that is apportioned measure for measure. However, the tradition informs us that [the assailant] should pay monetary compensation because of our inability to determine [the proper measure of punishment], lest we err and exaggerate the [true] measure of guilt.
>
> (com., loc. cit.)[5]

This principle is also implied by Rambam, regarding an analogous verse in VaYikra. He writes in *Mishneh Torah*:

> What is stated in the Torah, "If one inflicts injury on another person, so shall be done to him" (VaYikra 24:19), does not mean to injure this one as he injured his fellow, *but that he is worthy of losing a limb or being injured as he did [to his fellow]*. And therefore he pays monetary damages.
>
> (Hil. Chovel UMezik 1:3)

Another role of the nuances of *peshat* — even where they lack Halachic ramifications — is to reveal by allusion the reasoning of the Halachah itself. For example, in the laws governing the *chattath* (sin offering), the Torah states, "This is the law of the *chattath*: In the place where the *olah* [burnt offering] is slaughtered shall the *chattath* be slaughtered" (VaYikra 6:18). We note that the location is specified in the same verse as the heading, "This is the law of the *chattath*." By contrast, in the section discussing the *asham* (guilt offering), the first verse contains only the heading: "And this is the law of the *asham* ..." (ibid. 7:1). Only in the following verse is the location specified: "In the place where they slaughter the *olah* they shall slaughter the *asham* ..." (ibid. 7:2). This variation is understood by *Meshech Chochmah* as an allusion to the *reason* why the *chattath*, like the *olah*, is slaughtered in the north: to conceal the wrongdoing of the sinner bringing the *chattath*. Seeing the offering slaughtered in the north, the observer would assume that it was an *olah*, and not a *chattath* brought to atone for the misdeed of its owner:

> Hence, with regard to the *chattath*, which is brought for unintentional wrongdoing, Scripture was careful to write immediately [in the same verse], "in the place where the *olah* is slaughtered shall the *chattath* be slaughtered" (VaYikra 6:18). But with regard to the *asham*, which is brought for intentional transgressions [so that special consideration for the sinner is unjustified], Scripture did not state immediately [in the same verse], "in the place where they slaughter the *olah* they shall slaughter the *asham*" (ibid. 7:2).
>
> (com. on VaYikra 6:18, ד"ה קודש קדשים הוא)

On a more subtle level, the nuances of *peshat* may occasionally relate to a level of reasoning that reflects the period in which a certain *halachah* was stated. Thus, in *parashath Mishpatim*, the Torah commands, "If you see the donkey of *someone you hate* lying under its load ... you must unload it with him" (Shemoth 22:5). By contrast, in *parashath Ki-Thetzei*, an analogous law is stated regarding "the donkey of *your brother*" (Devarim 22:4). The Talmud, in discussing the former verse, asks, "Is it then permissible to hate [another Jew]? But it is written, 'Do not hate your brother in your heart' (VaYikra 19:17)!" (*Pesachim* 113b). The Talmud (ibid.) resolves this inconsistency by concluding that if one witnesses his fellow committing an immoral act, it is a *mitzvah* to hate him. But the inconsistency between the two verses — only one of which speaks of "someone you hate" — is perplexing. Based upon this Talmudic discussion, *Meshech Chochmah* explains the distinction in peshat between these two verses. Only prior to the sin of the golden calf (i.e., the verse in *parashath Mishpatim*) was Yisra'el at so lofty a spiritual level that hating a fellow Jew was justified if one witnessed his commission of a transgression. This was not the case after all the trials in which Yisra'el had sinned, whereupon if one were to notice his fellow's misdeeds, he could examine his own actions as well and find failings and questionable behavior in one or another detail. Hence — unless one were himself perfectly righteous in his behavior and scrupulous in avoidance of evil — it was forbidden to hate even such a person. Since so righteous a person is difficult to find, after the golden calf (i.e., the verse in *parashath Ki-Thetzei*), the Torah writes "your brother."[6]

Finally, the *peshat* — even where it explicitly contradicts the Halachah — may allude to a much deeper level of esoteric understanding of the Halachah. Perhaps the most forceful example of this phenomenon is *yibbum* (levirate marriage). We have previously noted Chazal's dictum that Scripture does not lose its plain meaning. In this case, however, regarding the verse, "The first-born son whom she bears shall stand up upon the name of his [father's] dead brother" (Devarim 25:6), the Talmud emphasizes, "Even though in the whole Torah, Scripture does not depart from its plain meaning, here a *gezerah shavah* [mode of Halachic exposition] comes and removes [the verse] entirely from its plain meaning" (*Yevamoth* 24a). Indeed, the Halachah completely negates the *peshat* here, as explained by Ramban:

> It is not [to be understood] according to the plain meaning, that they should call the first-born son by the name of the deceased, like "Re'uven" or "Shimon." For it is said similarly regarding Bo'az, "that the name of the deceased shall not be cut off from among his brothers and the gate of his place" (Ruth 4:10), yet he did not call [his son] "Machlon" [the name of Ruth's deceased husband]....
>
> (com., loc. cit.)

But Ramban explains that the plain meaning nevertheless has meaning — esoterically:

> This passage in the way of truth[7] is a promise, to be understood *according to its plain meaning.*
>
> (loc. cit.)[8]

In these and similar cases, the plain meaning of Scripture has no explicit relevance to the determination of the Halachah. Yet, as we can see, it would be inappropriate to surmise that the plain meaning is irrelevant, because it is specifically through the *peshat* that the ideas behind the Halachah are elucidated.

3. THE *PESHAT* AS AN ADDITIONAL BASIS
FOR HALACHAH

In addition to allusions to ideas that are behind the Halachah, the plain meaning can also have binding Halachic implications even where Chazal expound a verse not in accordance with its *peshat*. For example, the Torah states that "fathers shall not be put to death on account of [their] children, and children shall not be put to death on account of [their] fathers" (Devarim 24:16). The Talmud interprets this verse as a reference to the disqualification of relatives as witnesses: "Fathers shall not be put to death on account of *the testimony of* [their] children, and children shall not be put to death on account of *the testimony of* [their] fathers" (*Sanhedrin* 27b). Thus, the plain meaning of the text implies that fathers should not be put to death on account of their children's *sins*, while the Midrashic exposition concludes that fathers should not be put to death on account of their children's *testimony*.[9] Nevertheless, in reference to King Amatzyahu's execution of his father's assassins, it is stated, "The children of the assailants he did not put to death, as it is written in the book of the Torah of Mosheh[10] that G-d commanded: 'Fathers shall not be put to death on account of [their] children, and children shall not be put to death on account of [their] fathers, but every man shall be put to death for his own sin' " (Melachim II 14:6). Sefer Melachim, then, draws Halachic conclusions from the verse in Devarim according to its plain meaning and not according to the Midrashic exposition of Chazal. In *Chiddushei HaRan* on *Sanhedrin*, R. Nissim[11] explains:

> You may ask, is not the verse ["Fathers shall not be put to death on account of [their] children"] needed for its plain meaning, that fathers should not be put to death on account of the *sins* of their children, as is written regarding Amatzyahu, "The children of the assailants he did not put to death," etc.? One may respond that "Scripture does not depart from its plain meaning." And the plain meaning of the verse is that fathers should not be put to death on account of the *sins* of their children, while the Midrashic explanation is that they should not be put to death on account of the *testimony* of their children. Thus, a single verse splits into many interpretations, as it is written, "The L-rd has spoken one; I have heard two" (Tehillim 62:12).
>
> (*Chiddushei HaRan* on *Sanhedrin* 27b, ד"ה לא יומתו אבות בעדות בנים)

Ramban also considered the double meaning — both according to rabbinical tradition and according to *peshat* — of this verse.[12] Thus, we find among the *rishonim* (early rabbinical authorities) recognition of legitimate Halachic interpretation of a verse according to its plain meaning in addition to the Halachic exposition of the text by Chazal, where the plain meaning and the Midrashic interpretation do not contradict one another and both explanations may simultaneously be derived from the same verse.[13]

The *peshat* can have an additional function in the sphere of Halachah. Even where the plain meaning is not consistent with the Halachah as expounded by Chazal, it may nevertheless have Halachic significance in an historical sense. While it cannot be construed as permanently binding Halachah, the plain meaning may represent an aspect of Halachah that was temporarily in force. This significance of the *peshat* is also expressed in the works of the classic commentators.

A noteworthy example is provided by the Torah's statement, "And the *chelev* [hard fat] of an animal that dies of itself and the *chelev* of an animal that is fatally wounded may be used for any other purpose, but you shall in no way eat it" (VaYikra 7:24). The Torah has already instructed that "*all chelev* and all blood you shall not eat" (VaYikra 3:17). Regarding this reiteration of the prohibition against eating *chelev*, the Talmud explains, "What does the teaching [of this verse] imply? Said Rava: The Torah ordained that the prohibition against eating the flesh of an animal that dies of itself shall apply to the prohibition against eating *chelev*, and that the prohibition against eating the flesh of an animal that is fatally wounded shall apply to the prohibition against eating *chelev*" (*Chullin* 37a). Rava's explanation addresses an essential difficulty in the plain meaning of Scripture. Is the *chelev* of an animal that dies of itself or is fatally wounded not included in this prohibition against eating "*all chelev*"? Particularly, by what logic is it necessary for the Torah to specify that the *chelev* of such an animal — whose *flesh* one is also forbidden to eat — is not to be consumed? Could we conceive that the *chelev* of such an animal would be more permissible than that of an animal whose flesh may be eaten but whose *chelev* is still forbidden? Thus, there is no justification, even in terms of *peshat*, for the Torah's repetition of this prohibition. Hence, Rava concludes that the repetition teaches us that one who eats the *chelev* of such an animal is liable for having transgressed *both* prohibitions — against eating *chelev* and against eating of such an animal — in spite of the principle that "a prohibition is [generally] not applied to another prohibition" (*Pesachim* 35b, *Yevamoth* 13b, *Kiddushin* 77b).

Yet these questions still remain with respect to the plain meaning of the text. Since the prohibition against eating "*all chelev*" has already been articulated, why — in terms of *peshat* — is it restated with respect to animals whose very flesh is forbidden? Furthermore, if the *chelev* of an animal that dies of itself or is fatally wounded must be specifically banned, we might conclude that the flesh of such an animal was in fact permitted! Responds R. Naftali Tz.Y. Berlin:

> The Talmudic exposition [see *Chullin* 37a, quoted above] is well known. However, according to the plain meaning, this is astonishing, since in the case of an animal that dies of itself or is fatally wounded, even the flesh may not be eaten. It appears, then, that according to the plain meaning, mention here of an animal that dies of itself [i.e., without slaughter] is in reference to an animal killed by stabbing [and without proper ritual slaughter], whose flesh was permissible [during the forty years of wandering] in the wilderness [according to the view of R. Akiva].[14] Since such an animal was not ritually slaughtered, it is described as an animal that dies of itself and is nevertheless ritually fit [to be eaten].... Accordingly the Torah specified that eating the *chelev* is still forbidden [even though a special dispensation was granted to permit the otherwise forbidden flesh of such an animal]. The same rule [forbidding *chelev*] applies to ordinary meat nowadays, *but Scripture speaks of the wilderness period during which ritually slaughtered meat was eaten only as part of a sacrifice.*
>
> (*Ha'amek Davar* on VaYikra 7:24)

Thus, "Scripture does not depart from its plain meaning" (*Shabbath* 63a, Yevamoth 11b and 24a), and the peshat prohibition against eating the *chelev* of an animal that dies of itself or is fatally wounded is maintained. The plain meaning of this *halachah* is relevant, however, only during the wilderness period, in which consumption of an animal killed by stabbing without proper ritual slaughter

— here described as "an animal that dies of itself" (i.e., without slaughter) — was permitted.[15] Because of this special dispensation, the Torah was obliged to reiterate the prohibition against eating *chelev* with respect to such an animal for the benefit of the generation of the Exodus, for Scripture — at least on the level of *peshat* — "speaks of the wilderness period."

Even prior to R. Naftali Tz.Y. Berlin, the Vilna Ga'on had interpreted another Biblical passage similarly. The Torah states, "Aharon shall come to the Tent of Meeting and shall take off the linen vestments that he wore when he entered the sanctuary, and he shall leave them there. He shall immerse his body in water in the sanctified place and shall put on his [regular] vestments; he shall go out and shall complete his burnt offering and the burnt offering of the people and shall atone for himself and for the people" (VaYikra 16:23-24). In interpreting these verses, the Talmud explains, "Our rabbis taught: '*Aharon shall come to the Tent of Meeting*' — Why did he come? He came only to remove the censer and the coal pan. For the whole passage is reported in [chronological] order except for this verse" (*Yoma* 32a). The Talmud is constrained to interpret this passage not in accordance with its plain meaning, since according to the tradition of Chazal, the *kohen gadol* (high priest) performed five immersions (before he changed from golden to linen vestments and vice versa) and ten ablutions of his hands and feet (before and after each change) on Yom Kippur. Therefore, the verse describing the immersion, "He shall immerse his body in water ... he shall go out and shall complete his burnt offering and the burnt offering of the people and shall atone for himself and for the people" (ibid. 16:24), necessarily preceded "Aharon ... shall take off the linen vestments ... and he shall leave them there" (ibid. 16:23). Thus, according to the Midrashic exposition, the Talmud concludes that these verses are not in chronological order. But the plain meaning implies chronology in Scripture. How can both be valid?

R. Naftali Tz.Y. Berlin[16] and R. Avraham Danzig[17] respond, in the name of the Vilna Ga'on, in light of the approach cited in the Midrash[18] that Aharon himself could enter the inner sanctuary any day of the year (in addition to Yom Kippur) once he had undergone the preparation mandated in this chapter. Only subsequent *kohanim gedolim* were restricted to one occasion (on Yom

Kippur) each year.[19] The chronological inconsistency in *peshat* may then be resolved:

> *"Aharon shall come to the Tent of Meeting [and shall take off the linen vestments that he wore when he entered the sanctuary, and he shall leave them there.]"* (VaYikra 16:23) — According to the plain meaning, this reverts to the beginning of the subject, in which [Mosheh is commanded to] speak to Aharon alone. If he desired to come to the Tent of Meeting on any day of the year, [he could do so] after all these preparations. But all of this applies only to Aharon himself. However, for subsequent generations, Scripture is expounded to refer to the removal of the censer and the coal pan, as explained by the Gemara [cited above].
>
> (*Ha'amek Davar*, loc. cit.)

According to our understanding of this approach, we may conclude that the *halachah* that was temporarily in force during Aharon's tenure left its imprint on the language of *Torah shebikethav* (the written Torah). Were it not for such temporary Halachic realities, the Torah could have foregone — at least from a Halachic standpoint[20] — the reiteration of the prohibition of eating chelev (discussed above) and the lack of chronology in its description of the Yom Kippur service.

It appears that this approach has an even earlier precedent in Ramban, who also explained passages in the Torah based upon the principle that a temporary Halachic reality may determine the language of *Torah shebikethav*. Regarding the order and laws of inheritance, the Torah states: "And you shall speak to the children of Yisra'el: If a man dies without a son, you shall pass his inheritance to his daughter. And if he has no daughter, you shall give his inheritance to his brothers" (BeMidbar 27:8-9). Ramban comments:

> Our Rabbis received by tradition that the father inherits his son if [his son] dies without offspring. Scripture, however, does not mention this.... Perhaps this [situation] did not pertain to those who entered the land, *regarding whom [Scripture] speaks.*
>
> (com. on BeMidbar 27:9)

Thus, it was the temporary Halachic reality that deleted from the text of the Torah the law of the father inheriting his son, and it determined the manner in which Scripture was written.

While Ramban's explanation supports by implication the approach that we have attributed to the Vilna Ga'on and R. Naftali Tz.Y. Berlin, the explicit statement of R. Avraham b. Ezra concerning "the day after the Shabbath (ממחרת השבת)" (VaYikra 23:15) appears to be the foundation and primary source for this approach. The problem posed by the phrase "the day after the Shabbath" — which Chazal understand as referring to "the day after the first day of Pesach" — and the consequent dispute between Chazal and the Tzedukim are well known. Many have attempted to resolve the inconsistency between the plain meaning of the text[21] and the Midrash. R. Avraham b. Ezra writes:

> The believer could also respond that [Mosheh] knew through prophecy that the day of the Omer offering [that year] would occur on the Shabbath [and he therefore specified "the day after the Shabbath" (VaYikra 23:15)]. The evidence [that this did in fact occur on Shabbath] is from the arranging of the showbread [two weeks earlier],[22] which took place on Shabbath. *And Scripture recounted how the day was calculated during the first year.*
>
> (com., loc. cit.)

Thus, according to R. Avraham b. Ezra, the expression "the day after the Shabbath" reflects a temporary Halachic reality, applicable to the first year in which the Omer offering was brought. The permanent Halachah is deduced from the *principle* that the Omer was to be brought on the day after the first day of Pesach.

Summarizing the above, we could say that the plain meaning of the Halachah is what G-d *said*, while the Midrash Halachah is what G-d *says*. Just as one does not attend to the problems of temporary life while remaining oblivious to the problems of eternal life, so one should not focus on the temporary Halachah before deducing the permanent Halachah. Yet both "these and those are the words of the Living G-d" (*Gittin* 6b), and ultimately both provide instruction for all generations.[23]

4. CONCLUSIONS

As we have seen, then, study of the Halachic sections of the Torah includes two domains: one according to the Midrashic approach of Chazal, and the other according to the rules of *peshat*, the plain meaning. The Midrashim of Chazal play the chords of permanent, binding Halachah: the fabric of the Jewish way of life. Superimposed upon this is the domain of *peshat*, revealing all the other overtones: ideas behind the Halachah, inner meanings of the Halachah, *halachoth* in an historical context that no longer applies, etc. All these must be joined to provide a profound, comprehensive, and exhaustive analysis of the Torah of G-d, together with an appreciation of its eternity within the framework of the 613 *mitzvoth* and the infinite facets through which it is expounded.

NOTES

1. See Ramban in com. on *Sefer HaMitzvoth* (Rambam), *Shoresh* 2.

2. *Ed. note:* Chazal expound this verse as related to the multifaceted nature of Scripture. See, for example, *Sanhedrin* 34a (and *Shabbath* 88b): " '*Like a hammer that shatters a rock*' (Yirmeyahu 23:29) — Just as this hammer [causes the rock (Rashi)] to be split into several fragments, so too one [verse from] Scripture may diverge into several explanations." (See also *Yer. Nedarim* 3:2 [8a], *Yer. Shevu'oth* 3:8 [13a], and numerous Midrashic references.)

3. *Ed. note:* Ramban himself was an eminent student of Kabbalah and frequently refers to it in his *Commentary on the Torah* as "the way of truth." See also Ritva's assessment of Ramban's commentary in Ritva's *Sefer HaZikaron*.

4. *Ed. note:* See Ramban's introduction to his *Commentary on the Torah*.

5. It is noteworthy that this explanation, recognizing the possibility of error in human determination of the proper measure of punishment, is originally articulated by Chazal. Realizing the possibly fatal consequences of expounding the Halachah here literally and actually gouging out the assailant's eye, the Talmud notes, "[It is written,] 'an eye for an eye ... a life for a life,' and not 'a life and an eye for an eye.' And if you would think [that 'an eye for an eye' is to be understood] literally, occasionally one finds an eye and a life [paid] for an eye, because while blinding [the assailant as punishment], he died" (*Babba Kamma* 84a).

   Ed. note: Similarly, the Talmud observes, " 'An eye for an eye' [refers to] monetary [compensation]. You say, does it refer to money or to the actual eye? But if this one's eye were large and this one's eye were small, how can I describe [such punishment as] 'an eye for an eye'?" (ibid. 83b). It should be emphasized that the Talmud's discussion is *not* whether "an eye for an eye" is or is not to be understood literally, because it is universally recognized that according to the oral Torah the punishment is monetary. The discussion records the attempts of Chazal to discern how this posited assessment of the oral Torah is implied and even mandated in the words of the written Torah that ostensibly contradict it. Essentially, then, the discussion is an attempt to discern significance in the plain meaning of Scripture, even though it appears to be contradicted by the Halachah.

6. See also *Meshech Chochmah* on Devarim 16:7.

7. *Ed. note:* In Ramban's commentary, the phrase "the way of truth" consistently refers to the esoteric levels of meaning to which he frequently alludes.

8. *Ed. note:* Regarding the esoteric significance of *yibbum* according to Ramban, see also com. on BeReshith 38:8.

9. *Ed. note:* Nevertheless, it is noteworthy that the Talmud derives its conclusion not merely from Midrashic tradition but from textual analysis of the verse itself. (See *Sanhedrin* 27b, loc. cit.)

10. In the books of Nach, this is commonly a reference to Sefer Devarim. See *Meshech Chochmah* on Devarim 12:27.

11. *Ed. note:* It should be noted that according to R. Elchanan Wasserman these novellae on *Sanhedrin* are erroneously attributed to R. Nissim — a difficulty that frequently arises in the classification of manuscripts from the period of the *rishonim* (early rabbinical authorities).

12. See Ramban's *Mishpat HaCherem* and his com. on VaYikra 27:29.

13. For other examples in which classical commentators derive new *halachoth* from the plain meaning of Scripture, see *Ha'amek Davar* on Shemoth 28:31, ד"ה מעיל האפוד, on VaYikra 27:20, ד"ה ואם מכר, and on BeMidbar 35:30, ד"ה ועד אחד לא יענה. See also *Meshech Chochmah* on Devarim 21:7, ד"ה אשר ימצא לו, and on Devarim 22:2, ד"ה והשבתו לו. See also *HaKethav VeHaKabbalah* on Shemoth 12:14, on VaYikra 25:9, ד"ה והעברת שופר, and on Devarim 16:8, ד"ה ששת ימים.

Nevertheless, we note in contrast the principle invoked by *HaKethav VeHaKabbalah* that "*we are not permitted to innovate in a mitzvah*" any interpretation that has no basis stemming from [the Sages] who received the oral Torah" (com. on Devarim 17:18, ד"ה את משנה התורה).

14. See Chullin 17a.

15. See *Ha'amek Davar*, ibid., for an analogous explanation of the prohibition specified here against eating the *chelev* of a fatally wounded animal.

16. See *Ha'amek Davar* on VaYikra 16:23.

17. See the conclusion of *Chochmath Adam*.

18. See *VaY.R.* 21:7.

19. Therefore, Yom Kippur itself is not mentioned (as the date of this service) until the end of the chapter (ibid. 16:29), and the expression "the *kohen* [priest] shall atone" (ibid. 16:32) — without specifying Aharon — is employed only subsequently.

20. Of course, our discussion is only from a Halachic standpoint, regarding the *plain meaning* of Scripture, and has no relevance to the deeper significance of

each and every letter of the Torah on a more esoteric level.

21. It should nevertheless be noted that according to R. David Tz. Hoffman, only the term *"the day of* the Shabbath" refers to Shabbath in its plain meaning, so "the day after the Shabbath" — as opposed to "the day after *the day of* the Shabbath" — implies merely the day after a day of rest, without specifying which day. See also *Ha'amek Davar* and *HaKethav VeHaKabbalah*, loc. cit. Interestingly, the commentary of *HaKethav VeHaKabbalah* on "the day after the Shabbath" tends toward the explanation of R. Avraham b. Ezra (quoted in the text, below).

22. The arranging of the showbread took place on the day upon which the sanctuary was erected, the first day of Nisan. The first day of Pesach, which is the fifteenth of Nisan, is the same day of the week, two weeks later.

23. For other examples in which temporary *halachoth* are implied from the plain meaning of Scripture, see also *Meshech Chochmah* on VaYikra 3:1, ד"ה וזרקו בני אהרן את הדם, and ibid. 3:2, ד"ה ואם זבח שלמים קרבנו.

HAMAN'S BRIBE AND ITS ANTIDOTE:
Purim and the *Machatzith HaShekel*

Aryeh Naiman

1. INTRODUCTION

The Talmud states:

> It was known and revealed before the Creator of the world that in the future Haman would mete out *shekalim* against Yisra'el; therefore, He caused their *shekalim* to precede [Haman's].
>
> (*Megillah* 13b)

Thus, Chazal tell us that the *machatzith hashekel* (half *shekel*) that was contributed to the sanctuary by each of the members of *benei Yisra'el* who were counted in the wilderness, as well as the annual *machatzith hashekel* later given for the sanctuary and the Beith HaMikdash (*Mish. Shekalim* 1:1), served to protect the Jews from Haman's decree.

Yet the connection between these *shekalim* and the ten thousand silver talents offered by Haman to Achashverosh for permission to exterminate the Jews (Ester 3:9) seems elusive. What

ARYEH NAIMAN is an alumnus of the Hebrew Theological College of Skokie, Illinois, and of Yeshivat Keren BeYavneh and the Mir in Israel. A lawyer by profession, he resides in Yerushalayim, where he has done extensive research in *mishpat Ivri* (Hebraic law).

is there in the *mitzvah* of *machatzith hashekel* which could serve as an antidote for Haman's plan? Furthermore, the Talmud states that G-d "caused their *shekalim* to *precede* [Haman's]," indicating that the protection afforded by the *mitzvah* of *machatzith hashekel* was readied in advance because of what had already been contributed in the past. Why then did this protection prevent only the actual execution of Haman's decree, instead of preventing the decree altogether and sparing the Jews all of the anxiety that it caused? In addition, assuming (as Chazal did) that some deeper connection exists between the two sums, one would expect the sum donated by *benei Yisra'el* to the sanctuary to have comprised at least as much as Haman was prepared to donate for permission to destroy them. Why then did the relatively minimal amount of *machatzith hashekel* suffice to outweigh Haman's sum? All these *shekalim* combined amount to slightly more than one hundred silver talents (Shemoth 38:25), while Haman's proposed contribution to the king's coffers was one hundred times as much! Apparently, a deeper understanding both of the *mitzvah* of *machatzith hashekel* and of the decree of Haman is necessary.

2. THE EFFICACY OF THE *MACHATZITH HASHEKEL*

The power of the *machatzith hashekel* to protect is clearly indicated in the Torah itself, which states that the nation of Yisra'el was commanded to make this contribution so that "no plague may come upon them when they are counted" (Shemoth 30:12). But the Torah does not explain either how the census can precipitate a plague or how the *machatzith hashekel* can prevent it. Rashi explains that the potential source of the plague is the *ayin hara* (the so-called evil eye), which is "prevalent when a count is taken" (com., ibid.). From where, however, does this destructive capacity of the *ayin hara* derive?

Occasionally, a person may consider his friend's success with a dismay that is tinged with jealousy and wonder how his friend merited such good fortune. In order to prepare a response to these unstated accusations against divine justice, such critical questioning may arouse a closer scrutiny of the person enjoying this success by the heavenly court as well. It is here that danger lies, for G-d generally deals with us according to *middath harachamim*

(His attribute of compassion). The complaint against divine justice, however, necessitates a more precise, individual assessment, to ascertain whether such divine benevolence is in fact deserved. If it is not, and the accusations of the *ayin hara* demand reply, G-d may be constrained, as it were, to modify the situation in accord with *middath haddin* (His attribute of strict justice) and proceed to withhold the good fortune that had previously been enjoyed.

We may then conclude that *middath harachamim* does not *actively* dictate a favorable judgment in place of a negative one dictated by *middath haddin*. Instead, divine mercy is expressed in inaction: G-d may "ignore" (temporarily) the just punishment dictated by *middath haddin*, which would otherwise be executed immediately as the automatic consequence of sin. Yet how long can the demands of justice be ignored? The Torah expresses the limit on forbearance: until "the day of My accounting, [when] I shall bring them to account for their sins" (Shemoth 32:34). Thus, even without malicious intent, the critical *ayin hara* of one who questions his fellow's success demands an accounting — and an appeasement of *middath haddin*. Once the protection of divine mercy is withdrawn, divine judgment according to the letter of the law is activated.

Recognizing this function of the *ayin hara*, we can understand why it is especially "prevalent" when a count is taken. In reference to the *machatzith hashekel*, the Torah states, "This amount they shall give, each one who passes among the numbered" (Shemoth 30:13). Rashi explains that "the method of counting is to pass those being counted *one after another*" (com., ibid.). In a census, the individual is singled out; he is no longer part of the amorphous mass of the *kelal* (community).[1] Once the individual is no longer subsumed within the *kelal*, he must be treated *as an individual*. He can no longer be "ignored," nor can he benefit from any special mercy meted out to the community on account of collective merit. At the census, he stands exposed with only his own individual merits, without the concealment afforded by communal anonymity. Thus, by being counted, the individual stands in the focus of divine scrutiny — just as he does in the wake of the *ayin hara*.

It is noteworthy that, in the laws concerning the census, the Torah continually employs the root "פקד" (~ make accounting)

— rather than the usual "ספר" (~ count) — implying "settling accounts" with the counted and actualizing the results of these "accounts" for better or for worse. Thus, we find the root "פקד" in the context of the fulfillment of G-d's promise to Avraham: "And G-d *took account* (פקד) of Sarah as He had said" (BeReshith 21:1). Similarly, the Torah warns that G-d "*keeps account* (פקד) of the iniquity of fathers [bringing punishment] upon children" (Shemoth 34:7). Likewise, regarding Amalek, G-d states, "I *have taken account* (פקדתי) of what Amalek did to Yisra'el" (Shemu'el I 15:2). As we have noted, such "פקידה" ("accounting") marks the outer limit of *middath harachamim* — which is "slow to anger, abounding in kindness and faithfulness" (Shemoth 34:6) — beyond which, "on the day of *My accounting* (פקדי), *I shall bring them to account* (ופקדתי) for their sins" (Shemoth 32:34).

This interpretation of *machatzith hashekel* is explicit in the Torah commentary of R. Bachyai regarding the census:

> Scripture has revealed to us that the nation is reduced to its individual components during the count, each of whom is considered by divine providence, with all his actions scrutinized individually — at which point the plague occurs. This is not the case before [the census], when [the individual] was part of the many, but once everyone and his deeds are individualized, punishment is unavoidable. Thus, the Shunammith woman replied to Elisha, "*I dwell among my people*" (Melachim II 4:13). In other words, do not plead in my name before the king or the military commander; I prefer that my needs be included as part of the whole, lest I be singled out for punishment.
>
> (com. on Shemoth 30:12)

To spare us from these dangers of individualism, the Torah offered an antidote to the potential harm of the census and a way to restore the individual to the group. The *machatzith hashekel* was a uniform offering that negated individual identity: "The rich shall not add nor the poor detract" (Shemoth 30:15). No individual traits came to the fore in this commandment. In addition, the offering was specifically *half* of a *shekel*, not a whole one. This symbolized the desire of each person to be a part of something larger and more complete than himself.[2]

Finally, the sums collected were destined for public projects. From the coins given in the first census, the *adanim* (the bases of the beams of the sanctuary) were made. Furthermore, the *adanim* were produced by melting down the silver *shekalim*, "one hundred *adanim* from the one hundred talents" (Shemoth 38:27), each talent containing three thousand *shekalim*. The *separate* coins were collected and *fused* into bases, an expression of cleavage to the *kelal* at the expense of individual form and identity. Moreover, each base was but *half* of a pair on which each of the beams of the sanctuary stood. Similarly, the second census, taken in the second year on Rosh Chodesh Iyyar with the erection of the sanctuary (BeMidbar 1), served to fund the public sacrifices.[3] And during the time of the Beith HaMikdash, the annual *machatzith hashekel* levy supported the "donation for the treasury," used for the purchase of public offerings. All this emphasized the individual's desire to be subsumed within the *kelal* by sharing in the *community's* needs and participating in its *collective* atonement by means of the sacrifices.

The very wording of the Torah in *parashath Ki Thissa* suggests that the *machatzith hashekel* effects this transformation of the individual into part of the *kelal*. The Torah initially speaks of the numbered singly: "*Each one* [singular] shall pay an atonement offering for *himself* [singular]" (Shemoth 30:12). Ultimately, however, after the collection, it relates to them as part of a plural group: "It shall serve for *benei Yisra'el* [plural] as a remembrance before G-d to atone for *yourselves* [plural]" (ibid. 30:16).

3. THE INDIVIDUAL VERSUS THE COMMUNITY

Nevertheless, it appears that our conclusions regarding the *machatzith hashekel* are insufficient. One wonders why — if it is indeed so important for the individual to be subsumed within the *kelal* — a census with its inherent dangers of individualism is ordered altogether, only to have its possibly negative consequences neutralized retroactively. Obviously, G-d is not in need of a census to assess the size of Yisra'el.

In addition, when we compare the *mitzvah* of *machatzith hashekel* with the gifts solicited for the sanctuary in *parashath Terumah*, we find a very different emphasis: "They shall take Me an offering from *every person whose heart moves him to donate*" (Shemoth 25:2). The offerings expressed the individuality of the donor in both quantity (as much as his "heart moves him to donate") and type (whichever of the thirteen materials — "gold, silver, copper, sky-blue [wool], red [wool], crimson [wool]," etc. (ibid. 25:3-7) — contributed). The purpose of the gifts likewise depended on individual preference (for the holy vessels, the priestly vestments, or parts of the sanctuary). If the concealment of individualism is so important, why did the Torah not demand uniform offerings for the sanctuary as it did in the case of the *machatzith hashekel*?

It seems that implied here is a fundamental principle regarding the dual nature of proper service of G-d: Both aspects — the individual *and* the communal — have essential roles. Clearly, each and every one of us must dedicate himself on his earthly mission in accordance with his unique abilities and talents. One must sense the greatness of one's *personal* responsibility as an individual standing alone before G-d. The individual dare not excuse himself from his obligation to make the offering that is appropriate specifically *for him* by comparing himself to his fellow: "*If I am not for myself, who will be for me?*" (*Avoth* 1:14). At the same time, however, when we envision how G-d relates to *us*, we must labor to erase any trace of our individuality and to make ourselves part of the community as a whole; the individual dare not pride himself on his individuality to the point where he isolates himself from the *kelal*: "*When I am only for myself, what am I?*" (*Avoth* ibid.).

Both contributions — the offering to the sanctuary and the *machatzith hashekel* — highlight complementary aspects of this dual theme. Individualized donations to the sanctuary were intended to enhance in the donor the feeling that G-d dwelt in his midst. Thus, G-d emphasizes, "I shall dwell *in their midst*" (Shemoth 25:8): in the heart and soul of each and every one in Yisra'el.[4] Conversely, the levy of the *machatzith hashekel* served to make all the nation of Yisra'el into a single entity before G-d: "It shall serve for *benei Yisra'el* [collectively] as a remembrance *before G-d*" (ibid. 30:16).[5] Notwithstanding the importance of individual donations, they lack the communal dimension and thus the inherent grace (*middath harachamim*) that goes along with it. The Torah employs the term "an offering to G-d" three times in this *parashah*, alluding to the individual offerings to the sanctuary and the two *machatzith hashekel* contributions for the *adanim* and the public sacrifices. The expression "to atone for yourselves," however, appears only twice: for the two uniform *machatzith hashekel* contributions, but not for the individualized gifts brought to the sanctuary (Rashi on Shemoth 30:15).

In order to sense G-d in our midst, the personal offering is imperative. To this end, even the unspoken individual intentions of the donor are crucial: The contribution must be brought " 'for Me' (Shemoth 25:2) — [meaning,] in My name" (Rashi, ibid.). Those who lack this personal dimension in their offering will not succeed in attaining the goal of perceiving G-d "in their midst." Conversely, as we stand before G-d, we must realize that individual distinctions have no *true* significance. Therefore, the public sacrifices — which are intended to be acceptable on behalf of all Yisra'el "before G-d" — are purchased specifically through the *machatzith hashekel* contribution. Even before the personal contributions for the erection of the sanctuary were brought, the *shekalim* were solicited, emphasizing that the individual dimension in the sanctuary literally *rests* on the communal effort, symbolized by the *adanim* that were forged from the uniform *machatzith hashekel* contribution and served as the physical base of the entire sanctuary.

It is noteworthy that, with regard to the individual gifts to the sanctuary, we consistently find the root "לקח" (~ take) employed, as in, "They shall *take* (ויקחו) Me an offering; from every person whose heart moves him to donate, *take* (תקחו) My offering" (Shemoth 25:2). Regarding the donation of the shekalim, however, the Torah uses the root "נתן" (~ give), as in, "This amount they shall *give* (יתנו)" (Shemoth 30:13). The emphasis in "taking" is that there is a "Taker" (G-d). It is the donor's relationship with this "Taker" that both determines the size and type of gift and is affected by this act of giving. The goal, as discussed above, is that G-d should "dwell in their midst." Conversely, "giving" makes no reference to a receiver; the uniform gift of the *machatzith hashekel* is one-sided.[6]

We may conclude, then, that the individual must suppress his unique role and merge into the whole *only* in terms of how he wishes to be perceived by G-d, but *not* in expressing *his* relationship to G-d. On this latter level, he must continuously reaffirm the unique nature of his personal mission in life. Lest an individual adopt a posture of feigned humility to avoid such personal responsibility, the Torah commands him to be counted in the census — and thus stand before G-d — *as an individual*. One must sense how vital one's role is, as "one who passes among the numbered" (Shemoth 30:13). "Each and every one is *obligated* to say, '*For me the world was created*'" (*Mish. Sanhedrin* 4:5). At the same time, such an individual mission must not separate the person from the community. To the contrary, the uniqueness of the individual is the basis of *his role in the community*. Thus, the better the individual's performance, the stronger will be his bond to the community. Standing before G-d as an individual counted alone, he gives a *machatzith hashekel* as a tangible expression of his desire to be considered an integral part of *kelal Yisra'el*: as an individual component of the greater whole. With this understanding of the importance of collective unity, we can proceed to consider what really precipitated Haman's decree.

4. THE SIN OF THE JEWS IN THE TIME OF MORDECHAI AND ESTER

Haman described the Jews as being "scattered and divided among the nations" (Ester 3:8). According to R. Yeshayahu Horowitz ("*Derush for Parashath Zachor*"), this portrayal contained a legitimate indictment of the Jews, which was accepted in the divine court as tentative justification for their decreed destruction. Haman's assertion — "it is not worthwhile for *the king* to leave them alone" (ibid. 3:8) — should be read in light of the Midrash's conclusion that "wherever 'the king' is said in the *megillah* with no additional modifier, it refers to both the King — the Holy One Blessed be He — and the king — Achashverosh" (*Est.R.* 3:10). The Talmud, however, offers two other reasons why G-d sanctioned the decreed destruction of the Jews: either "because they partook of the banquet of the wicked [Achashverosh]" (*Megillah* 12a), or "because they bowed down to an idol [in the days of Nevuchadnetzar (Rashi)]" (ibid.). We can harmonize between R. Yeshayahu Horowitz's explanation and the Talmud's reasons by noting the Talmud's qualification that they did not actually serve idolatry, and "did so only for the sake of appearance," to be like their neighbors.[7] By trying to act like their diverse neighbors — there were one hundred twenty-seven different provinces within the Persian empire — the Jews lost their unique, unifying identity, making themselves perforce "scattered and divided among the nations."

Understanding this as the true, *underlying* sin of the Jews of that generation, the heavenly decree against them was indeed measure for measure. They did not preserve their national identity as Jews, so they were now to be treated as individuals. They could not rely on the *middath harachamim* — based on collective merit — that is reserved for the community as a whole.

In his plot, Haman "the Agagi" — descendant of Amalek — followed in the footsteps of his ancestors. Amalek knew well how to exploit divisiveness in the nation of Yisra'el in order to vanquish them as individuals. Thus the Torah describes the first encounter between Yisra'el and Amalek: "He cut off all the stragglers to your rear" (Devarim 25:18). Rashi explains "stragglers" as "those who were weak because they had sinned and were expelled by the cloud [of glory that surrounded the nation]" (com., ibid.); they had forfeited their connection with the *kelal*. The Midrash comments even more explicitly:

> "*He encountered you* (קרך)" (Devarim 25:18) — R. Nechemyah says: He literally called you ["קרך" is expounded as "קראך" ("he called you")]. What did Amalek do? ... He stood himself outside the cloud [of glory that surrounded the nation] and would call them, "Re'uven! Shimon! Levi! Come out for we are your brothers and we want to do business with you!" *When they would come out,* [Amalek] would kill them.

(Tan. Thetzei:9)

Perhaps the roots of this lack of unity are implied in the Torah itself, regarding the sin of *benei Yisra'el* in Refidim, which directly precipitated Amalek's attack.[8] The Torah relates, "The people thirsted there for water, and the people grumbled against Mosheh and said, 'Why did you bring *us* up from Mitzrayim to kill *me* and *my* children and *my* livestock with thirst?' " (Shemoth 17:3). At the beginning of the verse the people speak as one — "*us*" — but the end of the verse is expressed completely in the singular. Scripture implies that, in spite of the seemingly unified front presented in the demand for water, in reality everyone was concerned solely about himself and his possessions, oblivious to the needs of his fellows. Such an attitude destroys the communal whole and exposes Yisra'el to the assault — and indictment — of Amalek. Haman's campaign was essentially no different, and the repentance of Yisra'el was gauged by Yisra'el's ability to unite before G-d, a unity that is symbolized by the *machatzith hashekel*: the antidote for Haman's ten thousand silver talents.

5. THE ATONEMENT FOR THE SIN
— AND THE *MACHATZITH HASHEKEL*

To redress this sin and dispel the decree against the nation of Yisra'el, a united front before G-d was then necessary so that He would once again treat them communally. Appreciating this, Ester summoned the Jews to repentance by telling Mordechai, "Go and *gather all the Yehudim* in Shushan, and fast for me" (Ester 4:16). Likewise, in their letter effectively nullifying Haman's decree, Mordechai and Ester stress that the Jews must "*assemble together* to defend their lives" (ibid. 8:11). This they in fact did: "The Yehudim *assembled together* in their cities in all the provinces of the king Achashverosh" (ibid. 9:2). The threat of Haman precipitated their repentance, and — by gathering together — the decree of the divine court was revoked.[9]

This emphasis on unity appears manifest in the celebration of Purim as well. Perhaps the most vivid expression of the reunification of the Jewish nation was their celebration of the victory by "sending portions one to another and gifts to the poor" (ibid. 9:22). Such acts deepen the sense of relatedness and responsibility for others and increase the feeling of belonging to the *kelal*. The perpetuation of these acts as the *mitzvoth* of Purim stresses what was indeed the true miracle of Purim.[10] Perhaps the custom of masquerading on Purim expresses the same theme. As we saw in our interpretation of the *machatzith hashekel*, one may submerge oneself in the community by suppressing individual traits — even positive ones — that stress the distinctions between different people. While such conduct is not desirable on a regular basis, the Jews at the time of Purim were in need of radical measures to rectify their having been "scattered and divided." Similarly, a disguise hides the identity of the individual and renders him — at least externally — indistinguishable from his fellows.

On a more sublime level, *Zohar* notes a connection between Purim and Yom HaKippurim (which can be read as "יום הכפורים" ["a day that is *like* Purim"]),[11] even though these two days appear to have opposite characters and motifs. Perhaps this relationship can also be understood in terms of the theme of community that permeates both days. While Rosh HaShanah is a day of individual judgment for each and every person, when "all mankind pass before Him like *benei maron*"[12] (*Mish. Rosh HaShanah* 1:2), Yom Kippur is a day of atonement for the *kelal* as a national group, through which the nation of Yisra'el achieves collective atonement without a personal accounting for every individual. This may be at the root of the distinction that Ramban draws between Rosh HaShanah and Yom Kippur: "On Rosh HaShanah [G-d] is distinguished by *middath haddin* in guiding the world, and on Yom HaKippurim by *middath harachamim*" (com. on VaYikra 23:24, ד"ה זכרון תרועה). The mercy of Yom Kippur is expressed pre-eminently in the very fact that G-d relates to the nation as a *kelal* and not as individuals. Thus, the linkage between the ostensibly disparate days of Purim and Yom Kippur is that both stress the individual's attachment to *kelal Yisra'el*. Interestingly, we find a similar connection between Yom Kippur and the *machatzith hashekel*, which is also described in the Torah as "*kesef* hakippurim [money of *atonement*]" (Shemoth 30:16). Indeed, the first collection of *shekalim* to build the sanctuary was taken on the day after Yom Kippur.[13]

In this light, it is clear why the Talmud relates the events of Purim to the *mitzvah* to give *machatzith hashekel*, for these unifying *shekalim* were the proper counterbalance to the sum Haman was prepared to pay in order to bolster his indictment of the Jews as a people "scattered and divided among the nations" (Ester 3:8) and therefore lacking any sense of collective nationhood. In particular, the Tosafoth's explanation for the mathematical basis of Haman's offer of *ten thousand* talents to the king in exchange for permission to execute his plan amplifies this theme: "Ten thousand talents amount to fifty *shekalim*[14] for each of the six hundred thousand males who left Mitzrayim"[15] (com. on *Megillah* 16a, ד"ה ודחי עשרה אלפי ככרי כספא). These "fifty *shekalim*" are in accordance with the evaluation rate determined by the Torah: "The evaluation for a male from twenty to sixty years of age shall be fifty *shekalim* according to the sanctuary standard" (VaYikra 27:3). Haman thus related to each "scattered and divided" Jew as an individual, using the evaluation rates for each single person.[16] He therefore had to pay one hundred times as much as the Jews, who hastened to bring their unifying *machatzith hashekel* first as an antidote to his silver talents.

We may conclude that the connection between the themes of Purim and those of the *machatzith hashekel* is the basis of the current custom[17] to contribute money in remembrance of the *machatzith hashekel* prior to the reading of the *megillah*. Logically this remembrance should have been advanced to Rosh Chodesh Adar, when — in the time of the Beith HaMikdash — "they would proclaim [the imminent obligation to donate] the [*machatzith*] *hashekel*" (*Mish. Shekalim* 1:1), and indeed various commentators have struggled to elucidate the basis for the timing of our custom. Likewise, it is perhaps no coincidence that (in ordinary twelve-month years) the Torah reading of *parashath Ki Thissa* (which begins with the laws of the *machatzith hashekel*) invariably occurs on the Shabbath immediately following Purim or Shushan Purim. (In leap years, the same is true regarding Purim Katan.) Indeed, both Purim and the *mitzvah* of *machatzith hashekel* reiterate the same theme.

6. RECTIFYING THE SIN:
THE DUAL LEGACY OF BINYAMIN AND YEHUDAH

It remains for us to show why Mordechai and Ester were chosen to correct the flaw of "scattered and divided" by renewing the sense of nationhood that ultimately undermined Haman's decree. Ester sacrificed herself to a wicked, gentile king in deference to the wishes of her cousin Mordechai. She abnegated herself for the sake of the community, stressing her own passivity to the point that the Talmud concludes that "Ester was like natural ground" (*Sanhedrin* 74b). Even her name "Hadassah" (Ester 2:7) expressed her suppression of all her outstanding characteristics, "because she was ... intermediate like a *hadassah* (myrtle)" (*Megillah* 13a). Indeed, she is explicitly described as unassuming: "*Ester did not tell of her kindred or her people*" (Ester

2:20) — a description that Chazal regard as expressive of an inherent humility that may be traced back to her ancestors, Rachel and Sha'ul, both of whom concealed outstanding character traits or achievements that set them apart from their fellows.[18] Such suppression of *individual* characteristics certainly serves to enhance the communal dimension.

On a deeper level, both Mordechai and Ester, as descendants of the tribe of Binyamin (ibid. 2:5), were particularly fit for the role they were to play in the restoration of national unity among the Jews — a role played already by Binyamin himself. The Midrash links the sale of Yosef by his brothers with the events of Purim, regarding Haman's decree as the punishment for, or the natural outcome of, that sin:

> Said the Holy One Blessed be He to the tribes, "You sold your brother in the midst of eating and drinking, as it is said, '*They sat down to eat bread*' (BeReshith 37:25). Thus, Haman will come and seize you in the midst of eating and drinking, as it is written, '*And the king and Haman sat down to drink, and the city of Shushan was confounded*' (Ester 3:15)."
>
> (*Yal.Sh.* Ester:1056)

The seeds of divisiveness that precipitated Haman's decree against Yisra'el were sown by their ancestors, the sons of Ya'akov, progenitors of the tribes of Yisra'el.[19] From among the sons of Ya'akov, only Binyamin took no part in the sale of Yosef. Indeed, it was in Binyamin's presence (and indirectly *because* of his presence) that Yosef forgave his brothers and restored peace and unity among them, after witnessing the extent of his brothers' fraternal dedication to Binyamin.[20]

Binyamin and his descendants appear to have a unique propensity for harmonizing among the different components of the nation of Yisra'el. According to the Midrash, the color of Binyamin's stone in the breastplate of the *kohen gadol* (high priest), and similarly the color of his banner, "resembled all the twelve colors [of the other tribes]" (*BeM.R.* 2:7). Binyamin was able to live in peace with the individual character traits that each other tribe embodied; his color "resembled" each and every other color. This extraordinary capacity resulted from his readiness to tolerate in silence even personal suffering and pain, just for the sake of avoiding strife. Thus, the Midrash comments:

"He has no slander on his tongue" (Tehillim 15:3) — This is Binyamin son of Ya'akov, who knew of the sale of Yosef and did not reveal [it] to his father.

(*Yal. HaMachiri* on Tehillim 15:8)

He maintained this silence, in spite of the personal suffering that this caused him (as expressed in the names of his ten sons, "all of whom were called in Yosef's name" [*Sotah* 36b]). He realized that anyone with "slander on his tongue" — however justified — may precipitate hatred and divisiveness, just as his brothers' hatred of Yosef was rooted in slander (BeReshith 37:2). Binyamin, wary of repeating the same mistake, refrained from even the justified slander of reporting that his brothers had sold Yosef.[21]

Nevertheless, even silence, however virtuous, becomes vice when carried to an extreme. There are situations in which excessive silence and complacency are as dangerous as excessive speech. As we have seen (above), in discerning one's personal mission in serving G-d in the world, it is forbidden to hide behind collective anonymity and thus to avoid individual responsibility. Such appears to be implied in the Midrash's indictment of Binyamin himself:

Binyamin caused the tribes to tear their clothing [when Yosef's goblet was found in his sack]. And he was repaid in Shushan: "Mordechai tore his clothing [upon hearing of Haman's decree]" (Ester 4:1).

(*BeR.R.* 84:19)

The contention of the Midrash seems astounding: Binyamin was not the *cause*, but the involuntary *victim* of Yosef's plot! Apparently, Chazal are suggesting that Binyamin could have utilized his neutral position to reproach his brothers for the sale of Yosef and thus heal the festering wound of their enmity. By opting to remain silent and not to involve himself in the dispute, he is considered by Chazal to have shirked his *personal* responsibility, and thus indirectly caused the far more severe measures that Yosef had to employ later in order to rectify the wrong that had been perpetrated. Therefore, it is as if he caused these measures himself, resulting later in the tribes tearing their clothing on his account.

The duty to remain silent and the obligation to speak out and reproach actually both stem from a common source, for both are intended to prevent divisiveness and enhance unity among Jews. Silence should be motivated by a concern to avoid evil, just as reproach expresses a commitment to do good. Indeed, the obligation to reprimand is rooted in the principle that "all Yisra'el are responsible for one another" (*Shevu'oth* 39a). In this sense, that both reproacher and reproached are parts of an organic whole, the Midrash concludes, "Any love without chastisement is not [true] love.... Any peace without chastisement is not [true] peace" (*BeR.R.* 54:3).

We find a similar dichotomy, between the constructive and destructive aspects of silence, in King Sha'ul, who hailed from Binyamin as well. He too exercised modesty and reserve, de-emphasizing his own exceptional character traits. Scripture testifies that "Sha'ul was a choice young man and good, and there was no man in the nation of Yisra'el better than he; from his shoulders and upward, he was taller than all the people" (Shemu'el I 9:2). Nevertheless, when Shemu'el came to anoint him king, he protested, "Am I not a Binyamini, from the smallest of the tribes of Yisra'el, and [is] my family [not] the youngest of the families of the tribe of Binyamin?" (ibid. 9:21). Even at his coronation, he concealed his outstanding features, by "hiding among the vessels" (ibid. 10:22). This humility indeed furthered the unification of Yisra'el around its single leader. But exaggerated reserve was also King Sha'ul's downfall. There are situations which demand vociferous response, particularly from the leader. Thus, the Talmud explains:

> Why was Sha'ul punished [by being placed in a situation in which he would lose his monarchy (Rashi)]? [This was] because he waived his honor, as it is said, "And some base fellows said, 'How will this one save us?' ... but *he held his peace*" (Shemu'el I 10:27).
>
> (*Yoma* 22b)

Because King Sha'ul was silent when he should have spoken out, he eventually was "placed in a situation in which he would lose his monarchy."

We know to which "situation" Rashi is alluding. Sha'ul lost his monarchy by acquiescing in the people's desire not to annihilate Amalek as G-d commanded. He confessed to Shemu'el, "I transgressed G-d's will and your words, because *I feared the people and heeded their voice"* (Shemu'el I 15:24). But this was neither the time nor the place for humility and self-abnegation. Shemu'el reproached Sha'ul, "Even if you are small in your own eyes, you are the head of the tribes of Yisra'el; G-d has anointed you as king over Yisra'el" (ibid. 15:17). When the people sin, the king dares not remain silent; it is his responsibility to rebuke them and redress their sin. Because Sha'ul "held his peace," not only was he punished personally with the loss of his monarchy, but the nation of Yisra'el suffered collective punishment that Sha'ul could have prevented: "See what the Yemini [Sha'ul] paid me, by Sha'ul not killing Agag, who begat Haman, who persecuted Yisra'el" (*Megillah* 13a). Excessive silence — like unnecessary speech — can have disastrous repercussions.

Under analogous circumstances, we find very different conduct by Yehudah, who was characterized by his father as "the cub of a lion" (BeReshith 49:9) — meaning "that he was given the might of a lion and the brazenness of its cubs" (*BeR.R.* 98:12). He did not hesitate to speak, even when his harsh words were less than pleasing to his audience. He did so particularly where the collective needs of the *kelal* mandated such active involvement. Thus, he addressed himself to Yosef on behalf of his brothers: "Yehudah approached him and said, 'Please, my lord, let your servant speak before my lord, and do not be angered with your servant' " (BeReshith 44:18). Comments Rashi, "From here you learn that [Yehudah] spoke with [Yosef] harshly" (com., ibid.).[22]

Throughout Yehudah's descendants — in particular the lineage leading to David — we consistently find forceful characters who acted with initiative, even at personal risk, on behalf of the *kelal*. Thus, Kalev — great-grandson of Yehudah[23] and ancestor of David[24] — when confronting the slanderous report of the spies, "hushed the people for Mosheh and said, 'We shall by all means ascend and inherit the Land!' " (BeMidbar 13:30). Against the verbal calumnies of the spies, silence was of no avail, and Kalev was prepared to shout out.[25] Likewise, Chur — Kalev's son[26] — selflessly endeavored to prevent the sin of the golden calf (and according to Chazal he was actually killed in this attempt).[27] Similarly, Nachshon son of Aminadav — another direct ancestor of David[28] — jumped into the Red Sea before it split, as the nation of Yisra'el stood desperate on its bank.[29] Finally, King David himself, when only a young shepherd, confronted the giant Golyath, even though all the warriors of Yisra'el fled from him, in order to "remove shame from Yisra'el" (Shemu'el I 17:26), and so that "all the world may know that there is a G-d in Yisra'el" (ibid. 17:46).

Recognizing the challenge to Jewish leadership posed by Haman's decree, it is clear that the unassuming silence of Binyamin is — while indispensable to restore unity — insufficient. For a leader to succeed in correcting the flaw of "scattered and divided," he must also possess the brazenness of Yehudah in order to rouse the nation to repentance. Thus, the leadership of Mordechai, whose "father hailed from Binyamin and [whose] mother hailed from Yehudah" (Megillah 12b), was ideal given the circumstances: a Binyamini on the one hand and a Yehudi on the other, where both affiliations merge in reinforced dedication to unify the nation. Thus, he warns Ester, "If you *remain silent at this time*, relief and salvation will arise for the Yehudim from elsewhere, but you and your father's house will perish" (ibid. 4:14). "*At this time*" — as opposed to previously, when "Ester did not tell of her kindred or her people, *as Mordechai commanded her*" (ibid. 2:20) — the self-effacing silence of "your father's house," Binyamin, is inappropriate; if you "remain silent" now, "you and your father's house will perish," as befell your father's house previously because of the acquiescent silence of Sha'ul. By not being silent, but crying out "greatly and bitterly" (Ester 4:1) and selflessly struggling to "gather all the Yehudim in Shushan" (Ester 4:16), Mordechai and Ester succeeded in revoking the decree of Haman, by rectifying the ancestral sins of the tribes' divisiveness and Binyamin's silence, which were its ultimate cause.

7. CONCLUSION

In light of the above, we can also understand the following explanation of the *mitzvah* of *machatzith hashekel*, offered by Chazal:

> Said the Holy One Blessed be He to the tribes: You sold [Yosef] the son of Rachel "for twenty silver pieces" (BeReshith 37:28). Thus, the relative share for each of you is half [a *shekel*] per head, as it is written, "half [a *shekel*] per head, a *machatzith hashekel*" (Shemoth 38:26).
>
> (BeR.R. 84:18, Yer. Shekalim 2:3 [8b])

The *machatzith hashekel* donation — equivalent to two silver pieces — is intended to atone symbolically for the two silver pieces that each of the ten brothers received in exchange for the sale of Yosef. Indeed, as we have seen, the most effective means to combat the symptoms of divisiveness that originated in the sale of Yosef — and to reunify the nation of Yisra'el — is the *mitzvah* of *machatzith hashekel* and what it represents. This is the principal message of the miracle of Purim, which was above all the miracle of reunification of the nation of Yisra'el. Thus, observes the Midrash, " 'A people newly created' (Tehillim 102:19) — ... This is the generation of Mordechai, for they were created as a new creature" (*Mid. Tehillim* 102:3). Indeed, through their renewed unity, the Jewish *individuals* in the generation of Mordechai essentially re-created *kelal Yisra'el*: "a people newly created [that] shall praise G-d" (Tehillim ibid.).

NOTES

1. Compare the *halachah* that even where a forbidden food is diluted in sixty times its quantity, if it is "something countable" it is never considered negligible. Likewise, a forbidden food that is an "organic whole" is never considered negligible, since it signifies an autonomous unit. (See *Chullin* 100a.) According to the Talmud Yerushalmi, this latter rule — considering an "organic whole" as an autonomous unit — applies to the laws of final blessings on foods as well. (See *Yer. Berachoth* 6:1 [37b] and the Tosafoth on *Berachoth* 39a, ד"ה בצר ליה שיעורא.)

2. See also *HaTorah VeHaMitzvah* (Malbim) on Shemoth 30:12, where among the three explanations that Malbim provides for the linkage between the census and the plague, he submits: "As long as the people are united as one man, collective merit is very great. But when they are counted, whereupon each one is singled out and his deeds scrutinized, the plague may strike. To remedy this, [G-d] commanded that each person give a *machatzith hashekel*, which indicates the collective whole, for every individual is only a 'half' and not a complete unit, and he must be joined by another in order to become a complete unit."

3. See Rashi on Shemoth 30:15.

4. The Torah (ibid.) states, "They shall build Me a sanctuary, and I shall dwell *in their midst*" (referring to Yisra'el), not "in its midst" (as a reference to the sanctuary). See also *Or HaChayyim*, ibid., and Gra on Shir HaShirim 1:17.

5. The Talmud attributes to G-d a similar characterization of the nation of Yisra'el's reciprocal relationship with Him:

   You made Me [recognized as] a *single*, unique entity in this world, as it is said, "Hear, Yisra'el, G-d is our L-rd, G-d is *One*" (Devarim 6:4). And I shall make you a *single*, unique entity in the world, as it is said, "And who is like Your people, Yisra'el: a *single* nation in the world?" (Divrei HaYamim I 17:21).

(*Berachoth* 6a)

Note that while every member of Yisra'el is obligated individually to affirm the oneness of G-d, G-d's relationship, as it were, to Yisra'el is specifically collective (as a "single, unique entity").

6. It should be noted that the *machatzith hashekel* is also described repeatedly as "an offering *to G-d*" (Shemoth 30:13-15), thus specifying the "Taker." Nevertheless, the *personal* connection conveyed in the donations for the sanctuary, when G-d says *in first person*, "They shall take *Me* an offering; from every person whose heart moves him to donate, take *My* offering" (Shemoth 25:2), is absent.

7. See also the view advanced by R. Tam, "that the image of Nevuchadnetzar was not idolatrous but rather a monument erected in honor of the king" (Tosafoth on *Avodah Zarah* 3a, ד"ה שלא השתחוו לצלם).

8. See Shemoth 17:8 and Rashi, ibid.

9. It is indeed this unifying quality of their repentance that we celebrate on Purim in the liturgical hymn "*Shoshanath Ya'akov*," recited after the reading of the *megillah*: "The blossom of Ya'akov exulted and rejoiced when they saw *together* the [royal] blue vestments of Mordechai."

10. Regarding our contention that this reunification was the essence of the Purim miracle, see also Rashi's explanation of the Talmud's assertion that "the thirteenth [of Adar] is a time of assembly for all" (*Megillah* 2a): "All *assembled* then to take revenge on their enemies.... Thus ... the essence of the miracle was on that [day]" (com., ibid.). In other words, "the essence of the miracle" was not the miraculous success of the military venture but the miraculous success of the attempt to unite all the Jews; hence "the thirteenth is a time of assembly for all." (Compare, however, alternate explanations of the Gemara offered by Rosh in the name of Ri and R. Tam; see *Piskei HaRosh* 1:1.) Perhaps this is the justification for the Talmudic principle allowing village-dwellers to advance their reading of the *megillah* to the nearest "day of gathering (יום הכניסה)" (*Mish. Megillah* 1:1), since such a day is expressive of the same motif of *gathering* that is manifest in the original Purim as well. Furthermore, given that a holiday is generally not perpetuated in remembrance of "hidden miracles" that occur within the framework of nature, it appears that the decision to establish Purim as a permanent holiday was intended as commemoration not of the military victory but of the penitential measures taken that reunited the nation — "the records of the fasts and their cries" (Ester 9:31) — through which the miraculous victory was merited. (Indeed, the date of Purim does not even coincide with that of the military victory, but instead with the following day, when the Jews rested from battle.)

11. See *Tikkunei Zohar* 86.

12. The language of the *mishnah* is obviously reminiscent of the Torah's reference (quoted above) to the *individuals* in the census: "each one who *passes* among the numbered" (Shemoth 30:13), in particular considering Rashi's explanation that "the method of counting is to *pass* those being counted *one after another*" (com., ibid.). Regarding the focus of Rosh HaShanah on the individual, see also R. Bachyai on Shemoth 30:12.

　　Ed. note: Regarding the meaning of *benei maron* and the nature of the judgment of man as an individual and as part of a community on Rosh HaShanah, see also R. Beryl Gershenfeld, "Judgment on Rosh HaShanah," *Jewish Thought*, 1, No. 1, 29-45.

13. See *BeM.R.* 1:10.

14. The Tosafoth as printed (ibid.) actually reads, "Ten thousand talents amount to a *half shekel* (חצי שקל)" etc., which does not accord at all with the arithmetic calculations (see n. 15, below). It may be surmised that the original manuscript versions referred to "fifty *shekalim* (חמשים שקלים)" by the initials "ח"ש," which were incorrectly expanded in subsequent transcription as "a half *shekel* (חצי שקל)." Support for this supposition may be found in *Est.R.* 7:19 (which cites the calculation, specifying "fifty *shekalim*"); *Tosefoth HaRosh*, ibid. (which contains the correct version); and R. Bachyai on Shemoth 38:25 and in *Kad HaKemach*, "Purim." Compare, however, HaChizkuni on Shemoth 30:14.

15. Fifty *shekalim* for each of six hundred thousand males amounts to thirty million *shekalim*. Since three thousand silver *shekalim* are equivalent to one silver talent (see Rashi on Shemoth 38:26), these thirty million *shekalim* are equivalent to ten thousand silver talents.

16. In this light, we can elucidate Rashi's cryptic commentary on the verse "Mordechai related to [Hathach] all that had happened to him and *the sum of money* (פרשת הכסף) that Haman had promised to pay the king's treasuries against the Yehudim, to destroy them" (Ester 4:7): " 'The *sum* of money (פרשת הכסף)' [means] the *meaning* of the money (פירוש הכסף)" (com., ibid.). To what "meaning" is Rashi referring? Considering the deeper meaning of the question Ester posed, which Mordechai was answering — namely, what is the underlying cause of the decreed punishment against the Jews in the heavenly court (see Ester 4:5 and *Est.R.* 8:4) — the comment is clear. Mordechai wanted to clarify to Ester what the *meaning* of "the sum of money that Haman had promised to pay" was: It was an attempt to negate the Jews' communal strength by relating to them as "scattered and divided" individuals. Therefore, after being alerted by Mordechai to the underlying challenge posed by Haman — "the meaning of the money" — Ester instructed Mordechai to commence corrective measures: "Go and *gather all the Yehudim* in Shushan" (Ester 4:16).

17. See Rema on *Orach Chayyim* 694:1.

18. See *Megillah* 13b.

19. Indeed, even Ya'akov himself is reproached for his sibling rivalry — however justified — with Esav:

Ya'akov caused Esav to cry out once [BeReshith 27:34], and he was repaid in Shushan, as it is said, "[Mordechai] cried out greatly and bitterly" (Ester 4:1). (*BeR.R.* 16:14)

Although Ya'akov's actions against Esav can be justified, Chazal still find in them some basis for the divisiveness that subsequently surfaced in his progeny.

20. Therefore, Yosef gave Binyamin "*five* changes of clothing" (BeReshith 45:22): "hinting to him that he was destined to have a descendant [Mordechai] who would go forth from before the king [Achashverosh] in *five* royal vestments" (*Megillah* 16b, referring to Ester 8:15). Yosef thereby stressed that the renewal of brotherly love that was caused (indirectly) by Binyamin and spared the tribes of Yisra'el from the apparent decrees of Yosef would also be necessary to protect Yisra'el from the actual decrees of Achashverosh and Haman. Just as the tribes eventually recognized that their troubles were in retribution for the sin of divisiveness and the sale of Yosef — which Binyamin symbolically redressed — (see BeReshith 42:21), so too the Jews in Shushan would have to seek the underlying root of the decree against them in the lack of unity among them, striving to rectify it through "Binyamini" reunification.

21. It should be noted that this trait of reserve in speech contrasts markedly with the character of Haman: "No one could slander like Haman" (*Megillah* 13b). Far from wary of inadvertently eliciting hatred through slander, he exploited slander deliberately to generate hatred. It is particularly appropriate that his slanderous plot was thwarted by Mordechai and Ester: descendants of Binyamin, who "has no slander on his tongue."

22. See also *BeR.R.* 84:16 regarding the "three places where Yehudah spoke before his brothers."

23. See Divrei HaYamim I 2:3-5, 9, 18. See also *Sotah* 11b and *Sanhedrin* 69b.

24. See *Sotah* 11b and *Sanhedrin* 69b.

25. Therefore, the Torah principally credits Kalev with the opposition to the spies' report: "My servant Kalev ... had a different spirit and followed Me wholeheartedly ... " (BeMidbar 14:24; see Rashi, ibid.). Although Yehoshua — descended from Rachel — strove to achieve the same goal as Kalev, he is not singled out, since only Kalev spoke out vociferously. (For ample justification of Yehoshua's silence, however, see *Shemirath HaLashon*, II, ch. 19, in notes.)

26. Chur's father was Kalev; his mother was Miryam (sister of Aharon and Mosheh). See *Sotah* 11b and *Sanhedrin* 69b.

27. See *Sanhedrin* 7a and *Sh.R.* 41:7. (Obviously, the fact that Kalev's own son had lost his life under such circumstances emphasizes Kalev's selfless dedication in confronting the mob in his opposition to the spies only thirteen months later.)

28. See Ruth 4:18-22 and Divrei HaYamim I 2:4-15, where the ancestry of David, and Nachshon's position therein, is explicitly detailed.

29. See *BeM.R.* 13:7.

THE ANOINTMENT OF KING DAVID:
"Ruddy with Beautiful Eyes"

Yehoshua Bachrach

The essay that follows is based upon the source provided below:

[Shemu'el] said	ויאמר
[to the elders of Beith Lechem], "Peace,	שלום,
I have come to sacrifice to G-d.	לזבח לה' באתי,
Prepare yourselves,	התקדשו,
and come with me to the sacrifice."	ובאתם אתי בזבח;
He prepared Yishai and his sons,	ויקדש את־ישי ואת־בניו,
and he called them to the sacrifice.	ויקרא להם לזבח:
It happened when they came,	ויהי בבואם,
that he saw Eli'av.	וירא את־אליאב;
He said,	ויאמר,
"Surely before G-d is His anointed."	אך נגד ה' משיחו:

RABBI BACHRACH, a prolific writer on Nach, has written several major books, including *Imah shel Malchuth*, which was published in translation as *Mother of Royalty* (Yerushalayim: Feldheim, 1973). Through his numerous published works, he has had profound impact on the study of Nach in Israel. His essay *"Min HaRamathayim Tzofim"* appeared in the inaugural issue of *JT*.

"The Anointment of King David" was adapted (by Ch.Sh.E.) from *Yofyth Malchuth UZmiroth* (Jerusalem: Ariel, 1980), pp.20-32.

G-d said to Shemu'el,
  "Do not look at his appearance
  and at the height of his stature,
  for I have rejected him.
  For it is not as man sees:
  For man sees the external appearance,
  but G-d sees the heart."

ויאמר ה' אל־שמואל,
אל־תבט אל־מראהו
ואל־גבה קומתו,
כי מאסתיהו.
כי לא, אשר יראה האדם;
כי האדם יראה לעינים,
וה' יראה ללבב:

Yishai called Avinadav,
  and he had him pass before Shemu'el.
  He said,
  "Also this was not chosen by G-d."

ויקרא ישי אל־אבינדב,
ויעברהו לפני שמואל;
ויאמר,
גם־בזה לא־בחר ה':

Yishai had Shammah pass.
  He said,
  "Also this was not chosen by G-d."

ויעבר ישי שמה;
ויאמר,
גם־בזה לא־בחר ה':

Yishai had his seven sons pass
  before Shemu'el.
  Shemu'el said to Yishai,
  "G-d has not chosen these."

ויעבר ישי שבעת בניו,
לפני שמואל;
ויאמר שמואל אל־ישי,
לא־בחר ה' באלה:

Shemu'el said to Yishai,
  "Does this complete all your children?"
  He said, "The smallest still remains,
  and he is tending the sheep."
  Shemu'el said to Yishai,
  "Send and fetch him,
  for we shall not sit down to eat
  until he comes here!"

ויאמר שמואל אל־ישי,
התמו הנערים?
ויאמר, עוד שאר הקטן,
והנה רעה בצאן.
ויאמר שמואל אל־ישי
שלחה וקחנו,
כי לא־נסב
עד־באו פה:

He sent and brought him,
  and he was ruddy, with beautiful eyes,
  and good-looking.
  — G-d said,
  "Arise, anoint him, for this is he!"

וישלח ויביאהו
והוא אדמוני, עם־יפה עינים,
וטוב ראי.
— ויאמר ה'
קום משחהו, כי־זה הוא:

Shemu'el took the horn of oil,
  and he anointed him
  in the midst of his brothers.
  The spirit of G-d came upon David,
  from that day onward.
  Shemu'el arose, and he went to Ramah.

ויקח שמואל את־קרן השמן,
וימשח אתו
בקרב אחיו;
ותצלח רוח־ה' אל־דוד,
מהיום ההוא ומעלה.
ויקם שמואל, וילך הרמתה:

(Shemu'el I 16:5-13)

1. INTRODUCTION: THE SEER DOES NOT SEE

The anointment of King David stands out as an event fraught with tension and charged with emotion, as Shemu'el sets out humbly to fulfill G-d's command and anoint the replacement for his beloved King Sha'ul. Particularly striking is the singular ignorance that all of the principal characters display regarding the final outcome. Neither Shemu'el the prophet nor Yishai the father recognize G-d's anointed before G-d urges Shemu'el, practically in rebuke, "Arise, anoint him, *for this is he!*" (Shemu'el I 16:12). David emerges as a forsaken shepherd to become king: "The stone disdained by the builders has become the head cornerstone" (Tehillim 118:22). Indeed, in every sense, "This is G-d's doing; it is wondrous in our eyes" (ibid. 118:23).

Difficulties in the text abound. But what is perhaps most bothersome is the very unexpected quality of all that happens here. Scripture emphatically indicates to what extent no one, and especially not Shemu'el the seer, can truly see. Elsewhere, in the case of the prophecy of Mosheh, we have encountered similar limitations on a prophet's ability to know:

> "*Mosheh brought their case before G-d*" (BeMidbar 27:5) — There are those who say that [G-d] concealed [this law] from Mosheh, for there are *tzaddikim* who prided themselves on the performance of a *mitzvah*, and the Holy One Blessed be He weakened their power.
>
> (*BeM.R.* 21:22)

Similarly here, Shemu'el's concern and sorrow for Sha'ul[1] — because of the prophet's deep love for him — had weakened his power and reduced his prophetic capacity.[2] It is this concern that robbed him of happiness in the performance of the *mitzvah* that G-d had entrusted to him this day. Therefore, the seer did not see.[3]

Even on this day, while in Beith Lechem together with Yishai and his sons, Shemu'el did not cease to pray in his heart for Sha'ul:

> "*It happened when they came, that he saw Eli'av. He said, 'Surely before G-d is His anointed.'*" (Shemu'el I 16:6) — This means that [Shemu'el] said, either in his heart or in his mouth, that he thought that this one was the king that the L-rd had commanded him to anoint, since

he was the first-born of Yishai's sons. *In addition, [Shemu'el] saw in him the beautiful form and stature of Sha'ul.*

And others explain that when [Shemu'el] said, "Surely before G-d is His anointed," *he was still pleading for Sha'ul* [currently, still "His anointed"] — that sovereignty should not depart from him — when he saw that Eli'av was not as handsome as [Sha'ul]. And he entreated G-d not to replace Sha'ul with anyone else [i.e., to maintain him "before G-d"].

Therefore, the L-rd answered him, "Do not look at his appearance ... for I have rejected him" (ibid. 16:7). It was Sha'ul who was handsome in appearance and tall of stature.

(Radak, ibid.)

In any case, in his quest for G-d's anointed, Shemu'el — unlike G-d — did not see "the heart."

Typically, in the entire narrative, Scripture abbreviates. It does not describe how the father must have rejoiced in his offspring when the prophet disclosed his secret: that G-d had chosen one of Yishai's sons to be king. It also withholds from us any portrayal of whether Yishai noticed the seer's change of face when G-d rejected Eli'av and rebuked Shemu'el. With characteristic brevity, it tersely conveys the unfolding drama as Yishai's sons pass before the prophet:

Yishai called Avinadav, and he had him pass before Shemu'el.
He said, "Also this was not chosen by G-d."
Yishai had Shammah pass.
He said, "Also this was not chosen by G-d."

(Shemu'el I 16:8-9)

One by one, Yishai passed his sons before the prophet. Over each one of them he pondered, considered, and prayed, as they came and as they went. This procedure undoubtably lasted long and was fraught with tension.

During this time, did Yishai not think also of his young son, the one he had left behind tending the sheep?

Yishai had his seven sons pass before Shemu'el.
Shemu'el said to Yishai, "G-d has not chosen these."

(Shemu'el I 16:10)

Yishai hears Shemu'el's statement and his trembling and faltering voice. For now the prophet stood amazed and afraid: G-d had sent him to see,[4] and he sees not. Yishai sees all this, and yet Yishai is silent.

Finally, perhaps in desperation, Shemu'el turns to Yishai: *"Does this complete all your children?"* (Shemu'el I 16:11). One wonders how Shemu'el could still continue to ask Yishai. Did he believe in his question, that Yishai in fact had another son whom he was concealing? Perhaps in despair he poses this final question. And Yishai responds:

> He said, "The smallest still remains, and he is tending the sheep."
> (ibid.)

Weakly, Yishai replied, as if excusing himself. We note that Yishai is not mentioned here by name, even though properly his name should have been written. (Indeed, the clause "Shemu'el said to Yishai" is written three times in these two verses, but never once is it written, "Yishai said.") Also anomalously, both the question and the answer are presented in a single verse. With these words, Scripture introduces us to King David.

2. "THE SMALLEST STILL REMAINS"

"The Smallest"

Is it because David was small that his father had left him behind and deemed it unnecessary to bring him along to the prophet? Why then did Yishai bring along David's *younger* brother, Elihu, the *eighth* of his sons?[5] And if David were indeed small, why did his father appoint him to tend the sheep, as a shepherd in the wilderness — a place of danger, where the lion and the bear[6] lie in wait?

For this was the task for which Yishai had designated him from among all his father's family. He was the guarantor of the sheep, and he would be required throughout to care for them. Even while serving as Sha'ul's minstrel, "he would go to and fro ... to tend his father's sheep in Beith-Lechem" (Shemu'el I 17:15).

Indeed, thus did David's elder brother scold him when he saw him lingering on the battlefield:

Eli'av's anger burned against David,
and he said, "Why did you come down here?
And with whom did you abandon those few sheep in the wilderness?
I know your malicious intent and your evil desire...."

(ibid. 17:28)

"And with whom did you abandon those few sheep"? Were there not another four brothers who remained at home? But shepherding was not their responsibility. Therefore, it is written, "David rose early in the morning, and he left the sheep with a keeper" (ibid. 17:20).

According to *Seder Olam*, David was twenty-eight years old at this time. We are obliged then to understand why Yishai called him "the *smallest*," implying that he was the least worthy to be brought before the prophet.

"And He is Tending the Sheep"

The original Hebrew text inserts "וְהִנֵּה רֹעֶה בַּצֹּאן" (lit. "*and behold he is tending the sheep*"). I do not know how we are to read this "וְהִנֵּה" ("and behold"): whether as support for an excuse — as in "*And behold* (וְהִנֵּה) the smallest is with our father this day" (BeReshith 42:13) — or as a complaint against the subject — as in "*And behold* (וְהִנֵּה) a member of my household is my heir" (ibid. 15:3).

Shepherding had been favorably regarded in the days of the patriarchs. But now that the land had been settled, it was considered a despicable occupation, because of the ten conditions imposed by Yehoshua and his court when he apportioned the land among the tribes:

> One may not raise goats and sheep in Eretz Yisra'el, but one may raise [them] in Syria and in the wildernesses of Eretz Yisra'el.
>
> (*Babba Kamma* 79b, *Yad Hil. Nizkei Mamon* 5:2)

> Shepherds of goats and sheep in Eretz Yisra'el are disqualified as witnesses.
>
> (*Sanhedrin* 25b)

Apparently there was some reason in Yishai's household for which they subordinated David and sent him away to be a shepherd in the distant wilderness, estranged and separated from his brothers:

I am estranged to my brothers, and an alien to my mother's children.

(Tehillim 69:9)

He was despised by his father because as a child he would predict: "I am destined to destroy the Pelishti localities and to kill a great man from among them named Golyath. And I am destined to build the Beith HaMikdash." What did his father do? He left him to tend the sheep.

(Mid. HaGadol on Devarim 1:17)[7]

Thus, even when Shemu'el specifically "prepared Yishai and his sons, and he called them to the sacrifice" (Shemu'el I 16:5), David "the smallest" remained forsaken with the sheep.[8]

"Send and Fetch Him"

And even after the prophet's question, Yishai was still sitting and waiting. He did not rise up and say to the prophet, "By your leave, sir, I shall hurry and go, or send for him, and bring him." He remains silent, and it is Shemu'el who speaks:

Shemu'el said to Yishai, "Send and fetch him,
for we shall not sit down to eat until he comes here!"

(Shemu'el I 16:11)

Perhaps Shemu'el cast a glance at him, wondering why David had not been brought at the outset. Perhaps the exclamation burst forth from his lips: "Send and fetch him!" — a peremptory, urgent demand.

At that moment, Shemu'el recovered from his disappointment at being prevented from fulfilling his mission, to see what G-d had commanded him: "For I have seen among his sons a king for Me" (Shemu'el I 16:1). And here now he sits, waiting for this wondrous youth who had been concealed from him all that day.

We can only imagine the tension mounting in anticipation of David's arrival. In addition to the venerable prophet, the elders who had been invited to participate in the sacrificial feast remain waiting: They could not sit down to eat, since Shemu'el would not bless the sacrifice until David came. Yishai and his sons, too, sat and waited, revealing their astonishment to one another: The prophet had said regarding them all, "G-d has not chosen these." Would He then choose this one — David?

The Midrash comments on this wait for David:

> "*For we shall not sit down to eat until he comes here*" — Said R. Shemu'el
> b. Nachmani: Just as in this world, two great men — Shemu'el and
> Yishai — did not sit down to eat together until David sat in their
> midst, so in the hereafter there is not a single division of the just
> over which David does not preside.
>
> (*Mid. Shemu'el*, ibid.)

"He Sent and Brought Him"

Who sent? Who brought him? Did not Yishai, his father, send to bring him? Why then is his name not mentioned? Perhaps Scripture is alluding to the unmentioned One, Who has been manipulating all of the events that have led up to this moment. Yishai is the instrument, but not the One Who sent and brought David:

> "*And the chief butler did not remember Yosef; he forgot him*" (BeReshith
> 40:23) — Said the Holy One Blessed be He to Yosef, "The chief butler
> forgot you, but I shall not forget you."
>
> Who was waiting for Avraham and Sarah, who had grown old,
> that they bear a son?
>
> Who was waiting for Ya'akov, who crossed the Yarden with
> [only] his staff, that he prosper and become rich?
>
> Who was waiting for Yosef, who endured all these troubles, that
> he become king?
>
> Who was waiting for Mosheh, who had been cast into the Nile,
> that he become what he became?
>
> Who was waiting for Ruth, who was a proselyte, that she return
> to the royal house of Yisra'el?
>
> Who was waiting for David that he become king until the end
> of all generations?
>
> Who is waiting for the fallen tabernacle of David — that shall
> be raised by the Holy One Blessed be He, as it is said, "*On that day I
> shall raise the tabernacle of David that is fallen. I shall repair its breaches
> and raise its ruins. I shall rebuild it as in the days of old*" (Amos 9:11).
>
> (BeR.R. 88:7)

For my father and my mother have abandoned me,
and G-d will take me up.

(Tehillim 27:10)

Said R. Simon: Three "finds" were found by the Holy One Blessed be He:

Avraham — as it is written, "And You *found* his heart faithful before You" (Nechemyah 9:8);

David — as it is written, "I *found* David My servant; with My holy oil I anointed him" (Tehillim 89:21); [and]

Yisra'el — as it is written, "Like grapes in the wilderness, I *found* Yisra'el" (Hoshea 9:10).

(BeR.R. 29:3)

3. "HE WAS RUDDY, WITH BEAUTIFUL EYES, AND GOOD-LOOKING"

"Ruddy, with Beautiful Eyes"

In Sha'ul's outward appearance, only his stature was impressive: "from his shoulders and upward, he was taller than all the people" (Shemu'el I 9:2 and 10:23). And it is specifically in his height that Sha'ul is reckoned as "created as an abstract of the heavenly model" (*Sotah* 10a). In contrast, when David was brought from the sheep to Shemu'el, Scripture specifies a triad of characteristics, in his appearance and his eyes, that has no analogue in all the Bible. Each feature demands explanation, and the combination imposes an additional dimension.

We have encountered "אדמוני" ("ruddy") elsewhere in Scripture — in the Torah's description of Esav's birth:

> "*The first emerged* ruddy (אדמוני), *all of him like a hairy mantle. They called him Esav*." (BeReshith 25:25) — "*Ruddy*" occurs twice in the Massorah: here, and also, "He was *ruddy* (אדמוני), with beautiful eyes."
>
> (Ba'al HaTurim, ibid.)[9]

The Midrash, noting the marked contrast between the two individuals singularly identified in Scripture as ruddy, observes:

> "*Ruddy*" (ibid.) — Said R. Yehudah: If you see a person of ruddy complexion, [he is] either completely wicked like Esav, or completely righteous like David. Regarding Esav, it says, "The first emerged *ruddy* (אדמוני), *all of him like a hairy mantle*." Regarding David, it says, "[He was] *ruddy* (אדמוני), *with beautiful eyes*."
>
> (Mid. HaGadol, ibid.)

R. Yehudah deduced this from the continuation that is written regarding each of them.[10] We can similarly understand the following commentary in the Midrash:

> When Shemu'el saw that David was ruddy — as it is written, "He sent and brought him, and he was *ruddy*" (Shemu'el I 16:12) — he became fearful. He said, "This one too sheds blood like Esav?" Said the Holy One Blessed be He to him, "[He is] '*with beautiful eyes*' (ibid.)! Esav kills of his own volition, but this one kills only as authorized by the Sanhedrin."[11]
>
> (BeR.R. 63:8, Yal.Sh. Shemu'el:124)

Indeed, the Sanhedrin is called "*eyes*," as it is said, "If something is hidden from the *eyes* of the congregation ..." (VaYikra 4:13).[12]

Zohar perceives the eyes of David with comparable significance:

> David's eyes were composed of all manner of colors. There were no eyes in the world [as beautiful] to behold as were the eyes of David. All the colors of the world would sparkle in them. And all was suffused with love for those who fear sin, as it is said: "*Those who fear You will see me and be happy*" (Tehillim 119:74) — They are happy when they see me. And all the sinners [lit. guilty] would fear him.
>
> (Zohar, III, 206b)[13]

It seems to me that the source of this duality in Chazal's portrayal is implied in Ya'akov's dual blessing to Yehudah:
"*He washes his clothes in wine and his cloak in the blood of grapes*" (BeReshith 49:11) — This corresponds to "*ruddy.*"
"*His eyes are more sparkling than wine, and his teeth are whiter than milk*" (ibid. 49:12) — This corresponds to "*with beautiful eyes.*"

Indeed, thus these verses are expounded in *Targum Yonathan*:

> How beautiful is the King Mashiach who is destined to emerge from the house of Yehudah! He girds his sword and sets out to battle against his enemies. And kings are slain with their kingdoms, *reddening the rivers with the blood of the slain.*
> How beautiful are *the eyes of the King Mashiach, like pure wine....*
>
> (Tar. Yonathan, ibid. 49:11-12)

And thus summarizes *Sha'arei Orah*:

> It follows then that the wicked Esav was heir to the sword of bloodshed, while King David of blessed memory inherited the

kingdom to perform acts of loving-kindness and mercy and to kill only according to the law. Therefore, when David would don the attribute of "*ruddy*," he would fight the battles of G-d against the enemies of G-d, and he did not withdraw his sword unused. And when he would don [the attribute of] "*beautiful eyes*," he would provide for Yisra'el and generously mete out acts of loving-kindness to them. And when he would don [the attribute of] "*good-looking*," he would delve into the depths of the Halachah and the secrets of Torah.[14]

(loc. cit.)

The Vilna Ga'on, commenting on the verse "Educate the youth according to his way" (Mishlei 22:6), observes that this multiplicity of attributes in David derives from a supreme moral effort:

The matter here is that it is impossible for man to break "his way," in other words, the nature with which he was born. And if he was born with a bad nature, then regarding this he is given free choice; for he can utilize his nature for whatever he desires, to be either righteous or wicked or intermediate. Thus, it is written in tractate *Shabbath* [156a], "He who is [born] under Mars will be a shedder of blood. Said R. Ashi: [This means] either [a phlebotomist or] a robber or a butcher or a circumciser." This is the implication of the statement regarding David: "He was ruddy," [meaning that] he [was born] under Mars. Hence Shemu'el erred regarding him, when he saw David's countenance. But [David] controlled his attributes in everything.

(com. on Mishlei ibid.)

Indeed, in David's varied attributes, his description is reminiscent of the description of his Creator:[15] "My beloved is *pure* and *ruddy*" (Shir HaShirim 5:10):

"*Pure*" — [This means] that His actions are pure and pleasing to the pure.
"*And ruddy*" — [And they are ruddy] to those who provoke Him, as in, "Why is Your apparel *red*?" (Yeshayahu 63:2).

(R. Avraham b. Ezra, ibid.)[16]

"Adept at Playing [Music] ... and a Man of War"

By delineating these two profound character traits, Scripture reflected the soul of King David. Here we are accorded an insight into his whole life story, to apprehend his soul in all its many, many efforts and struggles.

We recall that David's soul was composed of two extreme, conflicting traits. This duality accompanied him throughout his stormy life. He struggled with himself and with many individuals who surrounded him, some in love and some in hatred.

In *love*, David attained the most treasured of loves, both with respect to his fellow man and with respect to his Creator. Consider the Bible's description of the aftermath of David's victory over Golyath, pervaded throughout by love of David: "Yehonathan *loved him* as his own soul" (Shemuel I 18:1). "And all Yisra'el and Yehudah *loved David*" (ibid. 18:15). "Sha'ul saw and he knew that G-d *was with David*, and Michal, Sha'ul's daughter, *loved him*" (ibid. 18:28). And in *hatred*, there was none like him who suffered from violent hatred and baseless persecution from the dawn of his life till his dying day.

To sustain both dimensions simultaneously, his soul had to be built with two such polarized forces: *"adept at playing [music] ... and a man of war"* (Shemu'el I 16:18). For the two were intertwined within him: the sword with the harp.

As for the *sword*, "his heart is as the heart of the lion,"[17] cruel and vindictive in his wars against the enemies of G-d and His people:

> I shall pursue my enemies and overtake them,
> and I shall not return until they are destroyed.
> I shall crush them so that they are unable to rise;
> they are fallen under my feet.
>
> (Tehillim 18:38-39)

And as for the *harp*, it is he who is the great supplicant, whose heart would melt within him like wax, while his soul, enrapt within him, yearned for its Creator in love:

> Surely I have steadied and quieted my soul
> like a weaned child upon his mother.
> Like a weaned child is my soul upon me.
>
> (ibid. 131:2)

These delicate and faithful chords of his heart have therefore become for all generations the possession of every soul who comes to seek the L-rd. This is the harp of David, "sweet singer of Yisra'el" (Shemu'el II 23:1).

This dichotomy is vividly depicted in the Talmud:

> *"This is Adino* (עדינו) *the Etzni* ([העצני [ק']*"* (Shemu'el II 23:8) — When David would sit and occupy himself in Torah study, he would make himself as pliant ["עדינו" is expounded as "מעדן" ("make pliant")] as a worm. And when he would sally forth to war, he would make himself as hard as a tree ["העצני" is expounded as "עץ" ("tree")].
>
> (*Mo'ed Katan* 16b)

In reality, both aspects are manifestations of David's true might:

> *"And these are the names of David's mighty men* (הגברים): *Yoshev BaSheveth* (ישב בשבת) *[the Tachkemoni* (תחכמני), *head of the captains* (ראש השלשי)*]"* (Shemu'el ibid.) — What does this say? Replied R. Abbahu: It says, "And these are the names of David's mighty *deeds* ['הגברים' is expounded as 'גבורות' ('mighty deeds')]:
>
> *"Yoshev BaSheveth* (ישב בשבת)*"* — When [David] would sit in the *yeshivah* ["ישב בשבת" is expounded as "יושב בישיבה" ("sit in the *yeshivah*")], he would sit not upon pillows and cushions but upon the ground. For as long as his teacher, Ira the Ya'iri, was alive, he would teach the rabbis [while seated] upon pillows and cushions. After he died, David would teach the rabbis [while] seated on the ground. They said to him, "The master should sit upon pillows and cushions." He did not heed them.
>
> *"Tachkemoni* (תחכמני)*"* — Said Rav: The Holy One Blessed be He said to him, "Since you have lowered yourself, you will be like Me ['תחכמני' is expounded as 'תהא כמוני' ('you will be like Me')]...."
>
> *"Head of the captains* (ראש השלשי)*"* — "You will be the head of the three ['השלשי' is expounded as 'לשלשת' ('of the three')] patriarchs."
>
> (*Mo'ed Katan* ibid.)

Furthermore, it is noteworthy that the cruelty of David was vented only in his wars against Mo'av and Ammon:

> David smote Mo'av,
> and he measured them with a line,
> forcing them to lie on the ground.
> He measured two lines to put to death

and one full line to keep alive.
> (Shemu'el II 8:2, Tehillim 60:10)

And the people who were inside [Rabbath *Ammon*]
he brought forth
and put them under saws and under harrows of iron
and under axes of iron,
and made them pass through the brick kiln.
> (Shemu'el II 12:31)

Indeed, according to the Midrash, the dichotomy that we find in David is partially rooted in the ancestral cruelty of these brother nations:

> Said R. Chisdai: Through her modesty, Ruth entered under the shelter of the divine presence, and from her David [her great-grandson] issued. The royal dynasty and the kings had perforce to emanate from the seed of David, so that they should be both compassionate and cruel: compassionate on the father's side and cruel on the mother's side,[18] both attributes perforce coexisting. Therefore the seed of David takes vengeance and bears grudges like a snake.[19]
>
> (*Mid. HaNe'elam* on Ruth, "*Keneseth Yisra'el*")

To comprehend the capacity of David to encompass these two conflicting traits, we note the Torah's allusion that, when G-d dispensed crafts to mankind, He distinguished between the archetypes represented by the sons of Lemech:

> Lemech took himself two wives,
> the one named Adah and the second named Tzillah.
> Adah bore Yaval;
> he was the father of all *tent dwellers with herds.*
> And his brother's name was Yuval;
> he was the father of all *who handle the harp and flute.*
> And Tzillah also bore Tuval Kayin,
> refiner of all forging of copper and iron implements
> [and he perfected the craft of Kayin by *making weapons for murderers* (Rashi)]....
>
> (BeReshith 4:19-22)

Within David's personality, he encompassed all these archetypes, harnessing them all in the course of his life.

A person's character traits, whatever they may be, derive

from his birth and heredity. They remain ingrained within him, unless he seizes them and molds them as he advances through life. Only in this manner will they be refined through the circumstances and actions of his life, which correspond with his "education according to his way" and prepare him for his life's mission.

4. "THIS ONE WARRANTS ANOINTMENT"

"It is good for man to bear a yoke in his youth."
(Eichah 3:27)

David's lot in his youth and his preoccupation with sheep developed within him and prepared for him both his instruments of war and his instruments of music. From this, he came to reach royalty:

> And now thus say to My servant to David,
> thus says the G-d of Hosts:
> I took you from the pasture, from following the sheep,
> to be ruler over My people, over Yisra'el.
> (Shemu'el II 7:8)

David followed the sheep, following the wilderness. There alone, he educated himself in solitude. To there he bore the shame of his youth, which he discarded, and from which he forged the strength of character to suffer hatred and strife all his life and to prevail. And there in the pasture, in the wilderness, he taught himself to free himself of these in reinforced trust in G-d — "As for me, I shall trust in You" (Tehillim 55:24) —

> Behold, then I would wander far;
> I would lodge in the wilderness. Selah.
> I would quickly devise a shelter for myself
> from stormy wind and from tempest.
> (Tehillim 55:8-9)

There, with the sheep in the wilderness, the youth would delight himself in the totality of Creation. There he would sing of the lofty mountains and of the valleys, of the rocks and of the plants and of every living thing. For he listened attentively to all their stirrings and would hear them also uttering perpetual song.

The youth lifted up his eyes to the broad, clear heavens and immersed his eyes in them, to purify them in the endless sky blue;

> For it has been taught, R. Me'ir said: What distinguishes *techeleth* (sky blue) [that the Torah mandated it for *tzitzith* (Rashi)] from all other colors? Because *techeleth* resembles [the color of] the sea, and [the color of] the sea resembles [the color of] the sky, and [the color of] the sky resembles [the color of] the sapphire stone, and [the color of] the sapphire stone resembles [the color of] the Throne of Glory.
>
> (*Chullin* 89a, *Menachoth* 43b)

> *Techeleth* is the throne of the house of David.
>
> (*Zohar*, III, 175a)

From his earliest youth, David rose to sing the song of man to his Creator. This is his everlasting song — "*O my soul, bless G-d!*" (Tehillim 104:1):

> David, while he tended the sheep in the wilderness, would gaze upon the wilderness and serve G-d. He would extol, "When I see Your heavens, the work of Your fingers ..." (Tehillim 8:4). And at night, while all were asleep in their beds, he would sit in the wilderness and gaze at the heavens, at the moon, at the stars and planets and the host of the heavens, and he would praise and extol the Holy One Blessed be He.
>
> (*Zohar Chadash*, Shir HaShirim, 67)

This youth, unwittingly deprived of the love of his father and mother, was abandoned by them to tend the sheep in the wilderness. Perhaps because he was perceived as strange to his brothers and as an alien to his mother's sons,[20] they distanced him from their midst at home.

Yet there in the wilderness his destiny confronted him, intimately with G-d, and kissed him and comforted him. For from the time that David kept company with the sheep, these innocent creatures became his friends and his beloved, and he gave to them all the faithful tenderness of his heart. He was their protective wall both by night and by day.[21]

Because of this occupation, his innermost self opened up there like fountains pouring forth compassion and kindness. And all this prepared his heart for his people, to be their faithful shepherd. There G-d saw him and tested him — and uplifted him:

> He chose David His servant;
> He took him from the sheepfolds (ממכלאת צאן).
> From following animals in need of care, He brought him,
> to shepherd Ya'akov His people and Yisra'el His inheritance.
> He shepherded them according to the integrity of his heart,
> and would guide them by the thorough discernment of his hands.
>
> (Tehillim 78:70-72)

> R. Yehoshua the Kohen [said] in the name of R. Yitzchak: What is [meant by] "from the sheepfolds" ("ממכלאת צאן")? [It means] that David made separate enclosures ["מכלאת" is from the same root as "כלא" ("enclose")] for the sheep. [First] he would bring out the kids and feed them the tips of the grasses, which are tender. [Then] he would bring out the [older] goats and feed them the middle parts of the grasses, which are intermediate. [Then] he would bring out the strong [lit. chosen] and feed them the roots of the grasses, which are hard. The Holy One Blessed be He said to him, "It follows that you are a faithful shepherd. Come and tend My sheep [Yisra'el]."
>
> (Sh.R. 2:2)

In order to understand the nature of David, one must first add to his portrait all that he endured in the "yoke in his youth," and all that he learned from them:

> Much have they persecuted me *from my youth*.
> (Tehillim 129:1, 2)

> O L-rd, You have taught me *from my youth*.
> (ibid. 71:17)

"In the Midst of His Brothers"

Once David has appeared, G-d's instructions are direct and abrupt:

> G-d said, "Arise, anoint him, for *this is he!*"
> (Shemu'el I 16:12)

> "*Arise, anoint him, for this is he!*" — This one warrants anointment and no other warrants anointment.
>
> (Horayoth 11b)

"For this is he" — According to its plain meaning, it states that *"this is he"* who will be king forever. And *"this is he"* who is "your fellow who is better than you" (Shemu'el I 15:28), who you said to Sha'ul [would replace him].

> (R. Yitzchak Abbarbanel on Shemu'el ibid.)

And under divine guidance, David the abandoned shepherd is anointed king of Yisra'el:

> Shemu'el took the horn of oil,
> and he anointed him in the midst of his brothers.
>
> (Shemu'el I 16:13)

The enigmatic addition, *"in the midst of his brothers,"* seems to offer a pithy supplement to that wondrous event, so dramatically — albeit concisely — portrayed:

> Said R. Shemu'el b. Nachmani in the name of R. Yonathan:
> David said, "I thank You, for You have answered me, and You have become my salvation" (Tehillim 118:21).
> Yishai said, "The stone disdained by the builders has become the head cornerstone" (ibid. 118:22).
> His brothers said, "This is G-d's doing; it is wondrous in our eyes" (ibid. 118:23).
> Shemu'el said, "This is the day that G-d has made; we will rejoice and be happy in Him" (ibid. 118:24).
>
> (Pesachim 119a)

Chazal sense the stirrings of the hearts of all present, and they express this through these verses of Tehillim, relating each to one of the principal participants in this drama, in accordance with his fears and wonderment.

What did David think in his heart when he was suddenly rushed away from the sheep, and when he came and saw Shemu'el the prophet at the head of those assembled, and his father and all his brothers in their midst? And behold, Shemu'el rises and takes the horn of oil and anoints him! Did he stand there dumbfounded, or as a dreamer beholding the dream of his affliction and his salvation together? *"I thank You, for You have answered me...."*

As for his father Yishai, did he delight this day in this "smallest" son of his, who rose to this greatness, from the root of royalty of his tribe, the tribe of Yehudah? Was his happiness complete, or marred by astonishment? Did he perhaps wonder regretfully about all the wrongs he had committed against this youth until now? *"The stone disdained by the builders has become the head cornerstone"* —

> In other words, [this refers to] David, who had always been a shepherd, and became head.
>
> (Rashi on *Pesachim* ibid.)

And what of his brothers? They, who had all passed before the prophet — and he had said, "G-d has not chosen these" — did they not feel jealous of this "smallest" brother who remained tending the sheep? Or did they perhaps stand there, anxious and fearful, before the inscrutable wonder? *"This is G-d's doing; it is wondrous in our eyes."*

As for the prophet Shemu'el himself, was he not as a person astonished, wondering why G-d had dealt with him thus on this day? Why had He confounded his prophetic vision until this youth came? Did he ask Yishai why he had left specifically this son with the sheep and not taken him along to the prophet? Or was Shemu'el perhaps preoccupied, with his thoughts drifting between Sha'ul and David? *"This is the day that G-d has made...."*

5. CONCLUSION: "THIS IS THE DAY THAT G-D HAS MADE"

Scripture implies to what extent all that took place on this fateful day was spurred specifically by G-d:

> *"G-d said, 'Arise, anoint him, for this is he!'"* (Shemu'el I 16:12) — *"Arise"* expresses urgency. And our rabbis expounded:[22] The Holy One Blessed be He said to him, "My Mashiach is standing, and you, holy one,[23] are sitting? *'Arise, anoint him!'*"
>
> (Radak, ibid.)

Apparently Shemu'el still hesitated and did not arise to anoint David, since he was not the principal in either the rejoicing or the action of the day.

The Midrash even more dramatically emphasizes G-d's hand in orchestrating the anointment itself:

> [Shemu'el] took the horn of oil and advanced to pour it out [in anointment] upon [Eli'av's] head, but the oil recoiled from him. When he saw this, he said, "Also this was not chosen by G-d." And

thus the oil behaved towards all of them.

When David came, the oil took note, rushed forward itself, and poured out on David's head. He said, "You have uplifted my horn like that of a *re'em*; I am anointed with fresh oil" (Tehillim 92:11).

And why did all this happen? Because the Holy One Blessed be He saw that David, by virtue of his deeds, was worthy to be anointed for royalty, as it is said, "You have loved justice and hated evil; therefore the L-rd, your L-rd, has anointed you with oil of gladness above your companions" (Tehillim 45:8).

(Yal.Sh. Shemu'el:124)

Thus, R. Mosheh Alshech concludes, all "would realize that the matter came from G-d, *for it was He Who anointed him*" (com. on Shemu'el ibid.). Indeed, "This is the day that G-d has made; we will rejoice and be happy in Him."

NOTES

1. *Ed. note:* See Shemu'el I 15:35 and 16:1.

2. *Ed. note:* See *Ha'amek Davar* on Shemoth 32:26. See also the author's *Mah Bein Sha'ul LeDavid* (Yerushalayim: Feldheim, 1980), pp. 16-19, regarding Shemu'el's love for Sha'ul, his consequent mourning over G-d's rejection of Sha'ul, and the resultant effect on Shemu'el's prophecy.

3. See Rambam's Introduction to Avoth (Shemonah Perakim), ch. 7.

4. *Ed. note:* See Shemu'el I 16:1: "G-d said to Shemu'el, '... Go, I shall send you to Yishai the Beith-Lachmi, for I have *seen* among his sons a king for Me.' "

5. See Divrei HaYamim I 2:15: "David was the *seventh*." See also com., ibid.:

> Having found the jewel [David], [Scripture] does not count the eighth [son], Elihu.
>
> (Rashi)

> Yet Scripture states, "His name was Yishai, and he had *eight* sons" (Shemu'el I 17:12). [Why then are only seven mentioned in Divrei Ha-Yamim?] According to the Midrash, the eighth son was Elihu. He is mentioned among the governors appointed by David over Yehudah: "Elihu, one of David's brothers" (Divrei HaYamim I 27:18). He was smaller than David. And what [Scripture] says, "And David was the smallest" (Shemu'el I 17:14), is because he would diminish himself.
>
> (Radak)

6. *Ed. note:* See Shemu'el I 17:34-37.

7. *Ed. note:* Parallels are clearly evident with the Torah's description of Yosef's

relationship with his brothers (BeReshith 37). Perhaps it was specifically the painful consequences of that rivalry that prompted Yishai to banish David to the distant wilderness, where contact with his brothers would be minimized. Obviously, in both cases, the will of G-d ultimately prevails. For further comparisons with the story of Yosef, see the author's *Yofyuth Malchuth UZmiroth* (*Yerushalayim: Ariel, 1980*), *pp. 59-60*.

8. See *Yal. HaMachiri* on Tehillim 118:28 for a much harsher explanation of David's subordination.

9. Actually, "ruddy" occurs once more in the Massorah, but also in reference to David. There are, however, certain variations between the two occurrences in reference to David:

> The Pelishti looked about, and he saw David, and he disdained him, for he was a youth and ruddy (ואדמני) with beautiful appearance.
> (Shemu'el I 17:42)

Note the differences: Here, "ואדמני" is written with the conjunctive *vav* ("*and* ruddy"). Also, this Pelishti was unworthy of seeing David's "*beautiful eyes*."

Ed. note: It should furthermore be noted that "אדמוני" ("ruddy") appears in the two references cited by *Ba'al HaTurim* with *malei* (plene) spelling, whereas in this remaining reference it appears "אדמני" with *chaser* (defective) spelling.

10. *Ed. note:* Clearly, it seems incongruous that so detailed a physical description of David follows G-d's rebuke of Shemu'el for noting Eli'av's physical appearance. Evidently this incongruity prompted Chazal to view this *physical* description of David as symbolizing his *spiritual* essence.

11. *Ed. note:* Perhaps it is the anomalous *sethumah* (section gap) inserted here in mid-verse, following the portrayal of David and preceding G-d's instruction to Shemu'el to anoint him, that prompted the Midrash's description of Shemu'el's hesitation and its insertion here of an additional dialogue between him and G-d.

12. *Ed. note:* Traditionally, the statement is understood as a reference to the Sanhedrin. See *Horayoth* 5a and Rashi, ibid., and on VaYikra ibid.

13. For a more comprehensive description of David, see also *Zohar*, II, 73.

14. *Ed. note:* David's ability to dispense justly both compassion and vengeance contrasts vividly with Chazal's indictment of King Sha'ul for unjustly showing compassion to Agag (Shemu'el I 15:8-9) and cruelty to Nov, the city of priests (ibid. 22:16-19). (See *Yoma* 22b and multiple Midrashic references.)

See also *Eruvin* 53a and *Sanhedrin* 93b (and com., loc. cit.), where King David's ability to derive Halachically appropriate conclusions is contrasted with King Sha'ul's deficiency in this area. For a more detailed treatment of this shortcoming in King Sha'ul, see "In Defense of Sha'ul," *Jewish Thought*, 1, No. 1, 107-111.

15. *Ed. note:* In this sense, just as the physical description of King Sha'ul — his

impressive height — alluded to the role of a human king as symbol of G-d's Kingdom (see above), so too the physical description of King David — combining the usually conflicting attributes of "ruddy" and "beautiful eyes" — alludes to his role as human symbol of G-d's Kingdom.

16. See also Rashi, ibid. and *BeR.R.* 75:4.

17. *Ed. note:* See Shemu'el II 17:10 and Ralbag, ibid.

18. *Ed. note:* The references to "father's side" and "mother's side" are obviously ancestral. "The father's side" refers to Bo'az, who married Ruth as an act of *compassion;* "the mother's side" refers to Ruth, descended from the *cruel* nation of Mo'av.

19. *Ed. note:* See also *Yoma* 22b: "Any Torah scholar who does not take vengeance and bear grudges like a snake is not a Torah scholar." It should be noted that this statement is cited as an indictment of King Sha'ul, who — unlike the seed of David — forewent the honor due him as king and was consequently punished. (See *Yoma* ibid.)

    See also *Iyyei HaYam* (cited in *Anaf Yosef,* ibid.), who explains the metaphor of a snake based upon the Talmud's conclusion that the snake symbolizes an animal that derives no personal pleasure from its attack (see *Ta'anith* 8a). Similarly, a Torah scholar should punish sinners through vengeance and grudges, not for any personal pleasure but because of his commitment to uphold the honor of Torah. Likewise, King David and his progeny use cruelty as an instrument of G-d's will, to crush the enemies of G-d and His people, not for personal benefit. See also the explanations of the metaphor offered by Maharsha (*Chiddushei Aggadoth* on *Yoma* ibid.) and by *Ramath Shemu'el* (cited in *Anaf Yosef* ibid.).

20. *Ed. note:* See Tehillim 69:9 and com., ibid.

21. See Shemu'el I 25:16.

22. See *Tan. VaYera*:6 and *Mid. Tehillim* 31:7, and see n. 23, below.

23. Radak presumably added "holy one" — which does not appear in the original Midrash cited (see n. 20, above) — in the spirit of Tehillim 22:4: "And You are *Holy,* Who *sits* upon the songs of praise of Yisra'el."

MOSHEH RABBEINU AND RABBI AKIVA:
Two Dimensions of Torah

Chaim Eisen

The essay that follows is based upon the source provided below:

אמר רב יהודה אמר רב:

בשעה שעלה משה למרום, מצאו להקדוש ברוך הוא שיושב וקושר כתרים לאותיות.

R. Yehudah said in the name of Rav:
When Mosheh ascended on high, he found the Holy One Blessed be He sitting and tying crowns [like the *tagin* (crownlets) of a *sefer Torah* (Rashi)] to the letters.

אמר לפניו, רבונו של עולם! מי מעכב על ידך? אמר לו, אדם אחד יש שעתיד להיות בסוף כמה דורות, ועקיבא בן יוסף שמו, שעתיד לדרוש על כל קוץ וקוץ תילין תילין של הלכות.

He said before Him, "Master of the universe! Who is detaining You [from presenting what You wrote such that You must yet add to it crowns (Rashi)]?" He said to him, "There is one man who will be after several generations in the future, named Akiva son of Yosef, who will expound upon each and every stroke mounds and mounds of *halachoth*."

RABBI EISEN, formerly of the faculty of the Yeshivat Hakotel, has lectured extensively in *machsheveth Yisra'el* and *parshanuth HaMikra* at post-secondary institutions in Israel. He teaches at Yeshivat Ohr Yerushalayim and at the OU-NCSY Israel Center, and he is an editor of *Jewish Thought*.

אמר לפניו, רבונו של עולם! הראהו לי. אמר לו, חזור לאחורך! הלך וישב בסוף שמונה
(ס"א: שמונה עשר) שורות ולא היה יודע מה הן אומרים. תשש כחו. כיון שהגיע לדבר
(אחד) – אמרו לו תלמידיו, רבי מנין לך – אמר להן, הלכה למשה מסיני, נתיישבה דעתו.
חזר (ובא) לפני הקדוש ברוך הוא; אמר לפניו, רבונו של עולם! יש לך אדם כזה ואתה
נותן תורה על ידי? אמר לו, שתוק! כך עלה במחשבה לפני.

He said before Him, "Master of the universe! Show him to me." He said to him,
"Turn backward!"
He went and sat at the end of eight (*alt. v.:* eighteen) rows and did not understand
what they were saying. His strength failed. When they reached a certain matter
[in need of explanation (Rashi)] — and R. Akiva's] students said to him, "Rabbi!
Whence do you [derive this]?" — [and] he said to them, "[It is] a *halachah* of
Mosheh from Sinai," [Mosheh's (Rashi)] mind became settled.
He returned before the Holy One Blessed be He [and] said before Him, "Master
of the universe! You have a man like this, and You give the Torah through me?"
He said to him, "Be still! Thus has the thought risen before Me."

אמר לפניו, רבונו של עולם! הראיתני תורתו; הראני שכרו. אמר לו, חזור [לאחורך]!
חזר לאחוריו; ראה ששוקלין בשרו במקולין.
אמר לפניו, רבונו של עולם! זו תורה וזו שכרה? אמר לו, שתוק! כך עלה במחשבה לפני.

He said before Him, "Master of the universe! You have shown me his Torah; show
me his reward." He said to him, "Turn backward!"
He turned backward [and] saw that they were weighing [Rabbi Akiva's] flesh in
the meat market [as it says in *Berachoth* (61b) that they flayed his flesh with iron
combs (Rashi)].
He said before Him, "Master of the universe! This is Torah, and this is its reward?"
He said to him, "Be still! Thus has the thought risen before Me."

(*Menachoth* 29b)

---

1. INTRODUCTION

Approaching Aggadah

It is with justified trepidation that one attempts to grapple
with the Aggadic encounter of Mosheh Rabbeinu and Rabbi
Akiva. While every student of the Talmud realizes that in Aggadah
far more is concealed than revealed,[1] many *aggadoth* provide

sufficient exoteric morals to allow discussion to proceed, albeit superficially,[2] at face value. But an aura of inviolable mystery hovers over an *aggadah* that juxtaposes the two greatest historic figures in the infusion of Torah into the world,[3] particularly considering the context (Mosheh's ascent to heaven) and the conclusion (Rabbi Akiva's macabre "reward").

More specifically, the passage before us appears saturated with enigma, almost every line replete with difficulties in both text and context. One senses that in this *aggadah*, the superficial meaning — if attainable — irrevocably draws the reader to a deeper level lurking within. It is our contention that only through consideration of the literal text may we hope to discover the lessons locked within it. If we are to uncover the underlying meaning, we must leave no stone unturned on the surface; we must demand resolution for every question and quandary that the text presents.

In essence, what we require is no different from the analytic inquiry to which every scholar — and certainly every student of the Talmud — is well accustomed. Such study presupposes that apparent textual difficulties are in fact signposts: the more we can find, the more we shall be able to proceed. Aggadah was not preserved as Talmudic storytelling, and its subtleties are not mere literary flourish. We therefore embark upon this quest for understanding armed with the conviction that the words of Chazal are to be taken seriously. It is through their choice of words and their mode of expression that they have confided to the serious student their intent.

"When Mosheh Ascended on High"

In its reference to Mosheh's ascent, our *aggadah* employs a phrase that occurs repeatedly in both Talmudic[4] and Midrashic[5] accounts of Mosheh's receipt of the Torah.[6] Nevertheless, regarding such "ascent" the Talmud asserts:

> Never did the Divine Presence descend below, *nor did Mosheh ... ascend on high,* as it is said, "The heavens are heavens of G-d, but the earth He has given to people" (Tehillim 115:16).
>
> (*Sukkah* 5a)

Moreover, the Talmud explicitly discusses the apparent contradiction posed by the case of Mosheh: "Did Mosheh ... not ascend on high? But it is written, 'Mosheh ascended to the L-rd' (Shemoth 19:3)! [He remained] below [a height of] ten [handbreadths]" (ibid.). While the deeper implications of Mosheh's "ascent" are beyond the scope of the present inquiry, clearly some explanation is necessary.

Halachically, ten handbreadths is the vertical extent of *reshuth harabbim*, the public domain.[7] In effect, ten handbreadths represents the realm of man.[8] Symbolically, beyond ten handbreadths commences an ontologically distinct domain (the realm of the divine), into which even Mosheh — in spite of his ascension — could not enter.[9] But if Mosheh did not truly "ascend on high," what was the nature of the ascension that Chazal persist in characterizing as "Mosheh ascended on high"?[4,5] Is this not a contradiction?[10] With respect to what did he ascend?

In Mosheh's first appearance in *Sefer HaKozari*, R. Yehudah HaLevi portrays him anonymously as "a person who goes through fire but is not burnt, who endures without food but does not hunger, whose face radiates light that the eye cannot bear to see, and who becomes neither ill nor infirm" (*HaKozari* 1:41). The description concludes rhetorically, "Is not this level essentially distinct from the level of people?" (ibid.). While we do not regard Mosheh's greatness as manifest principally in having the attributes of a superman, it is primarily those attributes that emphasize his transcendence of this world and of the physical limitations that normally circumscribe the human condition. In this sense, "Mosheh ascended on high." Although no man can enter the realm of the divine,[11] Mosheh *did* transcend the realm of man. As expressed in *Ein Ya'akov*, he reached "a domain supreme relative to us but subordinate with respect to heaven, a domain [nonetheless] at greatest proximity to heaven" (*HaKothev* on *Sukkah* ibid.).

Obviously, Mosheh's transcendence of this world is manifest not only in his superhuman attributes but in the extraordinary nature of his prophecy. The Talmud tersely characterizes the distinction between the levels of prophecy reached by all other prophets and the level attained by Mosheh: "We have learnt: All the [other] prophets gazed through unclear glass;[12] *Mosheh Rabbeinu gazed through clear glass*" (*Yevamoth* 49b).[13] Notwithstanding the profound depths of this assessment, it is apparent that for most of humanity the world is effectively opaque, concealing G-d's omnipresence from ordinary view.[14] The prophets are exceptions, who are able to gaze at an image, but the image is nevertheless obscured by "unclear glass": encumbered by an earthly clutter that precludes the unqualified perception of truth. In contrast, "*Mosheh Rabbeinu gazed through clear glass*": For him, the world is utterly transparent and can conceal nothing. His transcendence effectively negates any significance ascribed to a physical universe; for Mosheh, the world lacks any substance with which to obscure his image. In this sense, the unique intensity[15] of his encounter with G-d *is* an ascent on high.[16] The clarity of his vision is predicated upon utter transcendence of this world — transcendence that renders this world transparent to him.[17] Armed with this understanding of Mosheh's ascent "on high," we proceed in our *aggadah* to consider what he found there.

2. THE SETTING

"The Holy One Blessed be He
Sitting and Tying Crowns to the Letters"

Apart from the anthropomorphic portrayal of G-d that is characteristic of Aggadah, perplexities abound in the Talmud's description of His preoccupation here. Primarily, what is the nature of these "crowns," explained by Rashi as "like the *tagin* [crownlets] of a *sefer Torah*" (ibid.), and what are they intended to represent? Furthermore, appreciating the subtleties of Talmudic expression, since when does one "*tie*" a crown, especially one that is presumably to be *drawn* on a letter?

More generally, why does the Talmud depict G-d as — so to speak — behind schedule, such that Mosheh, upon ascending on high to receive the Torah, discovers that G-d has not yet finished writing it? Obviously He Who transcends time has not inadvertently run out of it. Moreover, numerous sources in the Talmud[18] and the Midrash[19] indicate that the Torah was already written — written, in fact, "before Creation."[20] What then is G-d portrayed as doing here altogether?

Finally, recognizing the conscientious precision of Talmudic expression, the insertion of G-d "*sitting*" seems superfluous (and excessively anthropomorphic). It appears, in addition, to contradict the Talmudic conclusion, derived from the verse "You *stand* here with Me" (Devarim 5:28), that study of Torah is to be conducted specifically while standing (*Megillah* 21a). And lest we erroneously presume that this conclusion is not intended to relate to G-d, the Gemara continues, "Said R. Abbahu: But for the written verse ['You *stand* here with *Me*'], it would be impossible to say it; as it were, even the Holy One Blessed be He is standing" (ibid.).[21] Why does our *aggadah* insert so problematic a reference to G-d "sitting" when the word could have been omitted entirely? Clearly, if we are to proceed, we must consider more thoroughly what the Talmud depicts G-d as doing here.

The Primeval Torah

While the Torah is repeatedly portrayed as the blueprint of the universe, predating Creation itself,[20] it is noteworthy that this primeval Torah is pictured as "inscribed upon white fire in black fire" (*Tan. BeReshith*:1, *Mid. Tehillim* 90:12, Rashi on Devarim 33:2).[22] The metaphor of fire is significant; G-d Himself is similarly described in the Torah: "For G-d your L-rd is [like] a *consuming fire*" (Devarim 4:24 and 9:3).[23] The symbolism appears related to fire's capacity to consume.[24] Terrestrial fire cannot be grasped, and the mere attempt to grasp it would *consume* the tools with which we physically grasp (our hands). Only from a distance can we be safely warmed. In likening G-d to a consuming fire, the Torah emphasizes that G-d cannot be grasped[11] — *intellectually* — and the mere attempt to comprehend G-d would *consume* the tool with which we *intellectually* grasp (our mind).[25] Similarly, while the Torah that is given to this world is tangibly inscribed upon white parchment in black ink, a Torah "inscribed upon white fire in black fire" is one that, in human terms, cannot be grasped.[26]

Indeed, the Midrash assumes such a distinction between the primeval, transcendent Torah (upon which the world's existence is predicated) and the material Torah (which is imparted to us as the basis for our lives in this world and thus implicitly presupposes the world's existence):

> "*No man knows [wisdom's] value*" (Iyyov 28:13) — Said R. Elazar: The sections of Torah were not given in order, for had they been given in order, anyone who would read them would be able to resurrect the dead and do miracles (*alt. v.:* immediately would be able to create

a world). Therefore the order of Torah was concealed. But it is revealed before the Holy One Blessed be He, as it is said, "*And who like Me can read and recount it and set it in order for Me*" (Yeshayahu 44:7).[27]

(*Mid. Tehillim* 3:2)

In its references to "order," were the Midrash alluding merely to questions of chronology, reading the unmodified version would obviously not enable "anyone ... to resurrect the dead and do miracles," much less "immediately ... be able to create a world." Evidently, the unmodified version relates to an ontologically different domain — the realm of the divine — in which the realities of this world (which normally exclude acts of resurrection, miracles, and creation) do not apply. This level of Torah, emphasizes the Midrash, was concealed from man, who by his very nature functions on a distinct, earthly level.

Expounding the same verse from Iyyov, the Talmud apparently regards this dichotomy as obvious — so obvious that it comments rhetorically:

Regarding the Torah, it is written, "[It is] *hidden* from the eyes of all living and concealed from the birds of the heavens" (Iyyov 28:21). [Are we to assume that "*hidden*"] implies that [Torah] was ever known? But it is written, "*No man knows [wisdom's] value*" (Iyyov 28:13)!

(*Shevu'oth* 5a)

Apropos of the Talmud's qualification of Mosheh's ascent (*Sukkah* 5a, quoted above), Maharal comments on this Gemara that even "Mosheh did not receive all of the Torah ... but *only received what it is possible to receive*" (*Derech HaChayyim* on *Avoth* 1:1, ד"ה משה קבל תורה מסיני).[28] Mosheh's receipt of Torah is the maximum possible specifically within these limitations. Thus, the Talmud affirms, "Fifty gates of understanding were created in the world, and *all were given to Mosheh save one*" (*Rosh HaShanah* 21b, *Nedarim* 38a).[9] Inasmuch as the number fifty symbolizes the absolute,[29] the distinction between fifty gates and forty-nine is the distinction between the absolute and the maximum level attainable in this world. *Tosefoth Yom Tov* cites this Gemara to verify "that all of the Torah was not delivered over to [Mosheh] ... but *only what was suitable for him to receive* he received from Sinai" (com. on *Avoth* 1:1, ד"ה ומסרה ליהושע).[28]

It should be emphasized that the implication of two distinct levels of Torah is not two different texts. Ramban cites a tradition that aptly characterizes our Torah:

> We are in possession of a true tradition[30] that the entire Torah is names of the Holy One Blessed be He, the words subdividing into names on a different level.... Therefore, a *sefer Torah* in which [the scribe] erred in the insertion or deletion of a single letter is unfit ... even though [the error] seems neither to add nor to detract [from the meaning].... And it appears that the Torah that was inscribed in black fire upon white fire was in the manner that we have mentioned: that the writing was continuous, without separation into words, and it was possible to interpret it in the manner of the names or in the manner of our reading regarding the *torah* [instruction] and the *mitzvah* [commandment]. And it was given to Mosheh Rabbeinu [in writing] in the manner of partition [in order to] read the *mitzvah*.
>
> (introduction to *Commentary on the Torah*)

R. Me'ir b. Gabbai amplifies Ramban's description of the Torah as names of G-d, and concludes, "This is the primeval Torah that predated the world" (*Avodath HaKodesh*, "*Chelek HaYichud*," ch. 21). While in principle it is also *our* Torah, it is clearly *not* the Torah as we perceive it. By analogy, we may imagine a child beginning to learn *alef-beith*, who is given a cryptic work of abstruse scholarship to use as a primer. The child may successfully use the book to practice his recognition of the letters. Yet even if the child is told that his primer alludes to profound mysteries, any attempt to discern them in his *alef-beith* will be misguided and futile. Given the child's level, we may truthfully say that they are not part of *his* book. Similarly, the level at which Torah is revealed to this world is specifically on physical parchment in material ink: palpable media presenting palpable instruction to earthly man on how to live in this world. From this world, the heavenly, fiery Torah of names — through which G-d created this world — cannot be grasped.[31]

Apparently, the Talmud presupposes these two levels as well, in the dispute between Mosheh and *malachei hashareth* (the ministering angels) regarding the descent of Torah into this world:

> *Malachei hashareth* said before the Holy One Blessed be He, "[The Torah is] ... a hidden treasure, cached for You nine hundred seventy-

four generations before the world was created. You wish to give it to flesh and blood? 'What is man that You remember him and a human that You take account of him?' (Tehillim 8:5). 'G-d our Master! How glorious is Your name in all the world, You Who *place Your majesty [the Torah] upon heaven!'* (ibid. 8:2)."

Said the Holy One Blessed be He to Mosheh, "Answer them!" ...

He said before Him, "Master of the universe! In the Torah that You are giving me, what is written? 'I am G-d your L-rd Who brought you forth from the land of Mitzrayim' (Shemoth 20:2)." He said to them, "You descended to Mitzrayim? You were subjugated to Paroh? Why should Torah be yours?"

(Shabbath 88b)[32]

Five additional challenges are leveled by Mosheh (ibid.), citing commandments revealed by G-d at Sinai and emphasizing their irrelevance to *malachei hashareth,* who presume to maintain Torah in heaven only. While they ultimately concede, the premise of the debate seems elusive. Given the content of the Torah, what motivated *malachei hashareth* to posit initially that it should be placed in heaven? Had they no familiarity with the treasure that they wished to possess so exclusively?

With our recognition of two distinct levels of Torah, the Talmud's message is evident. Obviously, in characterizing the Torah as "a *hidden* treasure" that preceded Creation, *malachei hashareth* were not referring to a Torah of inapplicable terrestrial commandments.[33] Their Torah "is inscribed not in the present, but in the primeval, order" (*Shenei Luchoth HaBerith* [R. Yeshayahu Horowitz], "*Masecheth Shavu'oth*" [p. 112a]); as such, it "is entirely unification and names of the Holy One Blessed be He" (*Me'or Einayim* [HaRif] on *Ein Ya'akov*, ibid.; *Shenei Luchoth HaBerith* ibid.). If they contend that Torah should be placed in heaven, it is because they perceive Torah as a transcendent secret, inappropriate to earthly man. It should therefore rightly be kept hidden in a transcendent realm — heaven.[33] Mosheh's decisive response is that there is, in addition to the *hidden* treasure, a *revealed* level of Torah that is relevant specifically to people and mandates the descent of Torah to this world.[33] While the transcendent Torah of white and black fire remains essentially in heaven, the terrestrial Torah of parchment and ink is consigned to man and revealed to the world at Sinai.

Recalling our *aggadah*, our primary concern is of course to elucidate what took place at Sinai. Since the Torah was already written "before Creation,"[20] what is G-d portrayed as doing there? In light of the foregoing, the resolution seems clear. As characterized by the Midrash, the giving of the Torah at Sinai was "a time for that which was placed beyond the heavens [the transcendent Torah] to be placed beneath the heavens" (*Koh.R.* 3:1). The Torah that predates Creation is the fiery Torah of the *malachim*, composed entirely of names of G-d and inaccessible to human grasp. In contrast, the Talmud asserts that our Torah "speaks in the language of people" (*Berachoth* 31b).[34] Indeed, the Midrash emphasizes that the Torah revealed at Sinai was specifically in accordance with man's ability to receive it: "With all of Yisra'el, each and every one [heard] according to his capacity" (*Sh.R.* 5:9).[35] For Torah to descend to this world, it must be concretized *corporeally*, transcribed into tangible ink on parchment. When Mosheh ascended on high, recounts our *aggadah*, he found G-d engaged in this act of transcription.

"Tying Crowns"

In spite of this conclusion, however, difficulties remain. Why does the Talmud depict G-d as — so to speak — behind schedule, still "*tying crowns* to the letters"? In particular, what do these "*crowns*" represent, and why is G-d "*tying*" them? Evidently we must clarify the enigma of the "crowns" before we can proceed. Maharal expounds their implication:

> Know that there are crowns and *tagin* on the letters of the Torah. For just as the bodies of the words in the Torah indicate the matters of Torah themselves, so the *tagin* that are *above* the letters in the Torah indicate subtle conceptions like mountains [dangling] by a thread emanating from the Torah itself — therefore indicated by the *tag*, which is as fine as a thread [and emanates from the body of the letter].... Because of the inaccessibility of their comprehension by man, this *tag* is *above* the letter. In addition, they are called "crowns" and "*tagin*," because the crown transcends its owner even though it is associated with him.[36] Similarly the conceptions that are indicated by these crowns transcend the conceptions of the Torah in their subtlety.
>
> (*Chiddushei Aggadoth*, ibid.; *Tifereth Yisra'el*, ch. 63 [p. 189])

Recognizing that Torah comprises both exoteric and esoteric dimensions, the "crowns," concludes Maharal, imply specifically the latter. While we regard all the *letters* of ink as earthly representations of the Torah of fire, it is the *crowns* that embody its most ethereal aspect. Although they are included in the Torah of ink on parchment, they involve a minimum of each; they are so minute as to appear functionally irrelevant to the proper, exoteric "reading" of the letters. Indeed, they are *literally* "between the lines," and their superscription — *crowning* the letters — suggests the inaccessibility of the realm to which they allude. Within the context of the terrestrial Torah, the crowns in particular resound with the echo of fiery transcendence.[37]

Given the profound nature of these "crowns," the anomalous "tying" of them to the letters may also be elucidated. Maharsha explains:

> The concept of tying is used [in reference to an act] that one does to recall something else lest it be forgotten, as it is written regarding [the *tying* of] *tzitzith*, "In order that you will *remember*," etc. (BeMidbar 15:40).[38] Thus, these ties of the letters are what allude to the sublime, transcendent matters in the Crown of [G-d] Blessed be He, to be recalled through them....
>
> (*Chiddushei Aggadoth*, ibid.)

Effectively, Maharal and Maharsha present compatible perspectives on the crowns of the letters. As representations of the most profound, supernal mysteries of the heavenly Torah of fire, the crowns are scarcely even *written* in the Torah of this world. They can only be *tied*[39] above the letters, by a stroke as fine as a thread, to *recall* a level so transcendent that — even when the Torah is transcribed into palpable ink on parchment — it can be at most implied.

"In Back and In Front"

With this appreciation of what "tying crowns" represents and what aspect of the transcendent Torah of heaven is transcribed as "crowns" in the terrestrial Torah of man, the outstanding problems regarding our *aggadah*'s portrayal of G-d appear soluble. The Talmud describes G-d as still tying crowns to the letters when Mosheh ascends to receive the Torah; one would expect the transcription of the Torah to have been completed already.

Realizing that the Creator of time is obviously not limited by it, one wonders why the crowns were transcribed so late. But on further reflection, it is the nature of the crowns themselves that necessitates this order.

In the context of G-d's other principal revelation to the world (Creation), we also encounter exceptional significance accorded to the final act. In the crescendo of Creation, man is the concluding note, emphasizing the greatness of both man and his responsibility. "When the Holy One Blessed be He created the First Man ... He said to him, 'See how becoming and praiseworthy My creations are! *And all that I have created, I created for you.* Pay attention that you not become corrupt and destroy My world' " (*Koh.R.* 7:13).[40] It is, therefore, not only man's prerogative but his mandate to realize his centrality: "Each and every one is *obligated* to say, '*For me the world was created*' " (*Mish. Sanhedrin* 4:5). Chazal, however, also discern an antithetical emphasis in the succession of Creation: "Man was created on the eve of Shabbath. And why was he created last? [This is] so that should he become overbearing, [G-d would] tell him, 'A mosquito preceded you in the work of Creation' " (*Tos. Sanhedrin* 8:3, *Sanhedrin* 38a). Given such ostensibly divergent assessments, we must consider more carefully the significance of the sequence of Creation as it relates to man.

The Midrash addresses this ambivalence in terms of the order in which transcendent conceptions are transposed into corporeal existence:

> "*In back and in front You formed me*" (Tehillim 139:5)[41] — ... Said R. Shimon b. Lakish: [This means that man was created] "*in back*" of the work of the last day [of Creation] and "*in front*" of the work of the first day [of Creation].
>
> This is [consistent with] the view of R. Shimon b. Lakish, who [also] said:
>
> "*A spirit of the L-rd hovered upon the water*" (BeReshith 1:2)[27] — This is the spirit of the King Mashiach [indicating that, since the King Mashiach is obviously human, the spirit of man *preceded* all of Creation, even though man was actually created *last*].... If a man is worthy, they tell him, "You preceded *malachei hashareth* (*alt. v.:* all of Creation). And if not, they tell him, "A fly preceded you; a mosquito preceded you; this slime preceded you."
>
> (*BeR.R.* 8:1, *VaY.R.* 14:1)[42]

The perspective of the Midrash seems perplexing. In light of the foregoing discussion emphasizing the *lag* in the creation of man, the Midrash's inference that the spirit of man was created *first* seems especially incongruous. Altogether, why should there be such a discrepancy between two such related acts of creation?

It appears that man's unique role in Creation mandates this duality. The *spirit* of man — and specifically *"the spirit of the King Mashiach"* — represents the ultimate destiny of the world and the final goal of Creation. As such, it must be envisioned as the *first* emanation from G-d, so to speak, in the unfolding of Creation: Everything is to be created within the context of this ideal as means to its realization. With the recognition that all of Creation is *means* to the realization of man, however, it is evident that the actualization of *everything* must precede that of man, so that the creation of man *as a corporeal reality* must be the *last* stage of Creation. The moral implications of this conclusion regarding man as expressed in the Midrash — basically, dependent on man's agreement with or rejection of this ideal[43] — are not relevant to the present discussion. The principle invoked, however, certainly is: That which is most essential is both the most transcendent, primeval ideal *and* the final component to be drawn down into a material reality. Because of its transcendence, everything else is predicated upon it; for the same reason, the intricate process of its *physical* realization depends upon everything else. Far from incongruous, both aspects are corresponding sides of the same coin.

With this understanding, the lag in the transcription of the "crowns" of the Torah is no longer enigmatic, but instead mandated by their very nature. As representations of the most transcendent aspect of the primeval Torah of black on white fire, they are necessarily the last element transcribed into the physical Torah of ink and parchment. They are the component of the heavenly Torah most intractable to materialization, most unyielding to *"tying"* down in the terrestrial Torah. Obviously, G-d was not behind schedule. Yet in light of the crowns and what they signify, their physical realization as minute strokes of ink necessarily occupies the final moments of the Torah's transcription into the palpable document that, once complete, is immediately presented to man.

"Sitting"

At this point, it is possible to resolve the final difficulty raised in analysis of our *aggadah*'s description of G-d. The Talmud (*Megillah* 21a, quoted above) teaches us that study of Torah — even, as it were, by G-d — is to be conducted specifically while standing.[21] Our *aggadah*'s portrayal of G-d "*sitting*" is ostensibly not only superfluous but inconsistent as well.

The Talmud (ibid.), nevertheless, does discuss circumstances that justified study of Torah while sitting. While the details of the discussion are not germane to our inquiry, the conclusion is: "Rava said: Easy matters [were studied] standing; hard matters [were studied] sitting." In light of the foregoing, the relevance of this conclusion is self-evident. In the process of transcribing the Torah of heaven into the Torah of this world, the component that may be regarded most as a "hard matter" is the "tying" of ethereal crowns down to ink on parchment. Because of their transcendence, they are the most incompatible with materialization. Obviously, in a literal sense, nothing is a "hard matter" for G-d. But inasmuch as our *aggadah* couches its message in anthropomorphisms, it describes G-d specifically as "*sitting*" when preoccupied with the "hard matter"[44] of "tying crowns to the letters."[45]

Mosheh finds G-d, so to speak, thus preoccupied. With our appreciation of what is involved in transcribing the transcendent Torah of the *malachim* into the terrestrial Torah of man, and our apprehension of what is implied in "the Holy One Blessed be He sitting and tying crowns to the letters," Mosheh's dismay can be readily understood: "*Master of the universe! Who is detaining You [from presenting what You wrote such that You must yet add to it crowns* (Rashi)*]?*" Effectively, Mosheh contends, You have already transcribed into the Torah of this world everything that relates to this world. The crowns allude to a level so supernal that, even in ink on parchment, it will remain beyond human grasp. It is only the "matters of Torah" themselves that must be transcribed into physical letters; the "subtle conceptions" indicated by the crowns ought to be left, untranscribed, in the Torah of heaven. They are so inaccessible to man as to be irrelevant to a physical Torah completely.[46]

Mosheh's argument seems so reasonable that, in contrast,

G-d's response is astounding: *"There is one man who will be after several generations in the future, named Akiva son of Yosef, who will expound upon each and every stroke mounds and mounds of* halachoth*."* In light of the meaning of the crowns, what could possibly be meant by deriving "mounds and mounds of *halachoth"* from them? Clearly, G-d's response is a reference not merely to one man, but to the novel approach embodied by that man. In order to comprehend this response, we must first elucidate both.

3. "ONE MAN ... NAMED AKIVA SON OF YOSEF"

"There is One Man Who Will Be after Several Generations"

Beyond the cryptic overtones evoked by depicting Rabbi Akiva as one "who will expound upon each and every stroke mounds and mounds of *halachoth,"* the implications of G-d's response seem incredible. Are we to conclude that Rabbi Akiva superseded Mosheh Rabbeinu in his mastery of Torah?[47] It is, after all, through Mosheh that the nation of Yisra'el — ultimately, including Rabbi Akiva — received the Torah.[48] Furthermore, the Torah itself affirms, "No prophet arose again in Yisra'el like Mosheh" (Devarim 34:10), an assessment that constitutes a fundamental principle of Jewish faith.[15]

In particular, the Talmud asserts that "later developments" of Torah are essentially not *later* developments at all:

> *"Upon [the two stone tablets] were as everything that G-d spoke with you on the mountain"* (Devarim 9:10) — [This] teaches that the Holy One Blessed be He showed Mosheh fine points of Torah and fine points of the scholars[49] and *whatever the scholars would innovate in the future.*
> *(Megillah* 19b)

Expounding the same verse, the Midrash is even more emphatic:

> [This teaches that] Scripture, Mishnah, Halachah, Talmud, *toseftoth, aggadoth,* and even what a faithful student is to instruct in the future were already said to Mosheh from Sinai. Thus it is written, "There are things about which one says, 'See this; it is new' " (Koheleth 1:10) — and his friend responds, "*It has already been forever before us"* (ibid.).
> *(Koh.R.* 1:9 [2] and 5:8 [2], *VaY.R.* 22:1)[50]

Still more generally, the Talmud emphasizes that the origin of *all* aspects of Torah inclusively is at Sinai, through Mosheh:

> "And I shall give you the tablets of stone and the torah [instruction] and the mitzvah [commandment] that I have written to instruct them" (Shemoth 24:12) — "Tablets" refers to the Ten Statements. "Torah" refers to Scripture [Chumash (Rashi)]. "And the mitzvah" refers to Mishnah. "That I have written" refers to Nevi'im and Kethuvim. "To instruct them" refers to Gemara. [This] teaches that all were given to Mosheh from Sinai.
>
> (Berachoth 5a)[51]

Given Chazal's repeated declarations that even the most innovative components of Torah really originated through Mosheh at Sinai, how are we to evaluate the significance G-d ascribes to Rabbi Akiva? Still more perplexing, how are we to comprehend Mosheh's inability to understand what Rabbi Akiva was expounding? The Midrash informs us explicitly, "Matters that were not revealed to Mosheh were revealed to Rabbi Akiva and his peers" (BeM.R. 19:6, Tan. Chukkath:8). Is this not a contradiction?

Upon further consideration, however, it is clear — even regardless of this glaring inconsistency — that Chazal could not have intended to suggest that Mosheh actually possessed every nuance of Torah, Nevi'im, Kethuvim, Mishnah, Talmud, Tosefta, Halachah, Aggadah, and every fine point of future scholarship in the forms in which they exist today. The Midrash emphasizes:

> And did Mosheh learn the whole Torah? It is written regarding the Torah, "Its measure is longer than the earth and broader than the sea" (Iyyov 11:9)! And in forty days Mosheh learned it? Instead, it was principles that the Holy One Blessed be He taught Mosheh.
>
> (Sh.R. 41:6, Tan. Thissa:16)

Maharzu elucidates the nature of these "principles": "These are the rules through which Torah is expounded, for each rule teaches countless [derivative conclusions]" (com., ibid.). By implication, then, the Midrash informs us that specifically in the sense of its underlying principles was the entire Torah received through Mosheh. Thus, we indeed regard Torah, Nevi'im, Kethuvim, Mishnah, Talmud, Tosefta, Halachah, Aggadah, and every fine point of future scholarship as originating with Mosheh from Sinai: not, of course, in the forms in which they exist today, but inasmuch as all are predicated upon the principles of Torah as

Mosheh received them from Sinai, all essentially originated with Mosheh.

In no domain of Torah scholarship is this perspective more indispensable than in the domain of Halachah. Rambam, in his discussion of rabbinical *mitzvoth* (particularly, the kindling of Chanukkah lights and the reading of Megillath Ester), states, "I cannot see that anyone would imagine or consider that it was said to Mosheh at Sinai that he should command us that when, at the end of our sovereignty, such and such will occur with the Greeks, we will be mandated to kindle Chanukkah lights" (*Sefer HaMitzvoth, Shoresh* 1). Nevertheless, certainly no one would question the inclusion of these *mitzvoth* in the corpus of Torah; indeed, the Gemara explicitly cites the reading of the *megillah* as having been shown to Mosheh.[52] Rambam himself notes this apparent difficulty and resolves it in terms that correspond to those we have already employed:

> In the Gemara *Shevu'oth* [39a, it is written], "[When Mosheh Rabbeinu had Yisra'el swear to fulfill the Torah,] we [know] that any *mitzvah* they accepted upon themselves from Mount Sinai [was included]. Whence [do we know that] *mitzvoth* that were to be innovated in the future, such as reading the *megillah* [were also included]? The teaching [of the text] implies, '[The Yehudim] fulfilled and accepted' (Ester 9:27): They fulfilled what they had already accepted." — *This [acceptance] means that they would believe in any* mitzvah *that the prophets and the scholars would ordain afterward.*
>
> (*Sefer HaMitzvoth* ibid.)[53]

Restated, Rambam concludes that it was not the *particular* acceptance of the later *mitzvah* that originated at Sinai but the *general principle* of acceptance, upon which the particular acceptance would later be based. Likewise, the Talmud explains:

> What does one bless [on Chanukkah lights]? "[You are Blessed, G-d, our L-rd, King of the universe,] Who sanctified us with His commandments and commanded us to kindle the Chanukkah light." And where did He command us? R. Ivya said: "[According to the teaching that they instruct you and according to the judgment that they declare to you, do.][54] Do not deviate from the matter that they tell you right or left" (Devarim 17:11).
>
> (*Shabbath* 23a, *Sukkah* 46a)[55]

Again, the commandment is rooted in the *general principle* that establishes rabbinical authority.[56] In this sense, all later developments of Torah truly derive from Sinai.[57]

Thus, in analyzing Chazal's derivations that all aspects of Torah actually originated through Mosheh, *Torah Temimah* concludes:

> The intent is that all the principles of the *halachoth* that the students are to innovate in the future by force of their reason and from allusions and subtleties in the Torah were all joined in the meaning of the Torah from its inception. But the intent is not that the actual [Talmudic] dialectics that would be innovated in the future were said to Mosheh.
>
> (com. on Shemoth 24:12, n. 28)

> The intent of this interpretation appears that [G-d] instructed [Mosheh] regarding the ways of interpretation and the rules that Chazal grasped with which to expound matters of Torah and to define it and explain it and deduce through those [rules] laws and innovations. Similarly, they found support for all rabbinical *mitzvoth* in the verse from *parashath Shofetim*, "Do not deviate," etc. (Devarim 17:11). Accordingly, there is a general basis for all rabbinical *mitzvoth* in the Torah.
>
> (com. on Devarim 9:10, n. 3)[58]

Mosheh, then, acquired the basis, but not the content, of all later developments of Torah.

Commenting in this spirit on the Gemara in *Megillah* 19b (quoted above), *Tosefoth Yom Tov* notes that the Talmud refers to G-d as having *shown* Mosheh "fine points of Torah and fine points of the scholars and whatever the scholars would innovate in the future." The reference is *not* to having *taught* these to Mosheh. The distinction, argues *Tosefoth Yom Tov*, is significant:

> The reference to having *shown* him is in the manner of sight only, not in the manner of delivery,[59] as one who shows something to his friend [for the latter] to see it, *without giving it to him*.
>
> (introduction to *Commentary on the Mishnah* and com. on *Avoth* 1:1)

Inasmuch as Mosheh was given the principles upon which all of Torah is based, he was *shown* all components of the Torah. This was, however, *not* "in the manner of delivery," since the actual components themselves, to be developed from the Torah only later, were not given.

At the heart of this ongoing process of development in Torah is the dynamism that characterizes the growth of *Torah shebe'al-peh* (the oral Torah) from its inception at Sinai. Just as Nevi'im and Kethuvim essentially "were given to Mosheh from Sinai" (*Berachoth* 5a),[51] inasmuch as the basic truths and principles that they elaborate originate in the Torah received by Mosheh, so does every aspect of these later developments of *Torah shebe'al-peh* derive from basic truths and principles from Sinai. And just as Nevi'im and Kethuvim as they appear before us represent the realization of these truths and principles unfolding through history, so too does the growth of *Torah shebe'al-peh* represent a process of historical development predicated upon the basic truths and principles of Torah, applied and reapplied throughout time. While these truths and principles are immutable and static, their applications are dynamic and endless.

"Named Akiva Son of Yosef"

Appreciating this distinction, we can begin to fathom both the dichotomy between Mosheh Rabbeinu and Rabbi Akiva and the singular greatness of each. Obviously, no one would contest Mosheh's pre-eminence in receiving all the truths and principles that Torah comprises. Maharal emphasizes that Mosheh's perception of Torah was on the level of *kelal*, the general principle,[60] through his prophetic capacity,[61] which was (as detailed above)[15, 16] unparalleled. On that level, "No prophet arose again in Yisra'el like Mosheh" (Devarim 34:10). Rabbi Akiva did not perceive Torah through prophecy.[62] But regarding this very uniqueness of Mosheh, *Iyyun Ya'akov* cites a crucial qualification:

> In reality, Rabbi Akiva is the foundation of *Torah shebe'al-peh*. And similarly it is [written] in the Midrash:[63] " 'No *prophet* arose again ... like Mosheh' (Devarim 34:10) — But among *scholars* one arose. And who is he? [He is] Rabbi Akiva."
>
> (com. on *Menachoth* 29b and on *Babba Bathra* 12a)

Of course we believe that the fundamental truths and principles, upon which all of *Torah shebe'al-peh* is predicated, originated through the *prophecy* of Mosheh from Sinai. However, it is the developmental process that continuously applies and reapplies

Torah shebe'al-peh to life that we regard as its true foundation. In this domain of human development, *scholarship* — not prophecy — reigns supreme, and Rabbi Akiva is its ultimate champion.

Moreover, in contrasting the principal vehicles through which Mosheh Rabbeinu and Rabbi Akiva perceived Torah — respectively, prophecy and scholarship — we note the principle established by the Talmud that "the scholar is preferable to the prophet" (*Babba Bathra* 12a, *Yal.Sh.* Tehillim:841).[64] Indeed, the Talmud (ibid.) likens the scholars to prophets and posits a prophetic dimension in scholarship as well. But this is clearly not prophecy in the sense that we usually intend. Ri b. Migash emphasizes that "while a prophet cannot say [anything] except what he heard and what was put in his mouth to say, a scholar can say what was said to Mosheh from Sinai *even though he did not hear it*" (cited in *Shittah Mekubbetzeth*, ibid.). Likewise, Ramban explains that the prophecy of prophets is through "images and visions" while the "prophecy" of scholars refers to "the way of scholarship ... knowing the truth through the divine inspiration *in their midst*" (com., ibid.). Obviously, both are referring to scholarly exercise of the mind, through which truths may be deduced and innovated within, even if not directly received. Thus, Ritva describes the "prophecy" of scholars as "perceiving *through their minds* many things" (com., ibid.). Still more explicitly, *Torath Chayyim* distinguishes this "prophecy" as one in which "the 'prophesier' *did not hear anything* from the Almighty, but instead *by dint of his great scholarship he innovates* and states laws and *halachoth* and corresponds to the truth *as if* delivered from Sinai" (cited in *Etz Yosef*, ibid.). This level, in which internal human effort and innovation — substituting for external revelation — figure so prominently, and in which the scholar says what he did not hear, is reckoned by the Talmud as superior to prophecy itself.

Regarding this level, the Talmud quotes approvingly the declaration that *keneseth Yisra'el* presents to G-d: "Master of the universe! The words of Your lovers [the scholars[49] (Rashi)] are more pleasing to me than the wine of Torah [the principal written Torah (Rashi)]" (*Avodah Zarah* 35a). *Etz Yosef* explains the metaphor: "*Torah shebikethav* [the written Torah] resembles [undiluted] wine ... [that is] unfit for drinking — because of its acute strength — unless mitigated by dilution with water. Similarly, because of its depth, the essence of *Torah shebikethav* is incomprehensible unless its words are 'diluted' with the 'waters' of *Torah shebe'al-peh*. For ... we would be unable to fulfill properly even one of the *mitzvoth* of *Torah shebikethav* without *Torah shebe'al-peh* ... to explain all the details[65] before us" (loc. cit.). In a similar vein, Chazal generalize that "words of scholars[49] are *more precious* than words of Torah" (*Yer. Berachoth* 1:4 [8b]).[66] Ultimately, while G-d may be more intensely revealed through the latter, it is solely through the former that *Torah shebe'al-peh* can develop and grow[67] as the basis of our lives.

Considering the relationship between the "external revelation" of prophecy and *Torah shebikethav* on the one hand and the "internal revelation" of scholarship in *Torah shebe'al-peh* on the other, we note that the Talmudic scholarship that Rabbi Akiva personified climaxed specifically during and immediately after the period of the second Beith HaMikdash,[68] in which prophecy ceased,[69] the complete transmission of Torah dwindled,[70] and — relative to the first Beith HaMikdash — the Shechinah (G-d's Presence) was absent.[71] From *Pirkei Heichaloth* we learn, "Even though the Shechinah did *not* dwell in the second Beith [HaMikdash], nevertheless the essence of the Torah and its splendor and glory were *only* in [the period of] the second Beith [HaMikdash]" (ch. 27). Characterized by R. E. Dessler, "this is the great revelation in the midst of the concealment, the exposure that comes through toil and painstaking" (*Michtav MeEliyyahu*, III, 53). The Midrash summarizes:

> This is *Torah shebe'al-peh*, which is difficult to learn and is accompanied by great agony *and is likened to darkness*, as it is said, *"The people who are going in darkness have seen great light"* (Yeshayahu 9:1) — These are the masters of Talmud, *who have seen great light*.
>
> (*Tan. Noach*:3)[72]

In that "light" — which is seen specifically by those who trudge and toil in darkness — *"matters that were not revealed to Mosheh were revealed to Rabbi Akiva and his peers"* (*BeM.R.* 19:6, *Tan. Chukkath*:8).[73]

"Upon Each and Every Stroke
Mounds and Mounds of *Halachoth*"

It is clearly not incidental that our *aggadah* juxtaposes Mosheh Rabbeinu, the pre-eminent prophet, with Rabbi Akiva, the pre-eminent scholar, for these two epitomize their respective — and distinct — approaches to Torah. Chazal emphasize that "the Holy One Blessed be He gave [Mosheh] the Torah as a gift" (*Sh.R.* 41:6, *Tan. Thissa*:16).[74] By contrast, no "gift" of Torah is readily forth-coming in Rabbi Akiva's well-known biography. Descended from converts[75] who traced their lineage back to the infamous Sisra,[76] Akiva began his life as an illiterate agricultural worker,[77] whose initial attitude toward Torah scholars was one of contemptuous hatred.[78] He only began to study Torah at age forty,[79] but eventually by dint of his extraordinary effort — virtually never inter-rupting his study[80] — he mastered the entire Torah[81] and became one of the chief determinants of Halachah.[82] His colleagues ulti-mately lauded him as one of the "fathers of the world" (*Yer. Shekalim* 3:1 [10b], *Yer. Rosh HaShanah* 1:1 [5a]), the very embodi-ment of the "wellsprings of wisdom" (*Sotah* 49b, *Yer. Sotah* 9:16 [45b]), without whom the Torah itself "would have been forgot-ten from Yisra'el" (*Sifrei* on Devarim 11:22).[83] This is Rabbi Akiva, emerging withal as "the foundation of *Torah shebe'al-peh*" (*Iyyun Ya'akov* on *Menachoth* 29b, quoted above).

With this understanding, we begin to appreciate the singular uniqueness of Rabbi Akiva, "who will expound upon each and every stroke mounds and mounds of *halachoth*." Recall our con-clusions regarding the significance of the "crowns" of the letters (see above). As representations of the most profound, supernal mysteries of the Torah of fire, the crowns are scarcely even written explicitly in the Torah of this world. They embody the most ethereal aspect of that heavenly Torah: a level so transcen-dent that — even when the Torah is transcribed into palpable ink on parchment — it can be at most implied. They are the compo-nent most intractable to materialization, most unyielding to "tying" down in the terrestrial Torah. In fact, posits Mosheh Rabbeinu, they appear so functionally irrelevant to the proper "reading" of the letters, so inaccessible to man, as to be com-pletely inappropriate to a physical Torah. Yet paradoxically, the implication of our *aggadah*, notes Maharsha, is "that not only do the 'ties' of the letters contain [allusions to] intimate matters, but also 'mounds and mounds of *halachoth*' depend upon them, which Rabbi Akiva expounded" (*Chiddushei Aggadoth*, ibid.). How can these *halachoth* be derived from crowns that are — from

Mosheh's perspective — inapplicable to man?

As we have seen, Mosheh's relationship with Torah is through an unparalleled level of prophecy.[61] By having "ascended on high" to receive G-d's Torah, he achieves maximum transcendence of this world and reaches the ultimate human proximity to the fiery Torah of G-d Himself.[9] For Mosheh, the world has become utterly transparent, lacking any significance with which to obscure his prophetic encounter with G-d. It is on this level that "he found the Holy One Blessed be He sitting and tying crowns to the letters." However, the very ethereality of this relationship with Torah confers a set of limitations of its own. Mosheh's perception of Torah is primarily on the level of the *kelal*, the general principle,[60] because inordinate focus on the particular details of terrestrial application of Torah is predicated upon an integral linkage to the earthly domain of that application. Thus, Mosheh — relating to the heavenly Torah of G-d — cannot accord this world sufficient significance for the crowns to be at all relevant to it. On his level — at which the world of man is itself reduced to inconsequential dust beneath Mosheh's feet — he regards the crowns as thoroughly inaccessible to man and inappropriate to an earthly Torah: "*Master of the universe! Who is detaining You [from presenting what You wrote such that You must yet add to it crowns (Rashi)]?*"

Yet in addition to the Torah of *G-d* that characterizes Mosheh's transcendent connection to Torah, there is another dimension, so to speak — the Torah of *man*:

> Said Rava: Initially, [the Torah] is ascribed to the Holy One Blessed be He, and ultimately it is ascribed *to him* [the student who labored in it (Rashi)]. As it is said, "His desire is in the Torah of *G-d*, and *his* [the student's] Torah he articulates day and night" (Tehillim 1:2).
>
> (*Avodah Zarah* 19a, *Yal.Sh.* Tehillim:614)[84]

Iyyun Ya'akov adds, "It is also possible to differentiate between *Torah shebikethav*, which belongs to the Holy One Blessed be He, as is not the case with *Torah shebe'al-peh*, which was *given to the scholars to innovate in it*" (loc. cit.). Rabbi Akiva, consummate scholar and "the foundation of *Torah shebe'al-peh*" (*Iyyun Ya'akov* on *Menachoth* 29b, quoted above), epitomizes this additional dimension of Torah that is ascribed to "the student who labored in it," a dimension that is indeed distinct from the sublime transcendence of Mosheh.[85]

In contrast to Mosheh, Rabbi Akiva does not receive the Torah by transcending the physical world. His relationship with Torah springs from the very depths of the physical and focuses on the particulars of physical application.[86] Perhaps for this reason, our *aggadah* refers to him by the patronymic "son of Yosef," emphasizing his inauspicious roots.[87] In context, it is these roots that allude to Rabbi Akiva's prodigious greatness and the distinct dimension of Torah that he epitomized. Comments *Iyyun Ya'akov*, "*Through Rabbi Akiva, who was descended from converts, Torah shebe'al-peh* was renewed" (loc. cit.). Nothing about Rabbi Akiva or his Torah in any way denies his corporeal existence. To the contrary, *from even the crowns* — the most ethereal, supernal aspect of Torah — he derives *halachoth*, the most earthly components of *Torah shebe'al-peh*. Moreover, these *halachoth* are described in terms of "mounds and mounds": tangible heaps of *matter*, into which even the crowns can be transmuted through the efforts of Rabbi Akiva.

4. TWO DIMENSIONS OF TORAH

"Turn backward!"

In effect, the juxtaposition of Mosheh Rabbeinu and Rabbi Akiva in our *aggadah* is the juxtaposition of not merely two individuals but two distinct dimensions of Torah. On the one hand, "no *prophet* arose again ... like Mosheh" (Devarim 34:10); on the other hand, "among *scholars* one arose ... Rabbi Akiva" (Midrash cited by *Iyyun Ya'akov*,[63] quoted above). Mosheh "ascended on high," transcending this world of particulars to receive as a gift the Torah of G-d on the level of principles. Rabbi Akiva "son of Yosef," from completely within this world, struggled on the level of particulars to acquire and extend *his* Torah, deriving from even the crowns "mounds and mounds of *halachoth*." The challenge of Mosheh is faithful, passive receipt of the Torah of G-d. The challenge of Rabbi Akiva is faithful, active exposition of the Torah given to men.

In these terms — recognizing the distinction of Rabbi Akiva's approach with respect to that of Mosheh — we readily understand Mosheh's reaction: "*He said before Him, 'Master of the universe! Show him to me.'*" Comments Maharal, "Each and every *tzaddik* has a unique level in reality, and [Mosheh] desired to apprehend [Rabbi Akiva's] level in the reality of the world" (*Chiddushei Aggadoth*, ibid.; *Tifereth Yisra'el*, ch. 63 [p. 190]). It is G-d's response that seems perplexing: "*He said to him, 'Turn backward!'*" Given that Rabbi Akiva lived nearly fifteen hundred years *after* Mosheh, the direction of motion is forward, to the future, not backward! On further reflection, however, we realize that the Talmud is concerned not with reiterating the obvious — that Rabbi Akiva "will be after several generations in the future" — but with emphasizing the themes it is teaching. Mosheh is conducting this dialogue with G-d by having "ascended on high." It is at this level that he asks to be shown Rabbi Akiva. G-d replies that, in order to apprehend the level of Rabbi Akiva, Mosheh must "*turn backward.*" At Mosheh's level of transcendence, the level of Rabbi Akiva — within this world — cannot be seen. Considering what Rabbi Akiva and his approach to Torah represent, it is only by turning backward, *to this world*, that Mosheh may be shown him.[88]

Our *aggadah* specifies further the relationship of Mosheh Rabbeinu with Rabbi Akiva — with numerical precision: "*He went and sat at the end of* eight (alt. v.: eighteen) *rows.*" Clearly, the Talmud is not concerned here with merely detailing the seating arrangement in Rabbi Akiva's study hall. With the conviction that the words of Chazal are to be taken seriously, we recognize that these numbers were not recorded incidentally; if we are to understand properly the relationship of Mosheh Rabbeinu with Rabbi Akiva, we are obliged to elucidate what they signify. Unfortunately, we are confronted here with a textual dilemma, since the Talmud, as recorded, presents us with two conflicting versions: "*eight* rows"[89] or "*eighteen* rows."[90] Inasmuch as we are unable to authenticate one version, we shall attempt to explicate both.

The number eight occurs in the Torah most obviously in reference to circumcision on the *eighth* day after birth[91] and Shemini Atzereth on the *eighth* day of Sukkoth.[92] We note also that the *kohen gadol* (high priest) would serve in the Beith Ha-Mikdash wearing *eight* vestments.[93] Significantly, Chanukkah was established as an *eight*-day holiday.[94] On a more cryptic note, the Talmud observes that there is reference in Tehillim to "the *eight*-stringed harp" (ibid. 6:1 and 12:1) and deduces, "The harp of the Temple had seven strings ... *and of the era of the Mashiach, eight ...* [and] of the world to come, ten" (*Arachin* 13b, Tos. *Arachin* 2:4).[95] In this context, Maharal — noting in addition the Talmud's conclusion that "after the seventh [year ends], the son of David comes" (*Megillah* 17b, *Sanhedrin* 97a) — comments, "Only the number that is after seven is appropriate for Mashiach ... because the level of the Mashiach is beyond this world, and this world is founded on seven.... For the whole concept of the Mashiach is on a divine level *that transcends nature*" (*Netzach Yisra'el*, ch. 32 [p. 148]).

Maharal elaborates elsewhere on the more general significance of the number eight as representative of that which transcends nature, particularly as it relates to the *eighth* day of circumcision, the *eight* days of Chanukkah, the *eight* vestments of the *kohen gadol*, and the overall supernatural dimension of Torah:

> The commandments of the Torah are on a greater and higher level than nature.[96] ... Thus, from the beginning of Mizmor [19, "The *heavens* relate the glory of the L-rd" (Tehillim 19:2),] until "The *Torah* of G-d is perfect" (ibid. 19:8), [there are] seven verses[97] ... because the natural order was created in the seven days of Creation, *whereas the Torah is beyond nature, and it is the eighth level*. For this reason, Mizmor [119] — which is founded on the Torah — comprises an octuple alphabetical acrostic,[98] because the Torah is the eighth level, which is beyond nature.... Similarly, *anything that is beyond nature and rectifies what is deficient in nature is after seven*.... Therefore, circumcision, which perfects man, was given on the eighth day,[99] because all perfection of man is beyond nature.
>
> (*Tifereth Yisra'el*, ch. 2 [pp. 10-11])

> Thus, [on Chanukkah] they kindled [the *menorah*] for eight days, *because that which is supremely holy is after seven, and this is the eighth*.[100] ... The natural order is subsumed under the number seven, since in seven days this natural world was created. *Therefore what is metaphysical is subsumed under the number eight*. Thus, circumcision, which is beyond nature — since the nature of man is to be born uncircumcised — ... is on the eighth day.... The Torah also was given after seven, for it is written, "Seven weeks count for yourself" etc. (Devarim

16:9), and after seven weeks, on the fiftieth day,[101] the Torah was given.... The Torah — which is light — is the eighth [level], and from there came the miracle of the eight lights of Chanukkah....

(Ner Mitzvah [p. 23])

The esoteric allusions here notwithstanding, we may conclude that — while a more extensive discussion of the symbolism in the number eight is beyond the scope of our discussion[102] — *"the number eight is completely beyond nature"* (*Chiddushei Aggadoth* on *Nedarim* 31b, ד"ה גדולה המילה שדוחה את השבת; *Ner Mitzvah* [p. 28]). Similarly, R. S.R. Hirsch — commenting on circumcision being associated with the eighth day — observes, in more concrete terms, that "the number eight is found as a symbol ... [of] freedom from those constraints imposed upon man by sensuality and the amenities of human society" (com. on Tehillim 6:1).[103] R. E. Dessler summarizes, "The concept of eight represents the spiritual level that cannot be perceived down below. This level is completely beyond our world" (*Michtav MeEliyyahu*, II, 115).

Returning to our *aggadah*, we can readily understand why the relationship between Mosheh Rabbeinu and Rabbi Akiva is described as a separation of *"eight* rows." Even after Mosheh heeds G-d's instruction to "turn backward," a gap of unbridgeable transcendence continues to interpose between him and "Akiva son of Yosef." Rabbi Akiva represents human scholarship that springs utterly from the depths of the physical world, a level at which even ethereal crowns are transformed into earthly "mounds and mounds of *halachoth*." By contrast, "Mosheh ascended on high" to receive the Torah of G-d by transcending this world at an unparalleled level of prophecy.[16,17] Recognizing their respective roles, it is certainly apropos that the number eight, signifying transcendence, characterizes their "relationship." Rabbi Akiva functions within nature; Mosheh — at eight removes from him — is indeed "completely beyond nature." Even after turning backward, he remains irrevocably distinct from Rabbi Akiva.

The alternate version of the text, however, specifies the separation between Mosheh and Rabbi Akiva as *"eighteen* rows." While the symbolic significance of the number eighteen is less obvious than that of the number eight, we nevertheless note its appearance in the Midrash: "Said R. Shimon b. Yochai: The celestial

Beith HaMikdash transcends the terrestrial Beith HaMikdash by only *eighteen mils*" (*BeR.R.* 69:7, *Yal.Sh.* BeReshith:120). Eighteen appears in various other contexts in the Bible, the Talmud, and the Midrash, most notably as the number of blessings (originally) in "*Shemoneh Esreh*," the number of references to G-d in "*Keri'ath Shema*" and in Mizmor 29, the number of references to "as G-d commanded" in the construction of the sanctuary (Shemoth 39-40), and the number of collective references to the three patriarchs in the Torah.[104] Maharal comments that "one finds G-d associated with the number eighteen" (*Chiddushei Aggadoth* on *Sanhedrin* 21a, 'ד"ה לא ירבה לו נשים וכו). Altogether, we observe the number eighteen repeatedly in the context of that which is divine or transcendent.[105]

We can clearly recognize this symbolism in our *aggadah*. Mosheh Rabbeinu represents the transcendent, celestial Beith HaMikdash, existing on a divine level; at eighteen removes, Rabbi Akiva represents the earthly, terrestrial Beith HaMikdash at the level of man. Their juxtaposition highlights the gap that separates them. Concludes Maharal, "[Mosheh] had no connection and association with Rabbi Akiva, and therefore sat at the end of eighteen rows" (*Chiddushei Aggadoth*, ibid.).

In the context of our *aggadah*, Mosheh's transcendence is evidently to his disadvantage: "He went and sat at the end of eight (*alt. v.*: eighteen) rows and *did not understand what they were saying*." Transcendence, it appears, is an insurmountable obstacle to comprehending Rabbi Akiva and his exposition of "mounds and mounds of *halachoth*."[106] Even after Mosheh turns backward, Rabbi Akiva's level — essentially distinct from Mosheh's ascension — remains for him an enigma.

"A *Halachah* of Mosheh from Sinai"

We readily appreciate Mosheh's reaction to his inability to grasp Rabbi Akiva's Torah: "*His strength failed.*" Similar reactions have doubtlessly been elicited in each of us by lectures that were beyond our ken. What seems, however, inconceivable is the basis of Mosheh's restoration: "When they reached a certain matter [in need of explanation (Rashi)] — [and R. Akiva's] students said to him, 'Rabbi! Whence do you [derive this]?' — [and] *he said to them,*

'[It is] a halachah *of Mosheh from Sinai,'* [Mosheh's (Rashi)] mind became settled." Can we imagine that, after not even apprehending the content of a lecture, our mind would become settled by mention of our name at its conclusion? Yet Rashi's explanation here appears only to compound our consternation: "Mosheh's mind became settled, *since [Rabbi Akiva] is saying [Torah] in his name,* even though [Mosheh] has not yet received it." Such behavior sounds like the pinnacle of egoism and conceit! Nevertheless, the man here described as reacting thus is one characterized by the Torah as the most self-effacing man in the world: "The man Mosheh was exceedingly humble, more so than all the people upon the face of the earth" (BeMidbar 12:3). Why, then, does Mosheh's mind become settled?

To understand properly Mosheh's restoration, we should re-examine his initial reaction to Rabbi Akiva's study hall. While incomprehension of Rabbi Akiva's discourse may be sufficient grounds for Mosheh's strength failing, another more trenchant factor appears significant in suggesting a deeper explanation of this response: No experience can be more jarring than one that negates a person's very essence, challenging the gestalt toward which one's every action and fiber has been dedicated. As we have seen, Mosheh Rabbeinu and Rabbi Akiva are archetypes — as pre-eminent prophet and pre-eminent scholar — of the two approaches to Torah that they respectively epitomize. Mosheh "ascended on high" to transcend this world and receive as a gift the Torah of G-d. Rabbi Akiva "son of Yosef" struggled within this world to acquire and extend *his* Torah. While the challenge of Rabbi Akiva was faithfully and *actively* to *expound* the Torah given to men, the challenge of Mosheh was faithfully and *passively* to *receive* the Torah of G-d. Our *aggadah* portrays Mosheh engaged in the quintessential fulfillment of his challenge. It is in the midst of this ultimate act of passive receipt that Mosheh is shown the fundamentally distinct level of Rabbi Akiva. And he is thereby confronted with the harrowing realization that Rabbi Akiva, through what is ostensibly an entirely different approach to Torah, has scaled heights that Mosheh — in spite of his ascension — cannot even understand, much less equal. *"His strength failed"*; for Mosheh, the supremely passive receiver, no experience could be more devastating.

In this light, we can reassess why "Mosheh's mind became settled." When in reply to his students' query — "Whence do you [derive this]?" — Rabbi Akiva invokes "a *halachah* of Mosheh from Sinai," its significance to Mosheh lies obviously not in the reference to his name. What Rabbi Akiva is affirming in his response is the role of Mosheh's passive receipt at Sinai as the indispensable foundation of Rabbi Akiva's active expositions. In particular, we note the specific connotation of "a *halachah* of Mosheh from Sinai," as explained by Rambam: " 'A *halachah* of Mosheh from Sinai' refers solely to something for which there is no allusion in Scripture ... and that *cannot be derived through any manner of reasoning*" (*Introduction to the Mishnah*, ch. 4). Similarly, Maharal avers that "those perceptions *cannot be attained by man except through G-d in prophecy*. And therefore this perception, which is 'a *halachah* of Mosheh from Sinai,' belonged specifically to Mosheh, who was the prophet of G-d and whose perception was through prophecy" (*Chiddushei Aggadoth*, ibid.; *Tifereth Yisra'el*, ch. 63 [p. 191]). It represents the elementary, irreducible, divine premise upon which human reason and scholarship operate.

Thus, Rabbi Akiva's approach to Torah neither denies nor supersedes that of Mosheh Rabbeinu; to the contrary, it is predicated upon it. If Mosheh's strength failed because he initially perceived in Rabbi Akiva's approach the negation of his essence, these words spoken by Rabbi Akiva are the ultimate reassurance: Rabbi Akiva's approach necessarily stands upon the shoulders of Mosheh's.[107] Rashi emphasizes, "Mosheh's mind became settled, since [Rabbi Akiva] is saying [Torah] in his name, *even though [Mosheh] has not yet received it.*" Especially at this juncture — as Mosheh readies himself for his most intensely *passive* moment as the consummate *receiver* of the Torah of G-d — nothing could be more settling than the recognition that both approaches to Torah derive from this initial act of supreme passivity: "a *halachah* of Mosheh from Sinai."

"Thus has the thought risen before Me."

In spite of this reassurance, Mosheh returns to G-d and humbly protests, "*Master of the universe! You have a man like this, and You give the Torah through me?*" While recognizing with renewed impact the central importance of his passive, prophetic receipt, Mosheh is nevertheless awed by the incomparable achievements of Rabbi Akiva's active, scholarly expositions. Why, he argues, must this development of Torah take place in two discrete stages (which are separated by nearly fifteen hundred years)? Since he cannot understand Rabbi Akiva's scholarship, Mosheh concludes that it is he who is superfluous. G-d should grant Mosheh's unique prophetic capacity to Rabbi Akiva — who would then singly embody both dimensions of Torah — and fuse both stages into one.[108]

Although Mosheh's contention seems reasonable, G-d's reply again does not: *"Be still! Thus has the thought risen before Me."* The rebuke evokes the image of an impatient teacher curtly retorting to a student's plea — certainly not the Talmud's intent in its depiction of G-d! Especially, G-d's expression, "Thus has the thought risen before Me," smacks of arbitrary authoritarianism. And were it the utterance of a human being — whose thoughts *are* inherently knowable — its implication would indeed be a dogmatic refusal to share one's thoughts and to respond rationally to a sincere proposal. Regarding the "thought" of G-d, however, we hear the echo of His admonition: *"For My thoughts are not your thoughts, neither are your ways My ways, says G-d. For as the heavens are elevated from the earth, so are My ways elevated from your ways and My thoughts from your thoughts"* (Yeshayahu 55:8-9). Given the ontological distinction between man's level and G-d's, the thought of G-d is *inherently unknowable,*[109] and thus, in principle, it cannot be communicated to any man. A bounded, finite creation can never comprehend its boundless, infinite Creator.

Likewise, G-d adjures Mosheh to "be still," obviously not in order to shut him up. But inasmuch as the divine thought is by definition beyond man's ken, Mosheh cannot understand it. Furthermore, in light of the limitations that intrinsically constrain the human condition, G-d counsels Mosheh to "be still," for under such circumstances the more said — the more he asserts himself as a person — the less understood. Conversely, silence is prescribed as the means to minimize human subjectivity and maximize man's ability at least to apprehend the thought of G-d. To grasp the divine thought is impossible; even to glimpse it demands silence.

It would be presumptuous, then, to attempt to explicate why the thought of G-d mandates the existence — and respective roles — of both Mosheh Rabbeinu and Rabbi Akiva. Ultimately, subsumed within this inscrutable thought are the structure and order of the world itself: "The *initial thought* [of G-d] is the final act [of Creation]" (*HaKozari* 3:73).[110] Man, from within this world, cannot grasp its basis. Yet, notes Maharal, our *aggadah* implies that "the structure of reality ordered by G-d *in His thought* and His wisdom mandates that the Torah be given not through Rabbi Akiva but through Mosheh" (*Chiddushei Aggadoth*, ibid.; *Tifereth Yisra'el*, ch. 63 [p. 191]). Given this world order, we may then at least venture to elucidate how the reality of two distinct dimensions of Torah, embodied by Mosheh and Rabbi Akiva, is consistent with it.

As discussed above, Torah is both the fundamental basis upon which the world is predicated and the final goal toward which the world is directed. As the primeval Torah of black on white fire, it is the blueprint of the universe, predating Creation;[20] everything that follows is based upon it and constitutes means to its physical realization. As the earthly Torah of ink on parchment, it presupposes the world's existence; its role is to guide us toward proper functioning in the world and proper utilization of all its contents. Without the transcendent Torah, the world could not have been created,[111] and without the terrestrial Torah, it could not continue to exist.

Thus — regarding the Torah given to this world from Sinai — the Midrash asserts, "Were it not for the Torah, the world would have already reverted to formless void" (*Dev.R.* 8:5), and "once [Yisra'el] said [at Sinai], 'We shall do and heed [all that G-d has spoken]' (*Shemoth* 24:7), the world became firmly established" (*Mid. Tehillim* 75:1).[112] Likewise, the Talmud concludes, "The Holy One Blessed be He made a condition with the work of Creation, stipulating, 'If Yisra'el accepts the Torah, you [continue to] exist, and if not, I shall return you to formless void' " (*Shabbath* 88a, *Avodah Zarah* 3a and 5a).[113] The implication here is certainly not that the continued existence of the world depends on divine caprice, but that the existence of the world from its inception could be justified only as raw materials to be elevated through Torah. A world that is left bereft of Torah would remain substance without form: hollow contents with no abiding context to order and uplift them. Similarly, Chazal characterize the first two millennia of this world's history — after Creation but prior to the millennia of Torah — as "two millennia of formless void" (*Sanhedrin* 97a, *Avodah Zarah* 9a),[114] *even though superficially the contents of the world were as ordered as they are today*, because "since Torah was not yet given, the world was *as if* formless" (Rashi on *Sanhedrin* ibid., ד"ה ב' אלפים היה תהו). Order versus formlessness is gauged not in terms of physical technicalities but in terms of an internal meaning that binds all the components together. Without Torah, the world would have never really left the state of formlessness.

For Torah to accomplish its mission in the world, two separate phases are critical. First, Torah's pre-eminent status as the guide of the world must be established. Otherwise, it will descend as but part of the world's substance, and not as the form that orders all substance. From the outset, its relationship with the world must be one of domination, for it is the redeeming message of Torah that must control the world, lest the world instead control and adulterate Torah's message. To effect this stage, the world must *passively receive* the Torah, accepting upon itself the Torah as its authority. Obviously, it is Mosheh — as unparalleled prophet who "ascended on high" and transcended this world — who mediates this phase.[115] But such a relationship with Torah is insufficient. To realize the ultimate goal of Torah in this world, it is imperative in addition to infuse Torah into every fiber of life. Otherwise, Torah's mastery of the world may remain of theoretical, but not practical, significance. Consequently, it is no less crucial to weave Torah into the fabric of the world, so that in principle nothing in the world may remain divorced from the sphere of Torah. To achieve this stage, Torah must be *actively merged* with every aspect of life, so that the aura of Torah may illuminate all of life itself. Rabbi Akiva "son of Yosef" — as unparalleled scholar who struggled within this ·world to expound heaps of earthly *halachoth* from even crowns — is designated to orchestrate this phase. If either stage is jeopardized, the object of the world — and of Torah — will remain unattainable.[116]

This, then, is perhaps G-d's reply to Mosheh. Every sincere student of Torah must *first* accept the Torah as conclusive guide and *then* grapple with it in a quest for a reasoned understanding of Torah as it relates to every aspect of life. Given the world as G-d created it, both phases are indispensable. Likewise, the nation of Yisra'el at Sinai declared *first*, "We shall *do*" (Shemoth 24:7), and only *subsequently*, "[we shall] *heed*" (ibid.). And thus the world requires *first* Mosheh, as a discrete stage in forging a relationship — through passive receipt — between it and the Torah, and only *afterward* Rabbi Akiva, to reinforce that bond — through active struggle — at every level in life. To be effective, each phase must be distinct; the "thought" of G-d mandates that the prophetic passivity of Mosheh Rabbeinu and the scholarly activity of Rabbi Akiva remain separate, to insure the integrity of each phase and its complete fruition. It is essential to have the first stage mediated by Mosheh, for whom the world of man is reduced to inconsequential dust beneath his feet, to guarantee initially the unqualified mastery of this world by Torah. It is no less essential to have the second stage mediated by Rabbi Akiva, who springs from the depths of the physical world, to guarantee ultimately the unqualified infusion of Torah into everything. Specifically the synthesis of both is the basis of the Torah's relationship with the world.[117]

5. THE REWARD OF RABBI AKIVA

"Show Me His Reward"

Mosheh, denied an explanation of G-d's thought and unable to understand Rabbi Akiva's discourse, nevertheless petitions G-d, "*Master of the universe! You have shown me his Torah; show me his reward.*" Obviously, this request — like Mosheh's previous request to be shown Rabbi Akiva — does not express mere intellectual curiosity. Mosheh recognizes that reward, like punishment, is "measure for measure"[118] and reflects, as a direct consequence, its recipient's true level.[119] Thus, by beseeching G-d to be shown Rabbi Akiva's reward, Mosheh attempts once more "to apprehend [Rabbi Akiva's] level in the reality of the world" (*Chiddushei Aggadoth* [Maharal], ibid.; *Tifereth Yisra'el*, ch. 63 [p. 190]): a level that has thus far eluded him.

Although we might have imagined that the reward dictated by absolute divine justice would be if anything more comprehensible when viewed from Mosheh's transcendent perspective,

G-d's response to Mosheh is again to *"turn backward."* Apparently, nothing about Rabbi Akiva — including his reward — can be properly understood in terms of Mosheh's ascension.[120] Rabbi Akiva's reward can be apprehended only from within the context of this world.

Indeed, when Mosheh complies, the grisly scene to which he is subjected is one that certainly would be incongruous with heavenly transcendence: *"He turned backward [and] saw that they were weighing [Rabbi Akiva's] flesh in the meat market [as it says in* Berachoth *(61b) that they flayed his flesh with iron combs* (Rashi)*]."* We cannot help wondering in horror: *This* is Rabbi Akiva's *reward?*

"Weighing His Flesh in the Meat Market"

Our *aggadah's* ghastly conclusion appears incomprehensible. We might have anticipated that Mosheh would be shown Rabbi Akiva's share in Gan Eden or in the world to come.[121] Even within the context of this world, is there no component of Rabbi Akiva's illustrious life that could more appropriately be considered his reward? Various aspects of Rabbi Akiva's biography certainly seem to be far more likely candidates for displaying his just deserts. On the most tangible level, he acquired vast wealth[122] and enjoyed extraordinary longevity.[123] On a more sublime level, certainly his accomplishments in the sphere of Torah scholarship were no mean reward. After twenty-four years of study, he returned home surrounded by twenty-four *thousand* students and acclaimed by all as an eminent scholar.[124] As recounted above, he ultimately rose to such prominence that his colleagues lauded him as one of the "fathers of the world" (*Yer. Shekalim* 3:1 [10b], *Yer. Rosh HaShanah* 1:1 [5a]), the very embodiment of the "wellsprings of wisdom" (*Sotah* 49b, *Yer. Sotah* 9:16 [45b]), without whom the Torah itself "would have been forgotten from Yisra'el" (*Sifrei* on Devarim 11:22).[83] Few scholars other than he are described as having mastered the entire Torah;[81] few have been as historically significant in the determination of Halachah.[82] Recall that specifically Rabbi Akiva became "the foundation of *Torah shebe'al-peh*" (*Iyyun Ya'akov* on *Menachoth* 29b, quoted above), and the Midrash affirms that "matters that were not revealed to

Mosheh were revealed to Rabbi Akiva and his peers" (*BeM.R.* 19:6, *Tan. Chukkath*:8). Is this not Rabbi Akiva's incomparable reward?

Evidently, Chazal regard all of the above as paltry compared with the supreme "reward" of "weighing [Rabbi Akiva's] flesh in the meat market." Clearly, in order to grasp our *aggadah*'s concluding message, we must understand how Rabbi Akiva's gruesome death heralds his unparalleled reward. We note that the Talmud, in confronting Rabbi Akiva's reward, blatantly ignores such transcendent issues as his share in Gan Eden or in the world to come. Inescapably, Chazal force us to resolve the fundamental question here: What is really meant by an individual's *supreme reward in this world*?

Were we asked to describe Mosheh Rabbeinu's reward *in this world*, we would probably resort to R. Yehudah HaLevi's portrayal of him as "a person who goes through fire but is not burnt, who endures without food but does not hunger, whose face radiates light that the eye cannot bear to see, and who becomes neither ill nor infirm" (*HaKozari* 1:41). Restated, the supreme reward possible in this world is *victory* over this world itself. The nature of Mosheh's victory is transcendence, for it is he who "ascended on high"; his victory over this world is his liberation from the physical limitations imposed by it. Thus, concludes Maharal, "Mosheh had dominion over this world" (*Chiddushei Aggadoth*, ibid.; *Tifereth Yisra'el*, ch. 63 [p. 190]).[125] Indeed, he asks rhetorically, "How could Mosheh not be principal in this world, inasmuch as he completed the world through the Torah that was given through him?" (ibid.).[126] Even in death — generally, the ultimate submission to the physical — Mosheh continues to defy normal constraints. Even as elementary a limitation as a well-defined physical location for his grave is lacking;[127] the Mishnah classifies Mosheh's grave itself among the *meta*physical creations of G-d.[128] In death as in life, Mosheh's victory over this world remains unabated.

Given that the supreme reward possible in this world is victory over this world itself, it is our contention that Rabbi Akiva was granted such reward as well, in his life and — even more so — in his death, in a victory of a very different nature, however, from that of Mosheh. The Talmud relates:

R. Akiva says: "*With all your soul*" (Devarim 6:5) [means] even if He takes your soul.

The Rabbis taught: Once, the wicked government [Rome] decreed that Yisra'el should not engage in [study of] the Torah.... [Nevertheless,] Rabbi Akiva would assemble public assemblies and engage in [study of] the Torah.... Not many days passed before they caught Rabbi Akiva and bound him in prison.... When they brought Rabbi Akiva out for execution, it was the time for the recitation of "*Shema.*" And they were flaying his flesh with iron combs, and he was accepting upon himself the yoke of the kingdom of heaven [through the recitation of "*Shema*"].

His students said to him, "Our master! *This far?*" ...

(Berachoth 61b)

I submit that we understand the question of Rabbi Akiva's students as painfully literal: In the midst of such inhumanly excruciating agony, how can you possibly concentrate on "the yoke of the kingdom of heaven"? Yet Rabbi Akiva's reply is *not* that he does so *in spite* of the circumstances or even *irrespective* of them:

... He responded to them, "All my life, I agonized over this verse: '*With all your soul*' [meaning] *even if He takes your soul.* I said, 'When will [the opportunity] come into my hands that I might fulfill this?' And now that [the opportunity] *has* come into my hands, shall I not fulfill it?"

He prolonged "[G-d is] *One*" until his soul departed on "*One.*"

A divine echo came forth, saying, "Happy are you, Rabbi Akiva, that your soul departed on '*One.*'"

(ibid.)

"*G-d is One*" is not merely Rabbi Akiva's death rattle; it is the culmination of his entire life. In affirming G-d's oneness, we emphasize the underlying unity of everything in the world, inextricably bound up with everything else as myriad creations of one Creator. Essentially, it is the recognition that everything in the world is a manifestation of G-d.[129] From his earthly roots, Rabbi Akiva emerged as the supreme unifier of this world. By infusing spirituality into every fiber of life, he left nothing in the physical world divorced from its spiritual source and nothing in the spiritual realm bereft of material application. It was Rabbi Akiva who expounded from inaccessible crowns of the transcendent Torah tangible heaps of terrestrial *halachoth*. His entire life is a testimonial to the oneness of G-d and the intrinsic unity of His Creation.

Herein lies Rabbi Akiva's victory over this world. Not only has he succeeded in transforming the totality of his life into fulfill-ment of his mission: Even his death — and such a death! — he has transformed as well. It is not *in spite* of his anguish that he affirms G-d's oneness in his dying gasps; it is *because* of it: to fulfill the precept that he himself expounded, to love G-d " 'with all your soul' [meaning] even if He takes your soul."[130] He has transformed even his suffering into an opportunity to reiterate with resounding might his conclusive victory over both tortures and torturers. Not only his life and death but even the inhuman torments of his final moments Rabbi Akiva uplifted to be an affirmation of the oneness of G-d and of the abiding value — as means to that oneness — of everything in the world He gave us. Can there be any more potent expression of victory over this world?

Evidently, the answer must be "yes," because our *aggadah* nevertheless refrains from depicting Rabbi Akiva's death and instead focuses on a lurid meat market scene where "they were weighing the flesh" of his dead body. Considering that the death scene itself was so appalling, one wonders why the Talmud insists on presenting the even more grotesque spectacle of the meat market. Specifically this, Chazal inform us, is Rabbi Akiva's supreme reward.

We conclude that Rabbi Akiva's victory over this world was so complete that it was expressed not only in his life and, in addition, in his death and the suffering that preceded it. So pervasive was his victory that it was manifest even in his inani-mate body. Even his flayed flesh, being weighed by the pound — the ultimate expression of separation and disunity — still testified to the unifying mission of its former owner. Even the dead body, bereft of the G-dly soul that had animated it, was still permeated by the spirit of Rabbi Akiva. It was not merely anon-ymous "flesh" that the Romans were weighing in the meat market; it was "*his* flesh." Even after murdering his body, the Roman empire remained utterly impotent against Rabbi Akiva's invincible spirit. No victory over this world could be more complete. Beaming forth from his mutilated body is indeed Rabbi Akiva's supreme reward in this world: a reward no less significant than that of Mosheh — except that it consumed its own recipient.

"This Is Its Reward": The Thought of G-d — Again

In spite of the magnitude of the reward manifest in Rabbi Akiva's fate, Mosheh Rabbeinu is overcome by the brutal cruelty of the fate itself. The faithful shepherd of Yisra'el gasps in protest, *"Master of the universe! This is Torah, and this is its reward?"* Only a heart of stone could respond differently to so dreadful a scene. Yet G-d replies, again, *"Be still! Thus has the thought risen before Me."* And with these terrifying words, echoing verbatim G-d's response to Mosheh's previous protest, our *aggadah* concludes. We are left, staring agape, struggling to grasp the Talmud's awesome message.

In confronting Rabbi Akiva's torturous end, the "thought risen" before G-d evokes, by association, the world's beginning, when "initially *the thought rose* to create it through *middath haddin* [the attribute of strict justice]" (Rashi on BeReshith 1:1, ד"ה ברא א־לקים).[131] *Nachalath Ya'akov* adds that this initial "thought" is still operative in judgment of the world, at least in principle (com. on Rashi ibid.).[132] In particular, avers *Be'er Mayim Chayyim*, the completely just "are still judged according to strict justice, as the thought that rose in the Creator of the world" (com. on Rashi ibid.).[133] It is tempting to explain Rabbi Akiva's extraordinary suffering as resulting from his exceptional righteousness — and his consequent subjection to the uncompromising assessment of *middath haddin*. The "thought" that rose before G-d would then refer to the original "thought" that rose in favor of basing the entire world on *middath haddin*.[134] Yet this explanation does not by itself resolve why *middath haddin* should dictate such a fate for Rabbi Akiva.

We recall, however, our conclusions regarding G-d's identical reply to Mosheh's previous protest: The inscrutable "thought" of G-d is the basis of the structure and order of the world itself. Regarding the divine thought that dictated Creation through *middath haddin*, Maharal comments, "This matter is the principal

secret of the *order* of the universe" (*Gur Aryeh* on Rashi ibid.).
Similarly, he notes that Rabbi Akiva's fate is "mandated by the
order established by G-d" (*Chiddushei Aggadoth* on *Menachoth* loc.
cit.; *Tifereth Yisra'el*, ch. 63 [p. 191]). We therefore quietly venture
— again — not to understand G-d's thought, but at least to
apprehend why this world order dictates Rabbi Akiva's macabre
"reward."

Ultimately, G-d's response to Mosheh must be a declarative
echo of his protest: Emphatically, "this *is* Torah, and this *is* its
reward." Mosheh was right in assuming an association between
the unique level of Rabbi Akiva's scholarship and his singular
reward. But if the supreme reward possible *in* this world is
victory *over* this world, it must be a victory with respect to the
challenge with which one was presented by life: "*According to the
suffering is the reward*" (*Avoth* 5:23, *T.DeV.Eli.Z.* 17). Since Mosheh
"ascended on high," passively receiving as a gift the Torah of G-d,
the nature of his victory is transcendence: liberation from the
physical constraints normally imposed by the world. By contrast,
the greatness of Rabbi Akiva lay in his active struggle with and
within this world to acquire and expound the Torah given to
men. Painfully, his victory over this world is likewise one of
struggle.

If the divine "thought" mandates the existence of a physical
world that needs to be pervaded by Torah and bestows upon man
the challenge to accomplish that pervasion, then the Torah of
Rabbi Akiva is indispensable, and his consequent "reward" is
inescapable. Without Rabbi Akiva and the scholarship that he
embodied, the Torah would have remained largely an abstrac-
tion, and the world would have largely remained devoid of
meaning. But to infuse Torah into an intractable world requires
descending into the trenches, illuminating the world by force if
necessary — even feeding the flames if necessary with one's own
body and soul. Rabbi Akiva's victory is the inevitable product of
this Torah of struggle, a victory in which life and death and a
divine echo — and even flayed flesh being weighed in the meat
market — all testify in resounding unison: "G-d is One!"[135]

6. CONCLUSION:
THE CHALLENGE OF THE TORAH AND THE WORLD

Our *aggadah*'s message for us is clear. For us to behold the singular greatness of Rabbi Akiva, we must also be prepared to bear witness to his grisly reward. A world spared his martyrdom would necessarily be deprived of his unique struggle for scholarship as well, for the one is inextricably bound up with the other. While the world must first be conquered by the principles of Torah as passively received by Mosheh Rabbeinu, such conquest is ultimately insufficient to realize either the goal of Torah or the goal of Creation. G-d cannot, so to speak, give the Torah without its crowns. Specifically the victory of Rabbi Akiva and of all the earthly *halachoth* he derives from these transcendent crowns is — while predicated upon the distinct victory of Mosheh — decisive. Because of it, the affirmation of G-d's oneness resonates throughout the world forever. "Through Rabbi Akiva, who was descended from converts, *Torah shebe'al-peh* was renewed" (*Iyyun Ya'akov* on *Menachoth* 29b). It is through his active scholarship, springing from the depths of the physical and unfathomably distant from Mosheh's ascension, that the world may be permeated with Torah.

For ourselves, obviously the challenge of Mosheh — functioning at a level of unparalleled prophecy — is unattainable. But the challenge of Rabbi Akiva — struggling in this world to extend the Torah of man — must be our own. While the Romans and their executioners faded long ago into twilight, the legacy of Rabbi Akiva, *who truly vanquished them*, lives on within us. As we grapple with his words and those of his peers, it is their innovative light that illuminates our darkness. " '*The people who are going in darkness have seen great light*' (Yeshayahu 9:1) — These are the masters of Talmud, who have seen great light" (*Tan. Noach*:3).[72] Through this revelation, emerging from the depths of concealment, "*matters that were not revealed to Mosheh were revealed to Rabbi Akiva and his peers*" (*BeM.R.* 19:6, *Tan. Chukkath*:8).

On an individual level, we too dare not satisfy ourselves with only the receipt of the Torah embodied by Mosheh Rabbeinu. While our relationship with Torah must originate in passive acceptance, it must terminate in struggle. The Midrash comments on the assertion of King Shelomoh, paragon of wisdom: " '*Even* (אף) my wisdom remained with me' (Koheleth 2:9) — Wisdom that I learned with *exertion* (אף) remained with me" (*Yal.Sh.* Koheleth:968).[136] Even more emphatically, the Talmud states, "Words of Torah endure only in he who *kills himself* over it" (*Berachoth* 63b).[137] True Torah without the struggle of innovation is a contradiction in terms: "It is *inconceivable* for a house of study to be without scholarly innovation" (*Chagigah* 3a).[138] It is our responsibility to execute the transition epitomized by Rabbi Akiva, champion of scholarship: "Initially, [the Torah] is ascribed to the Holy One Blessed be He, and ultimately it is ascribed *to him* [the student *who labored in it* (Rashi)]" (*Avodah Zarah* 19a, *Yal.Sh.* Tehillim:614).[84] While the stakes may not be as high, the essential challenge of Rabbi Akiva is ours as well.

NOTES

1. This perspective is emphasized in all classic commentaries on the Midrash and Aggadah. See, for example, *Introduction to Perek Chelek*, ch. 2, and the introduction to *Moreh HaNevochim* (Rambam); *Ma'amar al Odoth Derashoth Chazal* (R. Avraham b. Rambam); the introduction of Rashba to his commentary on Aggadah (cited in *Ein Ya'akov* on *Berachoth* 6a); the introduction to *Ein Ya'akov*; the introduction to *Chiddushei Aggadoth* (Maharsha); *Kelalei HaMidrash* and *Darchei HaAggadoth VeHaDerashoth* (R. Yeshayahu Horowitz); *Ma'amar al Aggadoth Chazal* (Ramchal); the introduction of *Yefeh To'ar* on *Midrash Rabbah*; the introduction of *Etz Yosef* on *Ein Ya'akov*; and *Mevo HaAggadoth* (Maharatz Chayyoth).

2. See Rambam's exposition of Mishlei 25:11 in the preface to *Moreh HaNevochim*. Rambam's approach is also echoed by Maharal in *Be'er HaGolah*, *Be'er* 5 (p. 88), and by Gra in com. on Mishlei ibid.

3. Mosheh's role in the infusion of Torah into the world is self-evident. Regarding Rabbi Akiva's equally central role, see in particular the sources cited in the text, below.

4. See *Shabbath* 88b and 89a, *Babba Metzi'a* 86b, *Sanhedrin* 111a, *Menachoth* 29b, and *Avoth DeRabbi Nathan* 2:3.

5. See *Sh.R.* 28:1; *BeM.R.* 19:7; *Dev.R.* 2:36; *Tan. Chukkath*:8; *Pes. Rabbathi* 14 (64b) and 20 (96b); *Mid. Tehillim* 7:6; and *Yal.Sh.* BeMidbar:752, 759, Devarim:853, and Tehillim:637, 641, 797.

6. It should be noted that *ascent* also figures prominently in Scripture's depictions of Mosheh's receipt of the Torah. See Shemoth 19:3, 20, 24, 24:1-2, 9, 12-13, 15, 18, and 34:2-4 and Devarim 9:9 and 10:1, 3.

7. See *Mish. Shabbath* 11:3 and *Shabbath* 7b and 96b. See also *Yad Hil. Shabbath* 14:18 and *Orach Chayyim* 345:12.

8. See also Ritva (cited by *HaKothev* on *Sukkah* ibid.) and Maharal (*Nethivoth Olam*, "*Nethiv HaAvodah*," ch. 14 [p. 122]; *Tifereth Yisra'el*, ch. 54 [p. 163]; *Netzach Yisra'el*, ch. 17 [p. 93]), who characterize similarly the realm that is "below ten."

9. Thus, the Talmud emphasizes, "Fifty gates of understanding were created in the world, and *all were given to Mosheh save one*" (*Rosh HaShanah* 21b, *Nedarim* 38a, *Yal.Sh.* Tehillim:641 — see discussion of this assertion in the text, below). See also *Sh.R.* 41:6, *Tan. Thissa*:16, and *Derech HaChayyim* and *Tosefoth Yom Tov* on *Avoth* 1:1 (discussed in the text, below), regarding Mosheh's limited receipt of the Torah. In addition, see nn. 11 and 28, below.

10. *Torah Temimah* notes the inconsistency between the Gemara's conclusion that Mosheh did *not* "ascend on high" and the implication in "several *aggadoth*" that he *did*. No resolution for the inconsistency is provided, however.

11. See Shemoth 33:20, 23 and com., loc. cit. See also *HaKozari* 4:3, בא"ד וכבוד ה'; *Shemonah Perakim*, ch. 7; *Yad Hil. Yesodei HaTorah* 1:10 and *Hil. Teshuvah* 5:5; and *Moreh HaNevochim* 1:21, 37, 54, 64. In addition, see *Megillah* 19b; *Yevamoth* 49b; *Kallah Rabbathi* 3:1; *Sifrei* on BeMidbar 12:8 and on Devarim 34:10; *BeM.R.* 14:22; *Tan. Tzav*:13; *Mid. Tehillim* 17:13 and 103:5; *Pir.DeR.E.* 34 and 46; and *Yal.Sh.* Shemoth:360, 396, VaYikra:431, BeMidbar:739, Devarim:966, Melachim:247, Yeshayahu:407, and Tehillim:671, 688, 857. See also nn. 25 and 109, below.

12. I have translated as "glass" the original "אספקלריא," which is derived — according to *Tifereth Yisra'el* — from "the Greek [i.e., Latin] *specularia*, meaning 'glass' or 'mirror' " (com. on *Kelim* 30:2). The exact connotation of the word as employed by Chazal is, however, subject to broad disagreement. Rach (cited by Ramban on *Yevamoth* ibid.) describes the vision of the other prophets as distorted, "like a person whose vision is weak and perceives the short as high and the one as two." Rashi (loc. cit.) explains seeing through "אספקלריא שאינה מאירה" (here trans. "unclear glass") as "they thought to see and did not see." Neither Rach nor Rashi, however, provides an explicit definition of "אספקלריא." Rambam (on *Kelim* ibid.) appears to describe "אספקלריא" either as a lens or as a curved mirror, made of glass or clear crystal, while R. Ovadyah Bartenurah (loc. cit.) defines "אספקלריא" as a glass mirror. *Tosefoth Yom Tov* (loc. cit.) cites both interpretations, concluding that Rambam would render "אספקלריא" as spectacles. *Tifereth Yisra'el* (loc. cit.) challenges *Tosefoth Yom Tov*'s explanation of Rambam on several counts, concluding that Rambam also defines "אספקלריא" as a glass mirror. *Tifereth Yisra'el* accepts this definition, as does *HaMethurgeman* (on *Ein Ya'akov* on *Yevamoth* ibid.). Others translate "אספקלריא" as window-glass.

13. See also *Tan. Tzav*:13 and *Yal.Sh.* Shemoth:360 and Melachim:247. In addition, see *VaY.R.* 1:14 and Ramban on BeReshith 18:1.

14. It is noteworthy that the Hebrew word for world is "עולם," derived from the

root "עלם" (~ hide — as in "נעלם" ["hidden"]). By implication, the nature of the world is concealment. See also *Pesachim* 50a, *Kiddushin* 71a, *Yal.Sh.* Shemoth:171, and Rashi on Shemoth 3:15. In addition, see *Pachad Yitzchak* (R. Yitzchak Hutner), "*Pesach*," *Reshimah* 4:6 (p. 304).

15. The uniqueness of Mosheh's prophetic capacity is affirmed explicitly in the Torah (see BeMidbar 12:7-8 and Devarim 34:10-12). See also Rambam on *Kelim* 30:2; Ramban on *Yevamoth* 49b (quoted in *Ein Ya'akov*); *Chiddushei Aggadoth* (Maharal), loc. cit.; *Etz Yosef* on *Tan. Tzav*:13; and the sources cited in nn. 13, 16, and 17. In addition, see *Shemonah Perakim*, ch. 7; *Yad Hil. Yesodei HaTorah* 1:10 and 7:6; *Moreh HaNevochim* 1:54, 63 and 2:33-35, 39, 45; Ramban on BeReshith 18:1, on Shemoth 6:2, on BeMidbar 12:6, and on Devarim 34:10; R. Ovadyah Seforno on Devarim 34:10-12; *Derech HaChayyim* on *Avoth* 3:14 (pp. 142-143); *Derech HaShem* 3:5; R. S.R. Hirsch on BeMidbar 12:8; and *HaTorah VeHaMitzvah* (Malbim) on Shemoth 33:11 and on BeMidbar 12:8.

   Belief in the qualitative supremacy of Mosheh's prophecy is one of the fundamental principles of Judaism, as listed among the "Thirteen Foundations" of Jewish faith by Rambam (see *Introduction to Perek Chelek, Yesod* 7). Moreover, the eternal significance of the Torah revealed through Mosheh derives specifically from the unique level of his prophecy. As a result, "no [other] prophet is authorized to innovate anything" to supersede the Torah of Mosheh (see *Shabbath* 104a, *Megillah* 2b, *Yoma* 80a, *Temurah* 16a, *Yer. Megillah* 1:5 [7a], and *Sifra* on VaYikra 27:34). Indeed, because of the essential difference between Mosheh (and the Torah given through him) and all other prophets (and the Nevi'im and Kethuvim given through them), "the Nevi'im and the Kethuvim will be nullified in the future, but the five volumes of Torah will not be nullified in the future" (*Yer. Megillah* ibid.). See also *Introduction to the Mishnah* (Rambam), ch. 2; *Introduction to Perek Chelek, Yesodoth* 8 and 9; *Yad Hil. Yesodei HaTorah* 8:1-3 and 9:1, 4; and *Moreh HaNevochim* 2:39. In addition, see R. Ovadyah Seforno, R. S.R. Hirsch, and *HaTorah VeHaMitzvah* (Malbim) on Devarim 34:10.

16. See *Moreh HaNevochim* 1:10, and Ramban and *HaTorah VeHaMitzvah* (Malbim) on "Mosheh *ascended* to the L-rd" (Shemoth 19:3, cited in *Sukkah* ibid.), who note the connection between Mosheh's ascension and his singular level of prophecy. Malbim emphasizes, "All the prophets who prophesied through 'unclear glass' [see *Yevamoth* 49b and the sources cited in n. 13, above] did not ascend 'to the L-rd' ... for they did not divest themselves completely of the material and earthliness ... except Mosheh, who divested himself of the material completely and ascended from the world and transcended the corporeal. This is implied in what is written: that he 'ascended to the L-rd' " (ibid.).

   This implication may further be suggested in the Talmud's cryptic reference to Mosheh having ascended "below ten." See *Ge'on Ya'akov* and *HaKothev in Ein Ya'akov on Sukkah* ibid., which offer profound insights on this subject.

17. In the context of our *aggadah* (*Menachoth* 29b), Maharal specifies that "to receive the Torah is impossible unless one ascends from the physical to a supernal level. This is what is written: 'When Mosheh ascended on high' " (*Chiddushei Aggadoth*, ibid.; *Tifereth Yisra'el*, ch. 63 [p. 189]).

18. See *Shabbath* 88b, *Pesachim* 54a, *Nedarim* 39b, *Zevachim* 116a, *Avoth DeRabbi Nathan* 31:3, and *Sanhedrin* 91b (and Rashi, ibid., ד"ה משֶׁשֶׁת ימי בראשית). See also nn. 20 and 111, below.

19. See *Sifrei* on Devarim 7:12; *BeR.R.* 1:1, 4, 8 and 8:2; *Sh.R.* 30:9 and 47:4; *VaY.R.* 19:1 and 35:4; *Sh.HaSh.R.* 5:11 (1); *Tan. BeReshith*:1, *VaYeshev*:4, *Naso*:11, and *VaYelech*:2; *Mid. Tehillim* 90:12 and 93:3; *T.DeV.Eli.R.* 31; *Pir.DeR.E.* 3; and *Yal.Sh.* BeReshith:2, 20, Shemoth:368, BeMidbar:743, 752, 764, Yirmeyahu:298, Tehillim:641, 710, Mishlei:942, 943, Iyyov:907, and Shir HaShirim:988. See also nn. 20 and 111, below.

20. Consistently, Chazal list Torah among the "things" that "were created before the world was created." (See *Pesachim* 54a; *Nedarim* 39b; *BeR.R.* 1:4; *Tan. Naso*:11; *Mid. Tehillim* 90:12 and 93:3; *T.DeV.Eli.R.* 31; *Pir.DeR.E.* 3; and *Yal.Sh.* BeReshith:20, Yirmeyahu:298, and Mishlei:942. See also *Sifrei* on Devarim 7:12, *Sh.R.* 30:9, and *Yal.Sh.* BeMidbar:743 and Mishlei:943. In addition, see *HaKozari* 3:73.) While the meaning of "before" — in the absence of time, which was created with the world — is elusive, Chazal further specify how long "before" the world Torah was created: "nine hundred seventy-four generations before the world was created" (*Shabbath* 88b, *Zevachim* 116a, *Avoth DeRabbi Nathan* 31:3, *Yal.Sh.* BeMidbar:752 and Tehillim:641, 710), or "two thousand years" (*BeR.R.* 8:2; *VaY.R.* 19:1; *Sh.HaSh.R.* 5:11 [1]; *Tan. VaYeshev*:4; *Mid. Tehillim* 90:12; *Yal.Sh.* Shemoth:368, Iyyov:907, and Shir HaShirim:988). The deeper significance of these numbers is not relevant to our discussion. That the Torah preceded the world does, however, indicate a causative relationship between them: In describing Creation, the Midrash tells us that "G-d would gaze into the Torah and create the world" (*BeR.R.* 1:1, *Tan. BeReshith*:1, *T.DeV.Eli.R.* 31, *Pir.DeR.E.* 3, *Yal.Sh.* BeReshith:2 and Mishlei:942; see also *BeR.R.* 1:8, *Sh.R.* 47:4, *VaY.R.* 35:4, and *Tan. VaYelech*:2). *See also nn. 18 and 19, above, and n. 111, below.*

21. Of course, the Talmud is not suggesting divine corporeity in describing G-d either as sitting in our *aggadah* or as standing in *Megillah*. As Rashi (on *Megillah* ibid., ד"ה כביכול) notes, "[This is] said with respect to the Holy One Blessed be He as with respect to man in whom [alone] it may be said [literally]." By implication, such anthropomorphisms are employed in order to convey a lesson for man.

22. See also *Yer. Shekalim* 6:1 (23a); *Yer. Sotah* 8:3 (35b); *Dev.R.* 3:12; *Sh.HaSh.R.* 5:11 (6); *Tan. Yithro*:16; and *Yal.Sh.* Shemoth:280, 368, Devarim:951, and Shir HaShirim:990. In addition, see Devarim 33:2 and Yirmeyahu 23:29 and com., loc. cit. See also *Ta'anith* 7a; *Mechilta* on Shemoth 19:18; *Sifrei* on Devarim 33:2; *Sh.R.* 51:7; *Sh.HaSh.R.* 1:10 (2); *Tan. Yithro*:12 and Pekudei:8; *Mid. Tehillim* 16:7, 38:2, and 52:8; and *Yal.Sh.* Yirmeyahu:306.

23. Note also the symbolism of fire in G-d's revelation to Avraham (BeReshith 15:17), to Mosheh (Shemoth 3:2), and to the nation of Yisra'el (e.g., Shemoth 13:21-22, 19:18, 24:17, and 40:38; BeMidbar 9:15-16 and 14:14; and Devarim 1:33, 4:11-12, 15, 33, 36, 5:4, 19, 20-22, 9:10, 15, and 10:4).

24. See also *Moreh HaNevochim* 1:30.

25. Consequently, in this world, "man cannot see Me [i.e., comprehend G-d] and live" (Shemoth 33:20). See also *Shemonah Perakim*, ch. 7; *Yad Hil. Yesodei HaTorah* 1:10 and *Hil. Teshuvah* 5:5; *Moreh HaNevochim* 1:21, 37, 54, 64; and the sources cited in n. 11, above, and n. 109, below.

It is clearly to this inherent limitation in the human condition — implied in the description of G-d as "a consuming fire" (Devarim 4:24) — that the Talmud alludes in commenting on the Torah's mandate to "go after G-d your L-rd" (Devarim 13:5): "Is it then possible for a person to go after the Shechinah? After all, it has already been said, 'For G-d your L-rd is a consuming fire'!" (*Sotah* 14a). It would certainly be ludicrous to imagine that Chazal related to either the mandate to "go after G-d" or the analogy of G-d to "a consuming fire" in physical terms. However, while they obviously posited an allegorical understanding of the mandate to follow G-d, they recognized the same implication in the analogy of G-d to fire. In effect, the Gemara asks, is it possible for a person to follow G-d in any meaningful intellectual quest to comprehend Him? After all, G-d is likened to a consuming fire, and any attempt to grasp the divine intellectually would be as ill-fated as an attempt to grasp fire physically. Thus, the Talmud replies, "Instead, '*go after*' the attributes of the Holy One Blessed be He: Just as He clothes the naked ... you too clothe the naked. The Holy One Blessed be He visited the sick ... you too visit the sick. The Holy One Blessed be He consoled mourners ... you too console mourners. The Holy One Blessed be He buried the dead ... you too bury the dead" (ibid.). In other words, while we can never comprehend what G-d *is*, we can apprehend how He *manifests* Himself *in this world* as the basis of our relationship with Him. See also Yirmeyahu 9:23 and com., ibid.; *HaKozari* 2:2; *Sefer HaMitzvoth* (Rambam), *Aseh* 8; *Yad Hil. Dei'oth* 1:6; and *Moreh HaNevochim* 1:21, 52-60.

This idea is expressed in other *midrashim* with somewhat variant but complementary emphases. See *Tan. VaYishlach*:10 and *Yal.Sh.* BeReshith:33, Devarim:873, 886, and Yeshayahu:452; see *Sifrei* on Devarim 11:22 and *Yal.Sh.* Devarim:873; see *Kethubboth* 111b, *Kallah Rabbathi* 4:1, BeM.R. 22:1, *Tan. Mattoth*:1, and *Yal.Sh.* BeMidbar:784, Devarim:824, and Yeshayahu:431; and see *VaY.R.* 25:3 and *Yal.Sh.* VaYikra:615.

26. Compare *Etz Yosef* on *Avodah Zarah* 35a, תורה של מיינה יותר ד"ה, which also relates the description of Torah as inscribed in fire to its incomprehensibility, from a somewhat different, but complementary, perspective.

It should be noted in addition that physically grasping a (terrestrial) *sefer Torah* is similarly forbidden (see *Shabbath* 14a, *Megillah* 32a, *Soferim* 3:16, *Yad Hil. Sefer Torah* 10:6, *Orach Chayyim* 147:1, and *Yoreh Dei'ah* 282:4). This proscription, however, is reverential and not expressive of an inherent, conceptual limitation. (See com., loc. cit.)

27. The translation employed is literal and corresponds to the meaning of the verse as implied by the Midrash. For the verse's contextual meaning, see com., ibid.

28. Both *Derech HaChayyim* and *Tosefoth Yom Tov*, ibid., find an allusion to Mosheh's limited receipt of Torah in the *mishnah's* distinction between "Mosheh *received* the Torah" — implying attenuation of the transmission because of the limited capacity of the receiver — and "*delivered* it to Yehoshua" — implying no attenuation because transmission is determined only by the deliverer.

   See also *Sh.R.* 41:6 and *Tan. Thissa*:16, which explicitly discuss Mosheh's limited receipt of the Torah. (See the discussion of this *midrash* in the text, below. In addition, see n. 9, above.)

29. This significance of the number fifty is expressed in the works of numerous classic thinkers, especially in reference to the counting of the *omer* (fifty days) and the *yovel* (fiftieth year). See, for example, Ramban (introduction to *Commentary on the Torah*, com. on VaYikra 25:2), R. Yeshayahu Horowitz (*Shenei Luchoth HaBerith*, "Masecheth Shavu'oth" [pp. 97a-98a]), Maharal (*Tifereth Yisra'el*, ch. 25 [p. 77]; *Chiddushei Aggadoth* on *Rosh HaShanah* 21b, 'וכו בינה שערי ה"ד), and Gra (com. on *Tikkunei Zohar*, 84).

30. Ramban's source is also found in *Zohar*: "The Torah is all the holy Name [of G-d], for there is not one word in the Torah that is not included in the holy Name" (II, 87a). See also Ramban's essay, "*Ma'aloth HaTorah VeYisra'el LeEinei HaAmim.*"

31. Extending this analogy further, it should be emphasized that the Torah of this world *is* related to the Torah of heaven, even if the very nature of the connection is beyond our ken in this world. Ultimately, we believe that the degree to which the transcendent Torah of Truth will be grasped in the world of Truth (the world *to come*) corresponds to the extent of one's dedication to understanding the terrestrial Torah during one's earthly sojourn (life in *this* world). While we recognize our bounds in this world, we appreciate the ultimate value of doing our utmost within them. Regarding the relationship between the Torah of this world and the Torah of the world to come, see also *Chagigah* 14a; *BeR.R.* 95:3; *Sh.HaSh.R.* 1:2 (4); *Koh.R.* 2:1 and 11:8; *Tan. VaYiggash*:11, *Ekev*:11, and *Tavo*:4; and *Yal.Sh.* Shemoth:273, Yeshayahu:479, Yirmeyahu:317, Iyyov:908, and Shir HaShirim:981.

32. See also *Sh.HaSh.R.* 8:11 (2), *Tan. BeChukkothai*:4, *Pes. Rabbathi* 25 (128a), *Mid. Tehillim* 8:2, *Pir.DeR.E.* 46, and *Yal.Sh.* BeMidbar:752 and Tehillim:639, 641.

33. See *Chiddushei Aggadoth* (Maharsha) and *Me'or Einayim* (HaRif) on *Ein Ya'akov*, ibid. See also *Shenei Luchoth HaBerith*, "Masecheth Shavu'oth" (p. 112a).

34. See also *Yevamoth* 71a; *Kethubboth* 67b; *Nedarim* 3a; *Gittin* 41b; *Kiddushin* 17b; *Babba Metzi'a* 31b and 94b; *Sanhedrin* 56a, 64b, 85b, and 90b; *Makkoth* 12a; *Avodah Zarah* 27a; *Zevachim* 108b; *Arachin* 3a; *Kerithoth* 11a; *Niddah* 32b and 44a; and *Sifra* on VaYikra 20:2. It should be noted that the principle that "the Torah speaks in the language of people" is explicitly articulated by the Talmud only in the context of linguistic analyses of the Torah. Rambam and other later commentators, however, apply this principle more broadly to the

manner in which the Torah presents abstract concepts that are beyond human ken. See *Introduction to Perek Chelek, Yesod* 3; *Yad Hil. Yesodei HaTorah* 1:9, 12; and *Moreh HaNevochim* 1:26, 33, 46. See also *Michtav MeEliyyahu*, II, 151.

35. It is noteworthy that the Midrash specifically emphasizes the *subjective* dimension in the revelation of Torah to the world:

> "*All the people saw the voices*" (Shemoth 20:15) — "The voice" is not written here but "*the voices.*" Said R. Yochanan: The voice would come forth and subdivide into seventy voices for seventy languages so that all the nations would hear. And each and every nation heard the voice in [its] own language.... Come and see how the voice came forth: With all of Yisra'el, each and every one [heard] according to his capacity. The elders [heard] according to their capacity, the youths according to their capacity, the children according to their capacity, and the infants according to their capacity, and the women according to their capacity. And even Mosheh [heard] according to his capacity, as it is said, "Mosheh would speak, and the L-rd would answer *him* with a voice" (Shemoth 19:19): with a voice that he could bear. And thus it says, "The voice of G-d is in strength" (Tehillim 29:4) — "In *His* strength" is not said but "in strength": according to the capacity [lit. in the strength] of each and every one.
>
> (*Sh.R.* 5:9)

Inasmuch as we live in a subjective realm, the terrestrial Torah is by definition subjective: Each person receives it according to his own subjective proficiency. Obviously, such subjectivity is excluded from the transcendent Torah of the world of Truth. A more detailed treatment of this subject is beyond the scope of the present discussion. See also *Shabbath* 88b; *Mechilta* on Shemoth 20:15; *Sh.R.* 28:6, 29:1 and 34:1; *BeM.R.* 10:1; *Tan. Shemoth*:25 and *Yithro*:11; *Pes. DeRav Kahana* 12 (110a); *Pes. Rabbathi* 21 (100b); and *Yal.Sh.* Shemoth:286, 300, Tehillim:795, and Iyyov:921.

36. In these terms, the connection of the crown with royalty implies that associated with the person of the monarch is a quality that transcends the individual — note that the crown is worn over the monarch's head — and represents the nation as a whole.

37. See also Ramban's reference to our *aggadah* and the significance of the crowns of the letters (introduction to *Commentary on the Torah*).

38. Perhaps the association of tying with recollection is conveyed graphically by the act of *tying* two objects together, whereby moving one drags the other along, even if the other had been forgotten. Interestingly, this implication is assumed idiomatically in English as well, in "tying a string around one's finger" as a memory device.

39. See also *Tifereth Yisra'el*, ch. 63 (p. 190).

40. Similarly, Chazal liken the progression of Creation to a king preparing a banquet and only afterward inviting guests — effectively regarding the entire world as

a banquet prepared for man. (See *Sanhedrin* 38a, *Tos. Sanhedrin* 8:3, and *Yal.Sh.* Mishlei:943. See also the "*Avodah*" section of the repetition of "*Musaf*" for Yom Kippur [Ashkenazi version].) In addition, it should be noted that the supremacy of man in the natural world is emphasized explicitly in Scripture. (See BeReshith 1:28 and 9:1-7 and Tehillim 8:6-9. See also *BeR.R.* 19:4.)

41. The translation employed is literal and corresponds to the meaning of the verse as implied by the Midrash. The verse's contextual meaning is debated among the commentaries.

    It should be noted that Mizmor 139 as a whole is traditionally attributed to Adam (see Rashi on *Babba Bathra* 14b, ד"ה על ידי אדם הראשון), and it is expounded homiletically in the Talmud and the Midrash as a description of his creation. See, for example, *Berachoth* 61a, *Eruvin* 18a, *Chagigah* 12a, *Sanhedrin* 38a and 38b, *Avodah Zarah* 5a and 8a, *Yer. Berachoth* 8:5 (54a), *Yer. Avodah Zarah* 1:2 (2a), *Avoth DeRabbi Nathan* 1:8 and 31:3, and numerous Midrashic references. See also com., loc. cit.

42. See also *Tan. Tazria*:1 and *Yal.Sh.* VaYikra:547 (on VaYikra 12).

43. In deference to the Midrash, at least brief consideration of the moral implications of our analysis, as articulated by the Midrash, seems necessary. In this sense, "*if a man is worthy*," he indicates his affinity for the ideal of man — "the spirit of the King Mashiach" — which precedes all of Creation and even *malachei hashareth*. The lag in man's physical creation is not to his detriment, since it merely emphasizes the progression necessary as a means to realize this ideal: "All that I have created, *I created for you*" (*Koh.R.* 7:13). On the other hand, "*should he become overbearing*," obsessed with himself and divorced from the ideal of man, he ceases to be a final stage — or any stage — in the realization of anything. The lag in man's physical creation, then, signifies nothing more than his own inconsequence: "A fly preceded you; a mosquito preceded you; this slime preceded you." The duality of man's creation is indeed the duality of man's nature: He may choose to be either worthy — focusing on the ideal of man — or overbearing — focusing on his own materialism to the exclusion of any ideal.

44. Regarding the "hard matter" implied here, compare *Iyyun Ya'akov*, loc. cit.

45. Apropos of the difficulty in tying down the crowns to the letters, Maharal notes that "because the crowns are utterly transcendent, He Who ties them must specifically be G-d, Who transcends everything" (*Tifereth Yisra'el*, ch. 63 [p. 190]).

46. See *Chiddushei Aggadoth* (Maharal) and *Chiddushei Aggadoth* (Maharsha), loc. cit., and *Tifereth Yisra'el*, ch. 63 (p. 190).

47. See *Chiddushei Aggadoth* (Maharal), loc. cit., and *Tifereth Yisra'el*, ch. 63 (p. 190).

48. See Devarim 1:5, 4:44, and 33:4; and com., loc. cit. Significantly, throughout Nach, the Torah is repeatedly ascribed to Mosheh, through whose agency we received it. (See Yehoshua 1:7, 8:31-32, and 23:6; Melachim I 2:3 and II 14:6, 18:6, 21:8, and 23:25; Malachi 3:22; Daniyyel 9:11, 13; Ezra 3:2, 6:18, and 7:6;

Nechemyah 1:7-8, 8:1, 14, 9:14, 10:30, and 13:1; and Divrei HaYamim I 22:13 and II 23:18, 25:4, 30:16, 33:8, 34:14, and 35:12.) See also *Avoth* 1:1 and *Avoth DeRabbi Nathan* 1:1-2.

49. I have translated as "scholars" the original "סופרים" (lit. "scribes"), which, in its strict sense, denotes the early scholars prior to the Tannaic period, commencing with Ezra. Indeed, the original usage of "סופר" during this period is in reference to Ezra himself. (See Ezra 7:6, 11, 12, 21 and Nechemyah 8:1, 4, 9, 13 and 12:26, 36.) Chazal employ the title generically in reference to the early scholars prior to the Tannaic period. (See *Kiddushin* 30a and com., ibid.) "סופרים" can also refer to teachers of young children. (See *Tos. Kiddushin* 5:10 and *Yer. Chagigah* 1:7 [5a].) In its broadest usage, however, "סופרים" refers to scholars in general. (See *Berachoth* 45b; *Yevamoth* 20a; *Chullin* 106a; *Temurah* 16a; *Yer. Shekalim* 5:1 [18b]; Radak and *Metzudoth* on Divrei HaYamim I 2:25; and *Metzudath Tziyyon* on Ezra 7:6, on Nechemyah 8:1, and on Divrei HaYamim I 27:32.) The term "דברי סופרים" ("words of scholars") similarly connotes words of the scholars in general. (See *Mish. Yevamoth* 2:4 and com., ibid.; *Mish. Sanhedrin* 11:3; *Mish. Yadayim* 3:2; *Rosh HaShanah* 19a; *Ta'anith* 17b; *Yevamoth* 20a and 85b; *Sanhedrin* 53b and 88b; *Yer. Berachoth* 1:4 [8b]; *Sefer HaMitzvoth* [Rambam], *Shoresh* 2, and com., ibid.; *Yad Hil. Ishuth* 1:2 and com., ibid.; and the sources cited in n. 66, below.) See also Rashi on *Megillah* 19b, loc. cit.

50. See also *Yer. Pei'ah* 2:4 (9b), *Yer. Megillah* 4:1 (27a), *Yer. Chagigah* 1:8 (6a), *Sh.R.* 47:1, and *Yal.Sh.* Shemoth:405 and Koheleth:971.

51. See also *Yal.Sh.* Shemoth:362. In addition, see references to this *derash* in Rambam (introduction to *Mishneh Torah*) and in Ramban (introduction to *Commentary on the Torah*).

52. See *Megillah* 19b, cited above.

53. Likewise, Ramban reinforces this aspect of Rambam's approach, explaining at length why Chazal refer to later components of Torah as having been "said to Mosheh at Sinai." See com. on *Sefer HaMitzvoth* ibid.

54. Regarding the inclusion of the bracketed component of the verse (which the Gemara omits), see *Yad Hil. Berachoth* 11:3 and *Kesef Mishneh*, ibid., and *Torah Temimah* on Devarim 17:11, n. 59.

55. More generally, the Talmud asserts, "All matters of rabbinical origin find support from the prohibition of 'Do not deviate' " (*Berachoth* 19b). See also *Sifrei*, ibid., *Yevamoth* 20a, *Chullin* 106a, *Tan. Naso*:29, and *Yal.Sh.* Devarim:911. See also nn. 56 and 66, below.

56. See *Sefer HaMitzvoth* ibid. and Ramban and com., loc. cit. In addition, see *HaKozari* 3:39; *Sefer HaMitzvoth, Aseh* 174 and *Lav* 312; *Yad Hil. Berachoth* 11:3 and *Hil. Mamrim* 1:1-2; Ramban on Devarim 17:11; *Chinuch, Mitzvoth* 492 and 508; and Ritva on *Rosh HaShanah* 16a, ד"ה תניא ר"ע. See also n. 55, above.

57. It should be noted that significant disagreement exists between Rambam and Ramban regarding the actual scope of the prohibition of "Do not deviate"

and of its positive counterpart ("You shall be careful to do all that they instruct you" [Devarim 17:10]) and the consequent status of rabbinical commandments and prohibitions. As indicated above, however, this disagreement does not pertain to the present discussion, regarding which they effectively agree. See *Sefer Ha-Mitzvoth, Shoresh* 1; Ramban and com., loc. cit.; and the sources cited in n. 56, above.

58. See also *Torah Temimah* on Koheleth 1:10, n. 47.

59. We must concede that the other references quoted above describe all the components of Torah as being "*said*" or "*given*" to Mosheh, certainly implying actual delivery. Nevertheless, *Tosefoth Yom Tov's* point certainly stands on its own merit, even if it is not implied in these other sources.

60. See *Sh.R.* 41:6 and *Tan. Thissa*:16 (quoted above). See also *Chiddushei Aggadoth* (Maharal) on *Menachoth* 29b (IV, 75, 77) and *Tifereth Yisra'el*, ch. 63 (pp. 189, 192).

61. See *Chiddushei Aggadoth* (Maharal) on *Menachoth* 29b (IV, 75-76).

62. See *Chiddushei Aggadoth* (Maharal) on *Menachoth* 29b (IV, 76).

63. While in the commentary on *Menachoth* 29b, *Iyyun Ya'akov* states merely "איתא" ("it is [written]") — which normally introduces a Talmudic or Midrashic citation — in the commentary on *Babba Bathra* 12a, "איתא במדרש" ("it is [written] *in the Midrash*") is stated explicitly. Nevertheless, I have thus far been unable to locate any earlier source of this *derash* in known Talmudic and Midrashic literature (even though its basic intent is certainly implied elsewhere). In deference to R. Y. Reischer (1670-1733), author of *Iyyun Ya'akov*, it is reasonable to assume that the reference is nevertheless to such an earlier source.

64. See also *Yer. Berachoth* 1:4 (8b), *Yer. Sanhedrin* 11:4 (40b), *Yer. Avodah Zarah* 2:7 (11a), and *Sh.HaSh.R.* 1:2b (2) for a related discussion. In addition, see *Zohar*, I, 7b and 183b; II, 5b; and III, 223a.

65. See also *Tan. Noach*:3, where the incomprehensibility of *Torah shebikethav* and its relationship with *Torah shebe'al-peh* are emphasized.

66. See also *Yer. Sanhedrin* 11:4 (40b), *Yer. Avodah Zarah* 2:7 (11a), *Sh.HaSh.R.* 1:2b (2), and *Yal.Sh.* Shir HaShirim:981. In addition, see *Eruvin* 21b, *Mish. Sanhedrin* 11:3, and *Pes. Rabbathi* 3 (8b).

67. Rambam discusses at length the irrelevance of prophecy to the development of *Torah shebe'al-peh* in his *Introduction to the Mishnah*, ch. 2. See also *Berachoth* 52a, *Eruvin* 7a, *Pesachim* 114a, *Yevamoth* 14a, *Babba Metzi'a* 59b, and *Chullin* 44a, and see com., loc. cit.

68. We obviously believe that *Torah shebe'al-peh* was extant in the period of the first Beith HaMikdash as well, having been given to us with *Torah shebikethav* from Sinai. Nevertheless, *Pirkei Heichaloth* (chs. 27 and 29) informs us that important levels of Torah were not available, and the principal secrets of Torah were not revealed, until the period of the second Beith HaMikdash. R. Tzadok HaKohen discusses this profound subject in depth. (See *Tzidkath HaTzaddik, chs. 93 and 256.*)

69. The Talmud states, "Chaggai, Zecharyah, and Malachi were the last of the prophets" (*Babba Bathra* 14b); after they died, "the holy spirit was withdrawn from Yisra'el" (*Yoma* 9b, *Sotah* 48b, *Sanhedrin* 11a, *Tos. Sotah* 13:4). Chaggai and Zecharyah prophesied during the return to Tziyyon and the reconstruction of the Beith HaMikdash, as evident both in the recorded dates heading their prophecies and in Ezra 5:1 and 6:14. Chazal cite opinions identifying Malachi alternately as Mordechai or as Ezra (see *Megillah* 15a and *Tar. Yonathan* on Malachi 1:1). The Talmud describes Chaggai, Zecharyah, and Malachi, together with Daniyyel, as contemporaries (see *Megillah* 3a and 15a and *Sanhedrin* 93b; see also *Nazir* 53a, *Zevachim* 62a, *Chullin* 137b, and *Bechoroth* 58a). In the transmission of *Torah shebe'al-peh*, "Chaggai, Zecharyah, and Malachi received from the [other] prophets; the men of the Great Assembly received from Chaggai, Zecharyah, and Malachi" (*Avoth DeRabbi Nathan* 1:3). Traditionally, the three were themselves members of the Great Assembly convened by Ezra (see *Megillah* 17b and com., ibid.; Rashi on *Babba Bathra* 15a, ד"ה אנשי כנסת הגדולה; and the introduction to *Mishneh Torah*) immediately prior to the Talmudic period (see *Avoth* 1, *Avoth DeRabbi Nathan* 4-5, and the introduction to *Mishneh Torah*).

    Regarding the cessation of prophecy at the beginning of the period of the second Beith HaMikdash, see also *HaKozari* 1:87, 2:23-24, and 3:39, 65 and *Tzidkath HaTzaddik*, ch. 256.

70. See *Derech HaChayyim* (Maharal) on *Avoth* 1:1, ד"ה משה קבל תורה מסיני: "From the [time of the] men of the Great Assembly, [the wisdom of] the generations began to diminish and dwindle.... [Each generation] would receive according to the capacity it had to receive." By contrast, concludes Maharal (ibid.), complete transmission of Torah typified all the previous periods, from Mosheh through the men of the Great Assembly. Similarly, avers *Tosefoth Yom Tov*, "Even though not all the [members of the Great] Assembly were prophets, the whole Torah was delivered over to them as it had been delivered to those who preceded them. But from then on, since [the level of] the generations dwindled, [the Torah] was not wholly delivered. Instead, each one received according to his capacity" (com. on *Avoth* 1:1, ד"ה ונביאים מסרוה לאנשי כנסת הגדולה).

    Thus, R. Eli'ezer — who among the sages is uniquely characterized by his mentor as "a limed pit that does not lose a drop" (*Avoth* 2:8) — conceded on his deathbed, "I learned much Torah, and I taught much Torah: I learned much Torah, and I did not take from my teachers even what a dog laps from the sea. I taught much Torah, and my students did not take from me more than a painting stick [dipped] in a tube [of mascara]" (*Sanhedrin* 68a). R. Eli'ezer regarded R. Akiva as his pre-eminent student (see ibid.).

71. See *Yoma* 9b and 21b, *Yal.Sh.* BeReshith:61 and Chaggai:567, and *Pirkei Heichaloth* 27 (quoted in text, below). See also *Yer. Ta'anith* 2:1 (8a); *Yer. Horayoth* 3:2 (12b) and *Penei Mosheh*, ibid., ד"ה ושמן המשחה ורוח הקדש; *BeM.R.* 15:10; *Sh.HaSh.R.* 8:9 (3); and *Tan.* BeHa'alothcha:6. In addition, see *HaKozari* 2:24, 3:65, and 4:3 and *Tzidkath HaTzaddik*, chs. 93 and 256.

72. We should add that, given this Midrashic perspective, we may perhaps understand why the Talmud Bavli seems to characterize itself so bleakly: " 'He has set me in darkness like the eternally dead' (Eichah 3:6) — Said R. Yirmeyah: This is the Talmud of Bavel" (Sanhedrin 24a; see also Pesachim 34b, Yoma 57a, Zevachim 60b, Menachoth 52a, and Bechoroth 25b). Significantly, Rashi understands this as implying that the Talmud Bavli "is deep" (com. on Chagigah 10a, ד"ה אפילו מש"ס לש"ס). See also Anaf Yosef on Sanhedrin ibid.: "[The Talmud Bavli] is our strength and light, but great painstaking is necessary to review one's learning lest forgetfulness prevail. And regarding all this, Chazal said, '[If a person says to you] I have toiled, and I have found — believe!' [Megillah 6b]." Similarly, Shenei Luchoth HaBerith relates this statement to the nature of Torah shebe'al-peh, which requires "painstaking to [be] acquired ... and killing oneself over it" ("Beith Chochmah," בא"ד נחזור לענין הרי מבואר [p. 16a]; "Sha'ar HaGadol," בא"ד ביתי"ן כפי" [p. 35b]). See Berachoth 63b and the sources cited in n. 137, below.

73. See Yedei Mosheh on BeM.R. 19:6, which cites a particularly profound comparison between the unsurpassed scholarly achievements of Rabbi Akiva and the prophetic achievements of Mosheh Rabbeinu. See also Michtav MeEliyyahu, III, 55. In addition, it is noteworthy that this midrash appears in Pesikta in somewhat altered form, exclusively in reference to Rabbi Akiva (see Pes. Rabbathi 14 [64b]).

74. See also Nedarim 38a, Yer. Horayoth 3:5 (14b), and Rashi on Shemoth 31:18, ד"ה ככלתו.

75. See Berachoth 27b, Yer. Berachoth 4:1 (29b), and the introduction to Mishneh Torah.

76. See R. Nissim Ga'on on Berachoth 27b. See also Iyyun Ya'akov on Berachoth 61b. Sisra was the commander in chief of Yavin, king of Kena'an, who harshly afflicted Yisra'el for twenty years (see Shofetim 4:1-3). Chazal state that "[individuals] from among the descendants of Sisra learned Torah in Yerushalayim" (Gittin 57b, Sanhedrin 96b, Yal.Sh. Yirmeyahu:335).

77. See Kethubboth 62b, Nedarim 50a, Avoth DeRabbi Nathan 6:2 and 21:2, Sifrei on Devarim 34:7, BeR.R. 100:10, and She'iltoth DeRav Acha Ga'on, She'ilta 40.

78. See Pesachim 49b.

79. See Avoth DeRabbi Nathan 6:2, Sifrei on Devarim 34:7, and BeR.R. 100:10.

80. See Pesachim 109a and Semachoth 8.

81. See Gittin 67a and Avoth DeRabbi Nathan 6:2 and 18:1.

82. See Eruvin 46b and Kethubboth 84b. See also Sanhedrin 86a and Yer. Shekalim 5:1 (18b). In addition, see Mevo HaTalmud (R. Shemu'el HaNagid), בא"ד סתם מתניתין ר"מ (46b).

83. See also the praises heaped upon Rabbi Akiva by R. Dosa b. Horkinas (Yevamoth 16a), by R. Tarfon (Kiddushin 66b, Zevachim 13a, Avoth DeRabbi Nathan 6:2), by R. Yehudah HaNasi (Avoth DeRabbi Nathan 18:1), and by Isi b. Yehudah (Gittin 67a).

84. See also *Kiddushin* 32b.

85. Regarding this additional dimension of Torah, see also the introduction to *Igroth Mosheh* (R. M. Feinstein) for a novel interpretation of the "crowns":

> The term "crowns" is appropriate because G-d made the letters of the Torah into kings, meaning that the scholar should operate by comparing cases and ruling according to *his* understanding of the meaning of the letters in the Torah ... even though it is possible that [the scholar] did not draw the true meaning.... Thus the letters of the Torah are kings, for one does according to whatever is concluded from the Torah by the scholars of the Torah, even though possibly this does not accord with G-d's understanding.

Differences notwithstanding, R. Feinstein also derives from our *aggadah* the significance of the "Torah of man" represented by Rabbi Akiva's efforts.

86. See *Chiddushei Aggadoth* (Maharal) on *Menachoth* 29b (IV, 77). See also nn. 75-79, above.

87. According to Rambam (introduction to *Mishneh Torah*), Yosef himself was a convert. See also *Berachoth* 27b and *Yer. Berachoth* 4:1 (29b).

88. See also *Tifereth Yisra'el*, ch. 63 (p. 190). In addition, see *Michtav MeEliyyahu*, III, 54.

89. "Eight rows" appears in the standard Vilna (Romm) edition of the Talmud Bavli and in *Ein Ya'akov*. Apparently, this version appeared in Maharsha's Talmud, since he comments exclusively on it (see *Chiddushei Aggadoth* [Maharsha], ibid.)

90. "Eighteen rows" is cited as an alternate version in *Shittah Mekubbetzeth*, ibid. It is also cited parenthetically in *Ein Ya'akov*. Apparently, this version appeared in Maharal's Talmud, since he comments exclusively on it (see *Chiddushei Aggadoth* [Maharal], ibid., and *Tifereth Yisra'el*, ch. 63 [p. 190]).

91. See BeReshith 17:12 and 21:4 and VaYikra 12:3.

92. See VaYikra 23:36 and BeMidbar 29:35.

93. See Shemoth 28, especially verses 4, 36, and 42 and com., loc. cit.

94. See *Shabbath* 21b. See also *Mid. Chanukkah, Beith HaMidrash* I, 134a, and *Sefer Chashmona'im II* 10:9-10, regarding the linkage between the *eight* days of Chanukkah and the *eight* days of Sukkoth. For a more detailed treatment of this linkage, see R. Gershon Kitzis, "Sukkoth and Chanukkah," *Jewish Thought*, 1, No. 1, 87-99.

95. See also *BeM.R.* 15:11; *Tan. BeHa'alothcha*:7; *Pes. Rabbathi* 21 (98b); *Mid. Tehillim* 81:3; *Yal.Sh.* Tehillim:634, 720, 831 and Shir HaShirim:980; *Sha'ar HaGemul* (Ramban), ד"ה ועכשיו נחזור לשכר הגדול בא"ד ובגמרא פרק אין נערכין; *Netzach Yisra'el* (Maharal), ch. 32 (p. 148); *Chiddushei Aggadoth* (Maharsha) on *Arachin* 13b; and R. S.R. Hirsch on Tehillim 6:1.

96. This motif — that the Torah transcends nature and therefore represents the eighth level — recurs frequently in Maharal. See also *Nethivoth Olam*, "*Nethiv HaAnavah*," ch. 7 (p. 15); *Ner Mitzvah* (p. 21); *Derech HaChayyim* on *Avoth* 6:2, ד"ה העוסק בתורה לשמה וכו'; and *Chiddushei Aggadoth* on *Shabbath* 21b, ד"ה כשנכנסו יונים להיכל.

97. Regarding Maharal's analysis of the motif of eight in Mizmor 19, see also *Ner Mitzvah* (p. 21) and *Derech HaChayyim* on *Avoth* 6:2, ד"ה העוסק בתורה לשמה וכו'.

98. Regarding Maharal's analysis of the motif of eight in Mizmor 119, see also *Nethivoth Olam*, "*Nethiv HaAnavah*," ch. 7 (p. 15); *Ner Mitzvah* (pp. 21, 23); *Derech HaChayyim* on *Avoth* 6:2, ד"ה העוסק בתורה לשמה וכו'; and *Chiddushei Aggadoth* on *Shabbath* 21b, ד"ה כשנכנסו יונים להיכל.

99. Regarding Maharal's analysis of the motif of eight in circumcision, see also *Chiddushei Aggadoth* on *Shabbath* 21b, ד"ה כשנכנסו יונים להיכל, on *Nedarim* 31b, ד"ה מושך בערלתו וכו', and on *Sanhedrin* 38b, ד"ה גדולה המילה שדוחה את השבת.

100. Regarding Maharal's analysis of the motif of eight in Chanukkah, see also *Ner Mitzvah* (pp. 21, 28) and *Chiddushei Aggadoth* on *Shabbath* 21b, ד"ה כשנכנסו יונים להיכל.

101. See also R. Avraham b. Ezra on VaYikra 23:16, who associates the number fifty — as "the number of Torah" — with the number eight.

   In addition, it is noteworthy that Shemini Atzereth — the *eighth* day of Sukkoth — is also singularly associated with the Torah (in its traditional role as Simchath Torah).

102. Maharal discusses the significance of the number eight in *Nethivoth Olam*, "*Nethiv HaAvodah*," ch. 11 (p. 113), and "*Nethiv HaAnavah*," ch. 7 (p. 15); *Gevuroth HaShem*, ch. 65 (p. 300); *Tifereth Yisra'el*, ch. 2 (pp. 10, 11 — quoted in the text, above); *Netzach Yisra'el*, chs. 7 (p. 43) and 32 (p. 148 — quoted in the text, above); *Ner Mitzvah* (pp. 21, 23, 28 — quoted in the text, above); *Derech HaChayyim* on *Avoth* 6:2, ד"ה העוסק בתורה לשמה וכו'; and *Chiddushei Aggadoth* on *Shabbath* 21b, ד"ה גדולה המילה שדוחה את השבת, on *Nedarim* 31b, ד"ה כשנכנסו יונים להיכל, on *Gittin* 57a, ד"ה אלו שמונים קרני מלחמה וכו', and on *Sanhedrin* 38b, ד"ה מושך בערלתו וכו'. See also R. Mosheh Tzuri'el, "*Misparim — Mashma'utham VeSimliyyutham LeFi Maharal*," *HaMa'ayan*, 18, No. 3 (5738), 14-20, and No. 4 (5738), 33-34, 39.

103. See also *Yeshurun* (R. S.R. Hirsch), V, 13.

104. See *Yer. Berachoth* 4:3 (30a), *Yer. Ta'anith* 2:2 (9a), *BeR.R.* 69:4, *Tan. VaYera*:1, and *Yal.Sh.* BeReshith:120. See also *Sukkah* 45b and *Avodah Zarah* 3b (and *Chiddushei Aggadoth* [Maharal], ibid., סד"ה י"ב שעות הוי היום וכו').

105. See *Tifereth Yisra'el*, ch. 63 (p. 190), and *Chiddushei Aggadoth* (Maharal) on *Avodah Zarah* 3b, סד"ה י"ב שעות הוי היום וכו', and on *Menachoth* 29b, loc. cit. (IV, 75). See also n. 104, above.

106. Maharal also infers a relationship between Mosheh's inability to understand what Rabbi Akiva was saying and the eighteen-row separation between them: "In attempting to fuse the level of Mosheh Rabbeinu to the level of Rabbi Akiva,

[the Talmud] says that [Mosheh] sat at the end of eighteen rows with respect to Rabbi Akiva. *For having said that [Mosheh] did not understand what they were saying, we can conclude that he had no connection and association with Rabbi Akiva"* (*Tifereth Yisra'el*, ch. 63 [p. 190]). (See also *Chiddushei Aggadoth*, loc. cit.)

107. Compare *Michtav MeEliyyahu*, I, 223.

108. Maharal explains Mosheh's argument similarly: Inasmuch as Mosheh's perception of Torah is at the level of the general principle and Rabbi Akiva's perception of Torah is at the level of the particulars (see text, above), G-d should give the Torah through Rabbi Akiva and thus synthesize a perception based upon *both* the general principle *and* the particulars. (See *Chiddushei Aggadoth* on *Menachoth* ibid.).

109. See also *Chiddushei Aggadoth* (Maharsha) on *Menachoth* ibid. and *Chazon Yeshayahu* (Malbim) on Yeshayahu ibid. In addition, see *HaKozari* 1:79, 98-99, 2:26, 60, 3:5, 23, 49, 53, and 4:5, 15; *Yad Hil. Yesodei HaTorah* 1:10 and 2:8, 10 and *Hil. Teshuvah* 5:5; *Moreh HaNevochim* 1:2, 31, 52-53, 56, 58-60, 68 and 3:20-21; and *Derech HaShem* 1:1 (2, 5). See also *Chagigah* 13a, *Yer. Chagigah* 2:1 (8a), *BeR.R.* 8:2, and *Yal.Sh.* Yechezkel:339 (based upon *Sefer Ben Sira* 3:21). See also nn. 11 and 25, above.

110. This concept is similarly expressed in the "*Lechah Dodi*" hymn by R. Shelomoh HaLevi Alkabetz: "The final act [of Creation] is [contained] in the *initial thought*" ("*Kabbalath Shabbath*" service). See also *Michtav MeEliyyahu*, III, 54. In addition, see *HaKozari* 4:25 regarding the divine thought as the essence of Creation itself.

111. As emphasized earlier, our intent here is not to imply the existence of objective constraints on G-d's act of Creation, but to recognize the principles of the world order contained in the "thought of G-d." In this sense, Chazal tell us that the world was created specifically through Torah: "G-d would gaze into the Torah and create the world" (*BeR.R.* 1:1, *Tan. BeReshith*:1, *T.DeV.Eli.R.* 31, *Pir.DeR.E.* 3, *Yal.Sh.* BeReshith:2 and Mishlei:942; see also *BeR.R.* 1:8, *Sh.R.* 47:4, *VaY.R.* 35:4, and *Tan. VaYelech*:2). This terse portrayal obviously does *not* teach us G-d's "technique" in Creation; it does emphasize, however, what — in G-d's order — is predicated upon what. See also *Shabbath* 88b; *Pesachim* 54a; *Nedarim* 39b; *Sanhedrin* 91b and Rashi, ibid., ד"ה משֶשֶת ימי בראשית; *Zevachim* 116a; *Avoth DeRabbi Nathan* 31:3; *Sifrei* on Devarim 7:12 and 11:22; *BeR.R.* 1:4, 10, 8:2, and 12:2; *Sh.R.* 30:9; *VaY.R.* 19:1 and 23:3; *BeM.R.* 14:12; *Sh.HaSh.R.* 5:11 (1, 4); *Tan. VaYeshev*:4, *Yithro*:14, *Naso*:11, and *Re'eh*:1; *Mid. Tehillim* 90:12 and 93:3; *Yal.Sh.* BeReshith:20, Shemoth:368, BeMidbar:743, 752, 764, Yirmeyahu:298, Tehillim:641, 710, Mishlei:943, Iyyov:907, and Shir HaShirim:988; and Rashi on BeReshith 1:1, ד"ה בראשית ברא. See also n. 20, above.

112. See also *Pesachim* 68b; *Nedarim* 32a; *BeR.R.* 66:2; *Sh.R.* 47:4; *VaY.R.* 23:3; *Sh.HaSh.R.* 1:9 (6), 2:2 (3), and 7:1; *Ru.R. Peth.*:1; *Tan. Yithro*:14, *Shemini*:6, and *Naso*:19; *Pes. Rabbathi* 21 (100a); *Yal.Sh.* Yirmeyahu:321; and Rashi on Tehillim 75:4.

113. See also *Tan. BeReshith*:1, *Yal.Sh.* Tehillim:811, and Rashi on BeReshith 1:31.

114. See also *T.DeV.Eli.R.* 2 and *Yal.Sh.* Yeshayahu:394 and Tehillim:888. The "two

millennia of formless void" actually terminated when Avraham was fifty-two years old, for reasons not germane to the present discussion. (See *Avodah Zarah* ibid. and com., loc. cit.)

115. Compare *Chiddushei Aggadoth* (Maharal), ibid. (IV, 76), which also emphasizes the need for Torah — as the "completion of this world" — to be given specifically through Mosheh and not Rabbi Akiva. See also *Tifereth Yisra'el*, ch. 63 (p. 191).

116. Compare *Michtav MeEliyyahu*, III, 54, which also explains that it is the final goal of Creation which mandates this order.

117. Maharal similarly argues that a single mediator of Torah comprising both dimensions would be inappropriate for the world's receipt of Torah. (See *Chiddushei Aggadoth* on *Menachoth* ibid.).

118. This principle is axiomatic in Judaism and cited repeatedly by Chazal. See, for example, *Shabbath* 105b, *Megillah* 12b, *Nedarim* 32a, *Sotah* 8b, *Sanhedrin* 90a, *Kallah Rabbathi* 1, *BeR.R.* 9:11, *BeM.R.* 10:2, and *Yal.Sh.* Devarim:940 (on Devarim 31).

119. This principle is articulated or suggested in numerous statements by Chazal, regarding both reward and punishment. Its broader implications are beyond the scope of our discussion here. See, for example, *Eruvin* 19a; *Yoma* 38b-39a; *Sukkah* 52b; *Ta'anith* 11a; *Chagigah* 16a; *Mish. Sotah* 1:7-9; *Sotah* 3b, 8b-9b, 11a, and 42a; *Gittin* 57a; *Babba Bathra* 16a; *Sanhedrin* 103a; *Avodah Zarah* 2a and 5a; *Avoth* 2:7 and 4:2, 11; *Avoth DeRabbi Nathan* 30:4; *Kallah Rabbathi* 3; *BeR.R.* 22:6, 41:7, and 50:8; *Sh.R.* 7:4 and 40:1; *Koh.R.* 3:9; *Tan. VaYera*:12; and *Mid. Tehillim* 92:14; and see com., loc. cit.

120. See also *Chiddushei Aggadoth* (Maharal), loc. cit., *Tifereth Yisra'el*, ch. 63 (p. 191), and *Michtav MeEliyyahu*, III, 54.

121. See Maharal's comment — in *Tifereth Yisra'el*, ch. 63 (p. 191) — that Mosheh "wanted to know what [Rabbi Akiva's] reward would be *in the world to come.*" Compare, however, an alternate view, also expressed by Maharal — in *Chiddushei Aggadoth*, loc. cit. — that Mosheh's request was to be shown Rabbi Akiva's "reward *in this world.*"

122. See *Nedarim* 50 and *Avoth DeRabbi Nathan* 6:2. See also *Avodah Zarah* 10b.

123. The Midrash lists four individuals who each lived to the age of one hundred twenty: "Mosheh, Hillel the Elder, R. Yochanan b. Zakkai, and R. Akiva" (*Sifrei* on Devarim 34:7). See also *BeR.R.* 100:10.

124. See *Kethubboth* 63a and *Nedarim* 50. See also *Yevamoth* 16a and 62b.

125. Maharal (ibid.) notes that this is symbolically indicated by Mosheh's supernatural victory over the Emori kings, Sichon and Og (BeMidbar 21), who epitomized worldly, physical greatness.

126. According to Maharal (ibid.), this is what Chazal imply in stating that "this world was created solely for Mosheh" (*Sanhedrin* 98b, *BeR.R.* 1:4, *VaY.R.* 36:4, *Yal.Sh.* BeReshith:2). Maharal also stresses the association between Mosheh's dominion over the world and his role as the giver of the Torah, which is to perfect this world.

127. Regarding the elusiveness of Mosheh's grave, see Devarim 34:6 and com., loc. cit. See also *Sotah* 13b-14a; *Mid. Tehillim* 9:2; and *Yal.Sh.* BeMidbar:787, Devarim:940, 965, and Yeshayahu:507.

128. See *Avoth* 5:6, *Pesachim* 54a, *Pir.DeR.E.* 19, and com., loc. cit.

129. See also *Nethivoth Olam*, "*Nethiv Ahavath HaShem*," ch. 1 (p. 39), regarding the association of everything with its source in G-d.

130. See also *Michtav MeEliyyahu*, III, 243-244, regarding Rabbi Akiva's level in his affirmation of G-d's oneness.

131. See also *BeR.R.* 12:15, 14:1, and 21:7; *Sh.R.* 30:13; and *Yal.Sh.* BeReshith:19 and Mishlei:962 (on Mishlei 29). It must be noted that none of these Midrashic sources refers explicitly to the "thought" of G-d as does Rashi, and Rashi's source — if extant — is unknown. See *Gur Aryeh* on Rashi ibid. Obviously, if Rashi's reference to "thought" is original, the association made by the commentaries (see n. 134, below) between it and our *aggadah* would be anachronistic.

132. See also *Gur Aryeh* on Rashi ibid., according to which the ideal remains *middath haddin* if man is capable of functioning on such a level.

133. See also *Etz Yosef* on *Menachoth* 29b, which quotes this explanation of *Be'er Mayim Chayyim*.

134. This interpretation is also advanced by *Iyyun Ya'akov* and *Etz Yosef*, loc. cit. In addition, see *Michtav MeEliyyahu*, III, 54.

135. See also *Michtav MeEliyyahu*, III, 54-55.

136. See also *Koh.R.* 2:9 and com., ibid. In addition, see Rambam on *Avoth* 5:23 and *Yad Hil. Talmud Torah* 3:12. See also *Torah Temimah* on Koheleth ibid., n. 40.

137. See also *Shabbath* 83b, *Gittin* 57b, *Tan. Noach:*3, and *Yal.Sh.* BeMidbar:762 and Tehillim:873. In addition, see *Avodah Zarah* 5b and *Yer. Berachoth* 5:1 (33b), and see *Yad Hil. Talmud Torah* 3:12 and *Yoreh Dei'ah* 246:21.

138. See also *Yer. Chagigah* 1:1 (1a), *Yer. Sotah* 3:4 (14b), *Tos. Sotah* 7:6, and *BeM.R.* 14:4. In addition, see *Avoth DeRabbi Nathan* 18:2 (*Nuschath HaGra*, ibid., n. 1) and *Mechilta* on Shemoth 13:2.

THE EMERGENCE OF MAN:
A Musar Approach to Mizmor 19

Hillel Goldberg

The essay that follows is based upon the source provided below:

LaMnatzeach, a *mizmor* of David.	:למנצח, מזמור לדוד
The heavens tell the glory of the L-rd, and His handiwork the sky recounts.	השמים מספרים כבוד־א־ל; ומעשה ידיו מגיד הרקיע:
Day to day expresses a statement, and night to night offers knowledge.	יום ליום יביע אמר; ולילה ללילה יחוה־דעת:
There is no statement and no words, without their voice being heard.	אין־אמר ואין דברים; בלי נשמע קולם:
Their line went forth throughout the earth, and their words to the end of the world; He has set a tent for the sun in them.	בכל־הארץ יצא קום, ובקצה תבל מליהם; לשמש, שם־אהל בהם:

HILLEL GOLDBERG is the editor of the *Intermountain Jewish News*. A well-known writer and lecturer, he has published several works on the Musar movement and Musar personalities, including *Israel Salanter: Text, structure, Idea* (New York: Ktav, 1982—Academic Book of the Year [*Choice*] and *The Fire Within: The Living Heritage of the Musar Movement* (New York: Mesorah, 1987).
The author acknowledges Rabbi Nathaniel Lauer, vice-principal of the Beth Jacob High School of Denver, for his illuminating comments on the penultimate draft of this article.

And it, like a groom,
  comes forth from its chamber;
  it will rejoice like a strong man,
  [eager] to run a course.

וְהוּא, כְּחָתָן,
יֵצֵא מֵחֻפָּתוֹ;
יָשִׂישׂ כְּגִבּוֹר,
לָרוּץ אֹרַח:

From the end of the heavens is its origin,
  and its circuit is upon their other ends,
  and there is nothing hidden from its heat.

מִקְצֵה הַשָּׁמַיִם מוֹצָאוֹ,
וּתְקוּפָתוֹ עַל־קְצוֹתָם;
וְאֵין נִסְתָּר, מֵחַמָּתוֹ:

The Torah of G-d is perfect,
  reviving the soul;
  the testimony of G-d is reliable,
  making the simple wise.

תּוֹרַת ה' תְּמִימָה,
מְשִׁיבַת נָפֶשׁ;
עֵדוּת ה' נֶאֱמָנָה,
מַחְכִּימַת פֶּתִי:

The mandates of G-d are upright,
  gladdening the heart;
  the commandment of G-d is clear,
  illuminating the eyes.

פִּקּוּדֵי ה' יְשָׁרִים,
מְשַׂמְּחֵי־לֵב;
מִצְוַת ה' בָּרָה,
מְאִירַת עֵינָיִם:

The fear of G-d is pure,
  abiding forever;
  the ordinances of G-d are true,
  coming together in integrity.

יִרְאַת ה' טְהוֹרָה,
עוֹמֶדֶת לָעַד;
מִשְׁפְּטֵי־ה' אֱמֶת,
צָדְקוּ יַחְדָּו:

They are more desirable
  than gold, than much fine gold,
  and are sweeter than honey
  and dripping of honeycombs.

הַנֶּחֱמָדִים,
מִזָּהָב וּמִפַּז רָב;
וּמְתוּקִים מִדְּבַשׁ,
וְנֹפֶת צוּפִים:

Your servant also is careful about them;
  in keeping them, there is much reward.

גַּם־עַבְדְּךָ, נִזְהָר בָּהֶם;
בְּשָׁמְרָם, עֵקֶב רָב:

Who can discern mistakes?
  Of hidden sins cleanse me.

שְׁגִיאוֹת מִי־יָבִין;
מִנִּסְתָּרוֹת נַקֵּנִי:

Also from intentional sins spare Your servant;
  let them not dominate me —
  whereupon I shall be flawless.
  Thus, I shall be clear of great transgression.

גַּם מִזֵּדִים חֲשֹׂךְ עַבְדֶּךָ,
אַל־יִמְשְׁלוּ־בִי
אָז אֵיתָם;
וְנִקֵּיתִי, מִפֶּשַׁע רָב:

May the words of my mouth
  and the meditation of my heart be pleasing
  before You,
  G-d, my Rock and my Redeemer.

יִהְיוּ לְרָצוֹן אִמְרֵי־פִי,
וְהֶגְיוֹן לִבִּי
לְפָנֶיךָ;
ה', צוּרִי וְגֹאֲלִי:

(Tehillim 19)

1. INTRODUCTION[1]

Mizmor 19 begins with a declaration: *"The heavens tell the glory of the L-rd, and His handiwork the sky recounts."* There is no reference in this opening verse, or in the several verses that follow, to the existence of human beings. We have, simply, a relationship between nature and G-d. By the end of the *mizmor*, human beings not only exist; they possess individuality. Indeed, they stand in intimate relationship with G-d: *"May the words of my mouth and the meditation of my heart be pleasing before You, G-d, my Rock and my Redeemer"* (ibid. 19:15).

The burden of the commentator on Mizmor 19 is to trace the emergence of man, standing in relationship with G-d, from out of a relationship obtaining between nature and G-d. In reading Tehillim generally, the commentator's burden is to recover the unstated progress and regress between and within verses. Tehillim's poetry is compressed, finely etched, often leaping from existential crisis or exultation to unpredictable heights and depths. These developments seem unpredictable because their arrival is seldom indicated by the verses themselves. Tehillim's inner logic is too rich to reach complete expression in words. Verses are often mere guideposts to subterranean rumblings and transformations of spirit. Crucial moments are not directly witnessed in words. It is for this reason that Tehillim retains a hold over the imagination in spite of its literary logic, which often seems strained. Tehillim's strength derives from its spiritual logic, its hinting at a world of spiritual confluences or explosions too volatile to be reduced to satisfying coherence.

Unarticulated moments between and within verses are best approximated by respecting Tehillim's bald meaning, including abrupt shifts in tense, voice, and person. Seemingly disjunctive, the bald meaning actually facilitates, not just necessitates, reconstruction and interpretation. Far from being loyal to the original Hebrew, the differentiated translation of *vav*, for example, as "however," "yet," "but," and "when," in addition to the basic "and," robs Tehillim's listeners (and readers) of the undifferentiated, bald communication of the original. In investigating Tehillim, it is by retaining the literal meaning, voice, tense, and person that shifts in intention have the best chance of being read out of rather than into the text, for all shifts reside in the Hebrew as it stands. Burden of proof rests on the commentator who would alter the bald communication.

In the Musar movement, I was taught to respond to the emotional-spiritual power of the Bible's verses, particularly in Tehillim: to allow verses to overcome my emotions and speak personally to my soul. Only from this intuitive, subjective level may I then proceed to literary, historical, or commentatorial perspectives. The hallmark of the Musar approach is paradox. By initially establishing a subjective link with a *mizmor*, I attune myself to its spiritual level of discourse, the precise nature of which will, under analysis, differentiate in ways sure to enlarge and possibly transcend (or even transgress) my initial response. Spurred by subjective attraction to particular verses in Mizmor 19 (especially verse 2 and verses 8-11), my commentary on the whole *mizmor* is an attempt to achieve an enlarged perspective — to retrieve the unspoken spiritual itinerary of King David as he retraces G-d's itinerary from nature to man to Torah.

In light of divergent approaches advanced by Chazal and classic commentators in expounding our *mizmor*, it should be emphasized that I do not by any means contend that mine is the only legitimate mode of interpretation. Mizmor 62:12 says, "G-d spoke one; I heard two." This means that no two Biblical verses can teach just one thing, but one verse can teach many things.[2] In interpreting Mizmor 19, I have chosen one method of interpretation: a Musar approach. Although I accept Chazal's interpretation of Tehillim as definitive, I am free to do so. "G-d spoke one; I heard two."

2. FROM NATURE TO TORAH THROUGH MAN

Both the opening and closing verses of Mizmor 19 have penetrated Jewish consciousness. The closing verse is recited at the conclusion of the "*Shemoneh Esreh*." R. Joseph B. Soloveitchik has observed that the "*Shemoneh Esreh*," formulated in the plural, infuses Jewish prayer with ethical responsibility.[3] Jews pray for others and for themselves simultaneously. Yet, R. Soloveitchik adds, prayer that is *only* ethical — that contains no intimate, personal request of G-d — is fundamentally deficient.[4] Accordingly, Halachah provides that, after the concluding blessing of the "*Shemoneh Esreh*," a person should articulate his personal prayers. Immediately after "ethical" prayer, the Jew must address G-d singularly: "May the words of *my* mouth and the meditation of *my* heart be pleasing before You, G-d, *my* Rock and *my* Redeemer." In contrast, the beginning of Mizmor 19, "The heavens tell the glory of the L-rd," taps the intuitive sense of the sacredness of glorious sunsets and mountain views. Mizmor 19 might seem to say that if prayer is essential to the relationship between man and G-d, response to nature is equally essential.

But is it? Mizmor 19 shifts from nature to man. Beginning with the heavens, the *mizmor* ends with the achievements, failures, and hopes of a "servant of G-d." Mizmor 19 lays down the roles of nature and man, and points to man's role as higher. Yes, the heavens tell the glory of the L-rd and nature induces reverence; yes, our *mizmor* esteems the religious response to nature. But Mizmor 19 is not satisfied with focusing on nature: It proceeds to man. In the beginning, too, G-d created nature, and then He created man as the pinnacle of Creation. Mizmor 19, however, goes even further. Building on BeReshith, it identifies how nature begs the existence of man: not only how G-d projects Himself through nature, but also how this is insufficient. Our *mizmor* is not bifurcated into two sub-*mizmorim* — verses 2-7, a paean to nature's testimony to G-d, and verses 8-15, a separate (and higher) paean to Torah's testimony to G-d. Instead, the *mizmor* as a whole is evolutionary. It is G-d's procession from expressing Himself through nature to finding His fullest expression through man's embodiment of Torah. In BeReshith, G-d creates Torah, creates nature, and witnesses man's rise. It is in this sense that Mizmor 19 acknowledges elements in the human condition that threaten to keep man from living up to Torah's potential, affirms man's ability to be self-critical, and records man's hope that self-criticism will actualize his — and Torah's — potential.

3. THE ACKNOWLEDGEMENT OF MAN

"*The heavens tell the glory of the L-rd, and His handiwork the sky recounts*" (ibid. 19:2). To whom do the heavens speak? To whom does the sky recount? This verse, seemingly a statement about G-d and nature, presumes the existence of man. From the very beginning, Mizmor 19 finds nature's reflection of G-d's glory insufficient. One might argue that when the heavens tell the glory of G-d, they tell it to G-d Himself, but the continuation of the *mizmor* makes it clear that it is man who is the recipient of nature's expressions. Man is the object of Mizmor 19.

"*Day to day expresses a statement, and night to night offers knowledge*" (ibid. 19:3). Day and night catalyze statements and knowledge, though both day and night, unlike man, have no auditory apparatus. Who, then, is listening to these statements and this knowledge? This verse, too, presumes the existence of man — and not only because man possesses an auditory apparatus. Our *mizmor's* opening verse speaks of day and night — of *time* — expressing G-d's glory. Time is primordial nature released in flux. Flux is the state of humanity — flux is man's bailiwick. Mizmor 19's shift from nature to time advances the acknowledgement of man.

The next verse comes still closer to making man explicit: "*There is no statement and no words, without their voice being heard*" (ibid. 19:4). It is man who hears this voice, since its locale is man's abode: "*Their line* [the line of the voice of time's expressions] *went forth throughout the earth, and their words to the end of the world*" (ibid. 19:5). The second half of verse 4 is amphibolous; "בלי נשמע קולם" is an exquisite double entendre. The verse could just as easily be translated, "There is no statement and no words; their voice is unheard." Indeed, the voice of time is not heard in any literal sense, as time (like nature) possesses no vocal apparatus. But the voice of time *is* heard in the same sense that nature conveys distinct, unmistakable messages about G-d. Literally, time's voice is not heard; optatively, it is heard. Attributing a voice to time's expressions, Mizmor 19 begs man's existence, since a voice implies an auditory apparatus — a human recipient.

As verse 5 ends, the gradual acknowledgement of man takes a qualitative leap, "*... He has set a tent for the sun in them*": in the expressions occasioned by day and night. Nature, represented by the sun, now not merely gives expression to G-d's glory or handiwork, or to unelaborated statements and knowledge; nature is not merely the location of the endless line of speech. Nature and nature's speech are now *confined*: "He has set a tent ... in them." For the endless, unrestricted character of speech to lodge itself ultimately in the mind of man — for nature's message to find itself ultimately received by man — speech is first confined. Nature — the sun — and its message are placed under a "tent," restricted to a clearly defined location.

As speech is confined — a listener of speech thus implied — joy bursts forth. It can only be the joy of a human being. Man enters the cosmos: "*And it, like a groom, comes forth from its chamber; it will rejoice like a strong man, [eager] to run a course*" (ibid. 19:6). The groom, whose life ascends to a new plane of existence by being confined to the *chuppah*, is compared to and thus explains the ascent of nature's speech to a new plane of existence by being confined to a "tent." Restricted to a tent, so to speak, nature's speech is finally able to find its audience: man. The metaphor is not of man as he is, but of man as he comes into existence — as a groom. Just as *chuppah* links two entities to create new existence, the tent — which captures speech — links nature's speech to its listener. It is this linkage of nature's speech to its listener that brings the listener into existence. The appearance of man in verse 6 proceeds from the containment of speech in verse 5.

Paradoxically, once speech has a home, once there is a human being to receive nature's expression of G-d's glory, speech is no longer contained. Speech unleashes its scope — "*From the end of the heavens is its origin ...*" — its endurance — "*... and its circuit is upon their other ends ...*" — and its comprehensiveness — "*... and there is nothing hidden from its heat*" (ibid. 19:7). Nature — the sun — initially contained, now witnesses speech's "heat," its power to raise all hidden matters to the level of expression.

Our *mizmor's* use of the sun to represent nature's containment is apt. More than all heavenly bodies (not to mention all other elements of nature), the sun bathes human existence in light. The sun, in its confinement that actualizes the human being, is the appropriate transitional metaphor for the second part of Mizmor 19, which bathes human existence in spiritual light — in Torah.

4. THE ASCENT OF MAN

As we have seen, nature and time express the glory of G-d, and their expressions are gradually confined until they finally find their reception in man. Called into existence by his receipt of these expressions, man possesses speech in its scope, its endurance, and its power to bring the inarticulate (the "hidden") to expression. Our *mizmor* now proceeds to levels of speech higher than the expressions of nature and time and to levels of human existence higher than the receipt of these expressions. While nature expresses G-d, and the receipt of this level of G-d's expression calls man into existence, Mizmor 19 summons man to a higher plane. The next verses enumerate six stages of man's ascent. The first four stages describe four new levels of expression by G-d, and their four respective effects on man.

The first stage is "*The Torah of G-d is perfect, reviving the soul ...*" (ibid. 19:8). "*Torah*" is the first new level of G-d's expression; "*revival*" is its effect. Torah meets an existential problem. If G-d communicates to man only through nature, life is fluid and fragmentary: a meaningless flow interrupted by rare, meaningful moments. Glorious sunsets and mountain views are few and far between. They are also amorphous. Eliciting deep emotion, they convey nothing concrete. "*The Torah of G-d,*" however, is perfect, not fragmentary; it is concrete, not amorphous. As man receives Torah — a perfection higher than nature and time — man revives.

The second stage is "*... the testimony of G-d is reliable, making the simple wise*" (ibid.). The reliability of G-d's testimony alleviates potential deficiencies in Torah's perfection. Revived by the perfection of Torah, man may remain skeptical, for many answers purport to be perfect. Many passing "perfections" ensnare humanity, from the idolatry of antiquity to the communism of modernity. G-d's testimony, however, is reliable; it is not a passing perfection. Thus, it not only revives but brings wisdom.

The third stage is "*The mandates of G-d are upright, gladdening the heart ...*" (ibid. 19:9). The uprightness of G-d's mandates alleviates potential deficiencies in the reliability of G-d's testimony. Made wise by the reliability of Torah, man may still remain skeptical, for wrong answers also seem to sustain themselves. Falsehood can persist for a long time. G-d's mandates, however, are upright. They are *correct*. They offer true, not false, reliability. Thus, they are not only reliable, but gladdening.

The fourth stage is "*... the commandment of G-d is clear, illuminating the eyes*" (ibid.). The clarity of G-d's commandment alleviates potential deficiencies in the uprightness of his mandates. Gladdened by the uprightness of Torah, man may nevertheless remain skeptical, for many answers seem correct but inaccessible. Truth can exist but remain esoteric, as the private preserve of a priesthood of believers. G-d's commandment, however, is clear — open — not the preserve of an elite. Thus, it is not only correct but illuminating.

These four higher levels of G-d's expression posit a separation between G-d and man. On the one hand, there is G-d's expression; on the other hand, there is man's response. G-d's Torah *is* — and man revives; G-d's testimony *is* — and man becomes wise; G-d's mandates *are* — and man is glad; G-d's commandment *is* — and man is illuminated. All are patterned as expressions of G-d to which man responds. In contrast, the fifth and sixth of the higher levels of G-d's expressions posit a oneness between G-d and man, since these expressions elicit no *response*. They have no *effect*; they *are*.

The fifth stage is *"The fear of G-d is pure, abiding forever ..."* (ibid. 19:10). The fear of G-d, which is pure, abides forever *within* man. Man does not *respond* to the fear of G-d (as he responds, for example, to Torah's perfection); he *embodies* the fear of G-d, he *is* the fear of G-d. In this sense he is one with G-d.

Similarly, the sixth stage is *"... the ordinances of G-d are true, coming together in integrity"* (ibid.). G-d's ordinances, which are Truth, come together *in*, and thus form, human integrity. Having responded to four higher levels of G-d's expression and having embodied the fifth level, man *becomes* the sixth level: the ordinances of G-d. They pull together all previous levels of ascent into an integral whole: the servant of G-d. Truth integrates all levels of G-d's speech as they come to expression in man. Man does not *respond* to the ordinances of G-d; they have no *effect* on him. Rather, he *is* the ordinances of G-d, he *embodies* them. In this sense man is one with G-d. Accordingly, the ordinances of G-d are "more desirable than gold, than much fine gold, and are sweeter than honey and dripping of honeycombs" (ibid. 19:11).

5. CONCLUSION: BEING HUMAN

Yet, alas, having climbed these heights, the human being remains — human. *"Your servant also is careful about them [G-d's ordinances] ..."* (ibid. 19:12). To embody the fear of G-d and the ordinances of G-d is no guarantee against backsliding. Even the servant of G-d must be careful; in so doing, "... *in keeping them, there is much reward*" (ibid.). Nevertheless, the higher levels of G-d's expression cannot always be "kept;" even G-d's servant does not always succeed in living up to, or embodying, them. They consist of conscious deeds and hidden commitments; their violation consists of objective mistakes and unconscious errors: "*Who can discern mistakes? Of hidden sins cleanse me. Also from intentional sins spare Your servant; let them not dominate me — whereupon I shall be flawless. Thus, I shall be clear of great transgression*" (ibid. 19:13-14).

Man has emerged. As the recipient of G-d's indirect speech, reflected through nature, man comes into existence. As the recipient of G-d's direct speech — Torah — man begins a path of ascent. It culminates in man becoming a servant of G-d. As such, he embodies the fear of G-d, which is pure, and the ordinances of G-d, which are true; but even at these high levels, man is subject to the backsliding of mistakes and hidden errors. Man must pray for divine help in understanding and avoiding them. For this, there is great reward and rescue from great transgression. Yes, prayer is essential for actualizing human potential. Man relates not merely to nature but — directly — to G-d Himself: "*May the words of my mouth*" — known intentions — "*and the meditation of my heart*" — hidden intentions — "*be pleasing before You, G-d, my Rock and my Redeemer*" (ibid. 19:15).

NOTES

1. Some of the ideas discussed in the introductory material for this essay are developed at greater length in my "Psalm 22: The Retrieval of Faith," *Tradition*, 24 (Winter 1989), 74-75.

2. See *Sanhedrin* 34a.

3. See R. Joseph B. Soloveitchik, "The Lonely Man of Faith," *Tradition*, 7 (Summer 1965), 37-38, and "The Community," *Tradition*, 17 (Spring 1978), 19-20.

4. This idea was emphasized by R. Soloveitchik during his *motza'ei Shabbath* lectures in *masecheth Berachoth*, given in Brookline, Massachusetts, ca. 5730. See also "The Community," p. 18.

JEWISH THOUGHT: A Journal of Torah Scholarship is a nonpartisan journal of traditional scholarship in *parshanuth HaMikra* (Biblical commentary and exegesis) and *machsheveth Yisra'el* (classic Jewish philosophy). It is a semiannual publication of the Union of Orthodox Jewish Congregations of America in conjunction with Yeshivat Ohr Yerushalayim in Israel.

Subscriptions are on an annual basis, two issues for $10, payable to *Jewish Thought*, c/o Orthodox Union, 333 Seventh Avenue, New York, NY 10001.

Appropriate scholarly essays in the areas of Biblical commentary and exegesis, Midrash, Aggadah, classic Jewish philosophy, and Jewish liturgy may be submitted for publication, contingent on the guidelines below.

GUIDE TO CONTRIBUTORS:

A) Content

1. Essays must be text-oriented, providing an analysis of either primary sources or specific topics illuminated by primary sources.
2. Essays must reflect original research, or adaptations or translations of research, hitherto unpublished in English.

B) Presentation

1. Essays must be written in a style suitable for an audience of both Torah scholars and learned laymen.
2. Essays must be prepared in conformity with *The MLA Style Sheet*. All sources must be properly referenced. Citations of quotations should be included parenthetically in the text, whereas more lengthy notes should be listed separately at the end of the essay.
3. Manuscripts should be approximately from ten to twenty-five pages long, double-spaced on one side of a page with adequate margins.

C) Editing

1. Essays accepted for publication may be edited. Authors will be notified about any significant changes.
2. All essays published will be synopsized in the table of contents and subdivided into subtitled sections. Authors may provide suggested abstracts and suggested subdivisions with their essays.